D1510866

The Mystery of Goodness

AND THE

POSITIVE MORAL CONSEQUENCES

OF PSYCHOTHERAPY

Mary W. Nicholas

C.I.S.W., Ph.D.

W. W. Norton & Company • New York • London

A NORTON PROFESSIONAL BOOK

Printed in the United States of America

First Edition

The text of this book was composed in 10/12 Palatino with display type set in Optima.
Composition by Bytheway Typesetting Services, Inc.

Book design by Justine Burkat Trubey

Library of Congress Cataloging-in-Publication Data

Nicholas, Mary W., 1945–
    The mystery of goodness and the positive moral consequences of
psychotherapy / Mary W. Nicholas.
        p.   cm.
    "A Norton professional book."
    ISBN 0-393-70166-2
    1. Ethical therapy. I. Title.
    [DNLM: 1. Psychotherapy. 2. Morals. 3. Behavior. 4. Ethics.
WM 420 N598m 1994]
RC489.E83N53 1994
616.89′14′01—dc20
DNLM/DLC   93-27992 CIP
for Library of Congress

W. W. Norton & Company, Inc., 500 Fifth Avenue, New York, NY 10110
W. W. Norton & Company, Ltd., 10 Coptic Street, London WC1A 1PU

1 2 3 4 5 6 7 8 9 0

CONTENTS

PREFACE:

ON THE TRAIL OF GOODNESS

Early in my practice, I had a client who occasionally paid me with large wads of cash, which I gradually realized were the proceeds from his selling marijuana.

This man had always impressed me as an unusually courageous and good-hearted individual. He stood by those he loved under very difficult circumstances and felt deeply for the misfortunes of others, always lending a hand to those in need. During the period of his therapy, a huge jetliner crashed in the Potomac River in Washington on a freezing cold night. Watching on television as impressive numbers of bystanders braved icy waters to save the drowning passengers, I remember thinking that, if my patient were on the scene, he would surely have been one of the first ones to dive in.

I sought consultation from my social work mentor, Bob, on how to address my client's selling marijuana.

"Simple," said Bob. "Tell him it's unethical, and that he can't get better if he does it. Unethical behavior and mental health are contradictory."

I had read no such thing in graduate school, nor in any of my psychotherapy textbooks; yet, it made perfect sense to me and, it turned out, to my client as well.

"You know, I really agree with you," my client said when I broke the news to him that selling pot and getting better were antithetical.

"Now that I have a kid, I cannot respect myself for doing this. I never did, really. How would I feel if someone sold my kid drugs? It's a lousy thing to be doing. I guess I needed you to say something. I'm going to stop." He did so immediately.

My client felt much better about himself after making this decision, and I began to think how odd and unfortunate it was that psychotherapy paid so little attention to matters of morality and goodness.

I was further stimulated to think about the relationship between therapy and morality during intense moral discussions that seemed to occur frequently in my therapy groups. In my groups, members regularly dig down to the ethical roots of one another's problems: To what extent is the "significant other" of an active drug user responsible for the actions of the addict? When, if ever, is having an abortion moral? Do clients have a moral responsibility to be honest in therapy or to try to be fair in their representation of people not present in the treatment? To what extent does one person have the right to judge another? Should friends excuse friends' or family members' irresponsible behavior, selfishness, prejudice, or dishonesty? Where does holding others accountable leave off and destructive blaming begin? Should one forgive one's oppressors even though they are unrepentent? These are just some of the moral questions that my groups have struggled with over the years.

It seems that whenever two or more people get together to discuss relationships in a personal way, it is not long before questions of relative goodness emerge and a kind of moral dialogue begins. While I recognized early on that group therapy was a fruitful context for the discussion of moral issues, it subsequently became obvious to me that individual and family treatment also provide considerable opportunity for patients and therapists to explore questions of what is valuable and meaningful in life.

I then began to wonder whether moral change takes place in patients as a consequence of psychotherapy, a question I had touched on in my earlier book, *Change in the Context of Group Therapy*, and, if so, what the mechanisms of therapy might be that fostered such changes.

By this time, I was well underway in my pursuit of the "mystery of goodness" in psychotherapy.

ACKNOWLEDGMENTS

I would like to acknowledge Dr. Hugh Mullan whose seminal writings on the inherent moral value of group therapy inspired me to start my exploration of goodness. I would like to thank my friends, family, and colleagues for their insights and encouragement: Richard Rubin and

David Johnson (whose perspectives are quoted in the book), Christine Harland, Jim Collins, Nancy Davidson, Grace Flight, Shalom Endleman, Mona Affinito, Gretchen Nicholas, Susan Nicholas, and my husband, Gene Eliasoph. (Gene's own goodness, as continually demonstrated through his support and devotion was probably the most basic and important inspiration for this enterprise.) Many thanks to Susan Barrows Munro, whom I have grown to appreciate over the years as an intellectual soulmate as well as a fine editor.

FORMAT

This book consists of three sections: The first section, *Mixing Apples and Oranges: Reconciling Goodness with Psychology and Psychotherapy*, begins the task of conceptualizing goodness in psychological terms. Chapter 1 poses the question of *Whatever Happened to Goodness?* in the fields of psychology and psychotherapy. In Chapter 2, *"Virtues" in Personality Assessment and Psychotherapy*, a theory of virtues in personality is presented, including a scale by which one can assess an individual's virtues—**altruism, responsibility, egalitarianism, justice,** and **honesty**—on the private and public levels. Anecdotes are presented that familiarize the reader with ways in which an individual's virtues can be enhanced through psychotherapy.

Section Two is entitled *The History of Goodness*. It contains five chapters that synthesize a variety of theories pertaining to goodness from the history of science, developmental psychology, behavioral and social psychology, psychoanalysis, and various other clinical perspectives. Anecdotes from psychotherapy are used to illuminate some of the concepts presented.

Chapters 3 and 4 explore the intellectual biases toward amorality that are inherent in Western culture and science, and, therefore, in therapists' training. These include: *the assumption of humans' separateness and alienation from one another and from the planet; positivism; Darwinism; and individualism.*

In Chapters 5 through 7, the complex topic of moral development is broken down into four parts: moral sensitivity, moral action, moral reasoning, and moral attitude. Moral sensitivity, the ability to make distinctions about what is morally right and wrong in interpersonal situations, and moral action, the ability to act on behalf of others, are discussed in Chapter 5, while the development of moral reasoning, the ability to reason out solutions to moral dilemmas is covered in Chapter 6. Chapter 7 brings both the Freudian and object relations psychoanalytic perspectives to bear on the question of what factors cause the development of a generally moral attitude in one's personality. First presented is Freud's theory of how we learn what *not* to do; second is the object relations view of how we learn what *to* do. In the object relations framework, positive morality is conceptualized as "the increased capacity to care."

Section Three, entitled *From Demoralization to Remoralization through Psychotherapy*, discusses the moral aspects of various mental and emotional illnesses and their treatment. Chapter 8 deals with the phenomena of *shame and guilt*—essential links between the moral and psychological experience. Chapters 9 through 11 describe the moral aspects of some of the problems people typically bring to psychotherapy—*depression; addictions and co-dependency; and the borderline and narcissistic personality disorders*. It will be shown that goodness is often enhanced when the psychotherapy of these problems is successful. Particular attention will be paid to how a therapist can address the ethical roots of a client's disorders or problem without causing shame, embarrassment, or undue guilt, and without imposing her personal moral views on the patient.

Chapter 12, *How Therapy Fosters Goodness*, discusses some of the ways that the process of therapy generates goodness. Therapy involves the pursuit of free and equal relationships, a search for truth, and a valuing of what is alive in each one of us. It can and usually does teach people how to love more and better. The therapist's choice of method and what kind of a person the therapist is are key factors in creating these moral changes.

Section One

MIXING APPLES AND ORANGES:
RECONCILING GOODNESS
WITH PSYCHOLOGY
AND PSYCHOTHERAPY

Chapter 1

WHATEVER HAPPENED

TO GOODNESS?

Goodness remains a mystery "even greater than the mystery of evil."

—Scott Peck, 1983, p. 41

At a time when violence, prejudice, and greed seem to be encroaching upon everyone's lives, it is shocking and unfortunate that so little information has yet emerged from psychology or psychotherapy on how to foster such generally agreed-upon "good things" as nonviolence, love, compassion, patience, fairness, truthfulness, peaceful dialogue, conflict resolution, egalitarian values, and unselfishness.

A flurry of concern about the fate of the human race after the Holocaust and World War II generated important thinking on morality by neo-analytic and humanistic clinicians Horney, Fromm, Frankl, and Maslow, but, by the early seventies, such interest had dwindled. In academic psychology the interest in goodness has been minimal with the notable exception of research by social psychologists on "prosocial" (helping) behavior and by cognitive developmentalists on stages of moral development (Piaget, Kohlberg, Gilligan).

Like the bad children in the class who eclipse the well-behaved ones, evil has gotten more of psychology's and psychotherapy's time and attention than goodness. Recently, psychiatrist Lifton and his research team (1986) isolated the psychological mechanisms that seemed to have allowed the "Nazi doctors" to have become "socialized to kill-

3

ing." Erwin Staub (1989), a social psychologist, has identified the social conditions that generate a genocidal mentality. Peck (1983), a psychiatrist and popular author dedicated to the integration of psychology and spirituality, pushed the traditional barrier of moral neutrality in psychotherapy by stating that some patients[1] are not just sick, but evil.

By contrast, goodness has been sparsely studied by psychologists, and has rarely received the attention of psychotherapists.

Goodness is defined here as *the capacity to behave with love and concern toward others*.

Two aspects of goodness are considered in this book: morality and virtue. *Morality* has to do with distinguishing between right and wrong, and *virtue* has to do with being and acting positively in the world.

A premise of this book is that the expression of five interpersonal virtues—**altruism**, **responsibility**, **egalitarianism**, **justice**, and **honesty** (meaning not lying, cheating or stealing)[2]—play an important role in personality. Each virtue operates along a spectrum from the private to the public domain. For example, one might be altruistic with one's spouse, but stingy with one's time and money in one's community, or vice versa.

Kitwood (1990) has stated

> Whatever their "presenting problem," the concern of those who look to psychotherapy often turns out to be to discover some richness of experience and relatedness, some *core of goodness*, which they feel has eluded them, but which they sense is their birthright as human beings. (p. 194, emphasis added)

As a therapist I have long observed that positive therapeutic and moral change are often inextricable. I have previously written (1984) that clients in group therapy seem to experience changes on the level of their beliefs and values—that the paradoxes occurring naturally in the group process force dramatic shifts in frame of reference regarding what people see as true, important, and good. In thinking more about this over the years, I have realized that, while a group is particularly likely to foster goodness, the basic processes that cause this to occur are a function of basic human interactions that also happen in individual, couples, and family therapy.

The message of this book is that psychotherapy, practiced competently in the context of a nurturing, interactive, and honest therapeutic

---

[1]The terms "patient" and "client" will be used interchangeably, as will male and female pronouns when gender is irrelevant.
[2]Hereafter, these virtues will be tagged in the text by means of bold print.

relationship can and often does bring the client closer to his inner ''core of goodness.''[3]

THE THERAPIST AS MORAL BEACON

While a ''client is not likely to come to a secularly oriented therapist complaining of bewilderment at the loss of values and moral standards'' (Lowe, 1969, p. 37), Fromm, among others, claimed that understanding and working through one's moral dilemmas are essential parts of therapy (1947). Victor Frankl (1969) agreed with Gordon Pleune whom he quotes as saying, ''the psychoanalytic practitioner is a moralist first and foremost'' and ''influences people in regard to their moral and ethical conduct'' (p. 15). While I do not think therapists are moralists *first and foremost*, it is hard to dispute that a great many people seek therapy not just for symptom relief but for help with basic ''problems of existence . . . [They feel] they do not know how to live'' (London, 1986, p. 151). While in previous generations, problems of existence, however they were defined, might lead one to seek the help of a religious figure, nowadays many individuals may view therapy and therapists as a kind of ''secular priesthood'' (London, 1986, p. 148).

These days it may not only be patients but society itself that is looking to therapists for moral guidance. Rollo May (1969) suggested that therapy patients are often the first to articulate society's incipient mental and moral illnesses. May (1962) also attributed most mental illness to the breakdown of values in society, ''causing the individuals in that society to founder on storm-shaken seas without solid mooring posts or even buoys and lighthouses which can be depended upon'' (p. 1). Lowe (1969) and Bellah et al. (1985) have suggested that patients not only are coming into therapy with confusion about their own individual morality, but are seeking to compensate for the lack of reliable and humane moral guideposts available in society as a whole.

The sheer volume of guidance fed by therapists to the general public on a daily basis via programs, such as *The Oprah Winfrey Show* and other media forums, is testimony to the credibility attributed to therapists today. The advice therapists are dispensing on the air and in print is as moral as it is psychological and sensationalistic. People are asking, ''How

[3]While the topic of goodness is, of course, linked to matters of spirituality and philosophy, this book will attempt to keep its language secular and psychological, for there is plenty to be said about goodness in this context alone. Morality in the sense of sexual behavior is not dealt with in this book, since to do so would take us into the area of *conventional morality* and away from the more universal ideas of interpersonal goodness, which are our central interest.

should we lead our lives?'' ''What will make me a 'better' wife, mother, boss?'' (The meaning of ''better'' often means, at least in part, more **responsible**, **altruistic**, **just**, and **honest**.)

It is highly ironic that therapists of all people should now find themselves called upon to provide moral leadership, given the fact that most therapists have been carefully trained to assiduously avoid the topic of morality and goodness, not only in their clinical work, but in their research and theoretical writings as well.

THE MYSTERIOUS AVOIDANCE OF GOODNESS IN PSYCHOTHERAPY

> Because the patient's morals in part result from his neurosis and in part contribute to its maintenance, the analyst has no choice but to be interested in them.
>
> —*Karen Horney, 1945*

Most psychotherapy treatments view as axiomatic the notion that an emotionally and/or psychologically distressed patient cannot ''get better''—i.e., achieve mental health—if any important areas of functioning are ignored, repressed, or suppressed. It is assumed that it is countertherapeutic for the therapist to collude with the patient to avoid discussing any aspect of the patient's world, for it might well be in this deleted area that the patient's greatest conflicts and difficulties reside. Given the high value placed on understanding all aspects of the patient in his world, the absence of consideration of patient morality is astonishing. How could therapists, for all these years, have omitted such a central area of human functioning and experience, one that is clearly of paramount concern to many of their patients, and to most of the therapists, themselves, personally, when they are not in the consulting room?

With the exception of Horney, Fromm, Frankl, and Maslow, the deletion of morality was fairly complete until just a few years ago. Therapists' moral judgments or even moral reflections when it comes to patient behavior have been assumed to have no rightful place in the consulting room. If therapists have opinions or feelings, positive or negative, about patient morality they are advised to seek supervision immediately in order that they may understand their countertransference and properly relegate what seemed a moral issue into a more clinically correct perspective. While I am always in favor of clinicians struggling with their own biases and agendas in supervision so as not to impose them on the client, I do think it is important for therapists to be able to make moral distinctions and articulate them in treatment.

A survey of counseling and psychotherapy texts in the mid-1980s (Grant, 1985) found that the overwhelming majority of 300- to 500-page textbooks contained not a single reference to the morality of the client or patient. What is it that accounts for the consistent avoidance of the topic of morality or virtue by psychotherapists? Personally, I do not think very many therapists really believe that goodness is irrelevant to therapy. Is it a matter of apathy, lack of imagination, or resistance? I doubt that, because the avoidance is just as pervasive among hard-working, well-meaning, well-trained, and skillful clinicians as it is by less competent and dedicated ones.

The first block to therapists' approaching the discussion of goodness may be the semantic limitations imposed by the framework of science, which forms the basis of most therapists' training. There seems to be little difference among the therapy professions with respect to their willingness to discuss the morality of the patient or other matters of goodness. All of them are quite wedded to the scientific ethos underlying their respective disciplines, which in each case seems to rule out attention to moral concerns, except as they apply to the professional behavior of the clinician.

Psychiatrists' training is rooted in the sciences, which orients them (to varying degrees) to remain dispassionate, to see people in terms of symptom complexes, and to conceptualize treatments in a systematic way that can be carefully documented. On the other hand, the thrust of psychiatrists' medical training is toward relieving patients of suffering regardless of their moral condition (London, 1986). Both the push to be scientific and the pragmatic pressure to alleviate suffering have mitigated against the likelihood of medically trained therapists (including psychiatric nurses) granting much if any consideration to patients' moral concerns.

Clinical psychologists are typically trained to perform a dual role— "scientist" and "practitioner"—neither of which implies any particular moral purpose. The stated mission of traditional academic psychology was to "predict and control" behavior. Translated into psychotherapy, the clinical psychologist is supposed to apply the knowledge of his science to helping the patient with "problems of living." For the most part, psychologists are taught, and pass on to their clients, the message that these problems of living are not supposed to include ethical dilemmas or a dissatisfaction with one's level of goodness. When faced with complaints having to do with morality, the clinical psychologist, like the psychiatrist, is trained to conceptualize them as symptoms of a more overriding problem that has a psychopathological basis.

Family therapy is based on a newer "scientific" model, namely systems theory. Systems theory holds that the motivations of the individuals in the system are subsumed by the needs of the larger system. The family, like other systems, strives toward acheiving balance or *homeostasis*. While the tendency of systems to seek homeostasis is highly adaptive, a family can get stuck in a balance that is dysfunctional and that renders its members miserable. Successful therapeutic interventions, therefore, are those that destabilize the system, allowing it to reorganize in a new and better way. While family systems theory presupposes a drive for some sort of greater good on the part of the system as a whole, the morality of the individual is given no relevance in and of itself. The **responsibility, justice, honesty**, or **altruism** of a given person are appreciated only in terms of the function they serve in the family system.

Social work derives its theory largely from sociology, which has typically seen problems in terms of norms and deviation from the norms. Siporin says social workers should teach their clients to conform to "the way people normally ought to act" (1975, p. 65), a strikingly amoral prescription for a profession with such high moral aspirations. While social work perceives its mission to be a "moral effort" that is supposed to "contribute to the betterment—not deterioration—of the human predicament" (Siporin, 1975, p. 64), in practice, social workers are not trained to concern themselves with the goodness or morality of their clients, although they are, to their credit, greatly concerned with the goodness and morality of the social work profession.

Unless they depart from the restrictions of the scientific method, therapists are stranded without even a vocabulary, much less a theory base from which to begin to formulate the questions that would spawn research and discussion. From my conversations with clinicians of all levels and disciplines, I am positive that the subject of morality in therapy is of enormous interest to them, but most do not seem to know how and where to begin discussing it. They seem to be worried, as I was at first, that in talking about morality with clients or with other clinicians they will be seen as unprofessional or unscientific. It is mystification and fear of embarrassment, not apathy or hard-heartedness, that has caused clinicians and scholars to hide defensively behind the empiricist tradition and "claim the privilege of ignorance" (London, 1986, p. 7) when it comes to the role of morality and goodness in personality, psychopathology, and psychotherapy.

While scientific values govern psychotherapists' conceptualization of their work, pragmatic and egoistic values often characterize their practice. Bergin's study of therapist values (1988) showed that therapists from all three of the major therapy professions espouse egoistic values over altruistic ones. Of the highest priority for clients to obtain through treatment, as therapists see it, are improved expression of *feelings, freedom and autonomy, coping, self-maintenance and physical fitness, self-awareness*, and *growth*. In terms of the virtues we are focusing on in this book, the study suggests that therapists do not seem to value highly the interpersonal values of **justice, egalitarianism**, or **altruism**. They do value **responsibility**, but more for the self than for others; they also admire **honesty**—in the context of therapy, particularly. In a recent study, experienced certified clinical social workers in private practice were found to place very little value, if any, on social justice or helping the poor, while placing a very high value on their own income, prestige, and autonomy (Seiz & Schwab, 1992). These studies' findings on therapists' worldly priorities match the unflattering perception of the profession arrived at by sociologist Bellah and his team of researchers in their seminal book, *Habits of the Heart* (1985). These investigators found that therapists communicate a highly individualistic and utilitarian ethic to their clients, thereby diverting their millions of therapy consumers away from community concerns and social responsibilities into the pursuit of self-satisfaction.

While I believe that therapists should question and remedy the insularity they have maintained from their communities and from the larger world, I have, in the course of my work, come to the conclusion that when you scratch the surface of the therapy process much goodness is inherent in it. As we will see in Chapters 8 through 12, successful therapy—truly successful, that is—does not increase egoism, but rather diminishes it. Underlying what may seem to be a preoccupation with the client's selfish interests, there usually runs a current of concern for others that is shared by the client and the therapist. That current may be obscured by fear, shame, depression, hurt, or anger, but it is running strong at some level, however deep. Liberating this underground flow of interpersonal goodness is indeed one of the most, if not the most, rewarding consequences of successful, in-depth treatment.

I think, were most therapist to be asked (which they have not been in any studies I have seen) they would say that they notice that as clients get better in therapy, they become less egocentric and more concerned about others. It has not escaped the notice of clinicians all these years that people are usually happier if they can "get out of themselves" and help others. Virtue can be, and often is, "its own reward" as the saying goes. Service to others, involving **altruism** and **responsibility** particularly, has always been considered a vital part of AA and twelve-step recovery programs. Almost all halfway houses include community service as part of their programs. People usually say they feel better when they volunteer, and Luks (1992) has claimed that such virtuous activity even relieves stress and bolsters the immune system. It is not that therapists and their clients do not care about goodness, nor that they do not notice it. They simply need permission to speak of it and a language with which to discuss it.

Besides scientism and the egoistic values which have seemed to prevail in therapy's conceptualization of itself, a third reason might account for therapists' apparent failure to attend to goodness in psychotherapy: guilt. George Weinberg, in his novel, *The Taboo Scarf* (1990), takes a hard look at his own reluctance to acknowledge the goodness in his patient, lamenting how quick the profession is to "pathologize" some of the best qualities of its clientele.

And I thought about Warren White, the exemplar of goodness on earth that must go forever unacknowledged, because the full recognition that there are such people, that they are not deranged in any way, would inform against us, showing the rest of us, the majority, to be devious, expedient, greedy. And we deny their existence, or, more diabolically, we deny them their goodness, ascribing other, baser motives to them. And psychoanalysts, blinded by their light, charging patients for every hour missed, has led the curse against them, by inventing secret, self-serving motives for them. According to psychoanalysis, they are covering their hidden rage, or seeking power by giving pleasure, or playing God. (p. 105)

GETTING BEYOND NEUTRALITY

One crucial artifact of the scientific tradition in psychotherapy is the concept of neutrality. While neutrality has its rightful conceptual and technical place in therapy, the weight it has been given in therapeutic practice has often proved problematic. This is particularly true when therapists are confronted with difficult moral dilemmas within the treatment context. Therapists often feel constrained from discussing patients' moral failures and from recognizing and admiring their virtues because they are afraid of committing the unpardonable "sin" of having a moral opinion or, worse yet, making a value judgment in the presence of their patients. In some cases, the therapists may lack a system of values themselves and consequently be unable to grasp, much less address, moral questions when they arise in the therapy.

Not infrequently, however, the dilemma a client brings to therapy is an explicitly moral one. A typical example is when a woman comes for help with her decision about whether or not to get an abortion. The therapist will be of no help to the client if she feels she may not or does not know how to discuss the moral aspects of this decision. While the therapist has no right to impose her own opinions about abortion on the client (if she is not pro "choice" she should not be discussing "choice" with the patient), she is obligated to help the client sort out her own moral views of the situation. The reality is that either decision the woman makes is likely to be fraught with moral consequences—for herself and for others in her life. If the woman is to feel comfortable with her decision afterwards, she needs to cover all the moral bases before she makes her decision. I have seen many cases where a woman experienced considerable emotional difficulties after choosing either to have or not to have an abortion: not because she was sure she had done the wrong thing, but because she did not feel she had given the matter enough consideration on the moral level beforehand to be confident that her choice was the right one. By contrast, women who really thought the whole matter through, facing the moral issues head on, were much better able to deal with the inevitable doubts and regrets that came later.

Some moral problems brought to therapists ethically require the therapist to take action, such as reporting child abuse or threatened violence toward another. Others, like the abortion example, simply require the therapist to engage with the patient in resolving the moral dilemma. Other typical moral dilemmas presented to therapists include "Should I have an affair with this man I love while I am still married?" "Do I have a right to punish my father now for the way he treated me when I was younger?" "Is it my moral responsibility to have my son arrested for drunken driving?" For the therapist to demur from discussing the oughts and shoulds of these genuine moral concerns is insulting to and frustrating for the patient. What is more, the therapist's feigning neutrality or avoiding the issue will likely result in the patient's projecting a judgmental opinion onto the therapist anyway, which will only serve to increase the client's confusion and anxiety.

The biggest moral challenge for the therapist is not when the client is already explicitly and consciously grappling with a moral issue, but when the therapist perceives a moral aspect to what the client is presenting, which the client either does not see or clearly does not want to talk about. The therapist is then faced with two choices: She can try to point out that a wrong may have been committed by the client himself or by someone of whom he is protective, thereby taking the chance that she will be perceived as judgmental by the patient; or she can hold fast to the tenet of moral neutrality as a ready-made excuse for ducking the issue. Both choices carry positives and negatives.

There are three important reasons, all interrelated, for not confronting patient immorality. Such an intervention may cause shame; it may undermine trust in the therapeutic relationship; and/or it may abrogate the patient's self-determination.

According to Helen Block Lewis (1971), shame in the treatment situation is the greatest cause of treatment failure. The pain of feeling that one's therapist is disgusted or shocked by what one has done is never therapeutic. Causing the client more shame than he already has must be avoided by the therapist at all costs.

In addition to causing shame, feeling judged by the therapist will certainly erode the patient's trust in the therapist. This will lead to the patient either fleeing or just not opening up to the therapist, either of which means that the treatment has failed. While we will make the case that the therapist has to make moral distinctions in order to do effective therapy, he should never judge the client as a whole person. The adage that there is good and bad in everyone should always be kept in mind.

In a relationship that is unequal in terms of power—which is certainly the case in psychotherapy—it is indeed unethical for the therapist to use her considerable influence to try to get the client to do what she (the therapist) thinks is morally right. The purpose of confronting a client's immoral behavior is not to persuade the client to "do the right thing," but to give her a chance to explore with the therapist the moral ramifications of her actions. If the patient uses the discussion simply to figure out what the therapist wants of her, the confrontation cannot be considered a useful intervention.

Given sensitivity and respect for the patient and an absence of a specific moral agenda on the part of the therapist, and given rapport and trust in the therapeutic relationship, the arguments against therapist's making moral judgments begin to fall away. In fact, there are compelling reasons why the therapist should learn to make moral distinctions in the context of therapy.

1. *Therapists cannot be all that neutral anyway.* Neutrality is basically a myth, because therapists' moral biases come through to patients no matter how much we try to hide them. As London says, all therapies and all therapists value certain behaviors and ways of being in the world over others.

> . . . much of the material with which they deal, as clinicians, is neither intelligible or usable without thought to some system of values. . . . Moral considerations may largely dictate how they define their clients' needs, how they operate in the therapeutic ses-

sion, and how they define "treatment" and "cure" and even "reality." (London, 1986, p. 6)

I have long since realized I could never be completely neutral on moral issues no matter how hard I might try. It irritates me when people, my clients included, cheat the I.R.S., shoplift, figure out ways to avoid paying their alimony or child support, or declare bankruptcy when they don't really have to. I tend to dislike people who routinely abuse others. I like unselfish people better than selfish ones, and egalitarian and socially concerned individuals better than those who are racist, sexist, age-ist, or homophobic. Much as I would like to retain an attitude of pure beneficence when it comes to my clients, I have to admit these distinctions apply to them also. I generally prefer patients who tell the truth over those who are habitual liars. Giving unvirtuous clients a clinical diagnosis such as "sociopath" or "narcissistic personality," legitimate as that diagnosis may be, only slightly distances me from my feelings of distaste when a client tries to cheat me out of my payment, makes menacing phone calls to me in the middle of the night, or spreads false rumors about me in a fit of pique.

When I feel antipathy toward a patient, it is my job as a therapist to work through this dislike if I am to continue to treat him. Only if I accept the person fully can I hope to address some of his moral or immoral behaviors with equanimity. Usually it is not that hard for me to achieve empathy with a client. If I can listen carefully to the client and appreciate the nature of the particular psychic pain that plagues her, I can approach the moral issues in her story without rancor. I can bring up the moral concerns as part—just a part—of the fabric of her life that she and I both need to understand better if we are going to help her.

2. *While they may fear being judged, patients will not trust a therapist who condones all their behavior.* The assumption that clients want all their behavior, no matter how immoral, to be "unconditionally accepted" by their therapist is a fallacy. While some clients might feel mortified if their therapist "caught them" in some immoral act, others feel abandoned and uncared for if the therapist fail to comment on an immoral action. The therapist who refrains from commenting on the patient's immoral behavior will, on some level, be viewed with distrust, if not contempt, by the patient. For the therapist to be neutral when the client is being immoral conveys to the client that the therapist does not have the courage of his convictions to risk the patient's outrage and defensiveness and confront an immorality. Given such modeling by the thera-

pist, how can the patient be expected to develop the courage to look at his own behavior in the context of treatment?

3. *To suspend such opinions is to create a lie in the therapeutic relationship, which, in essence, invalidates the entire treatment.* Any inauthenticity in the therapeutic relationship damages the chances for the patient's recovery. While the therapist probably should not burden the client with details about her life, information relating to her perceptions of and reactions to the client are of paramount importance to the client's therapeutic learning. On some level, the patient will *always* know that the therapist is not being truthful, even if the moral judgments are locked away in the therapist's subconscious.

4. *Sometimes moral issues are at the heart of the dilemmas clients bring to therapy, even though they may not realize it.* The therapist is required to deal with the patient's whole self, not just the part (or problem) the patient chooses to present. For the therapist to ignore or withhold her observations about the client's moral self can be as egregious an omission as overlooking his sexuality or his professional aspirations. Sometimes the patient's immorality is at the very root of his interpersonal difficulties. A patient who continually abuses others or neglects their needs will be perpetually disliked and disdained. Neither his popularity nor his self-esteem will improve until he gets a handle on his moral responsibilities and becomes a "better" (in the sense of more virtuous), person, one who can gain others' trust and respect. To help a person stop lying, cheating, stealing, neglecting his responsibilities, or abusing others is not an abrogation of his self-determination, but rather is a necessary step in helping that patient learn to feel peace and pride within himself and to live in harmony and connectedness with others.

While it is important for therapists to be able to make moral judgments about patients' behavior, they should work very hard not to have opinions about things that are not moral. Many decisions clients face are difficult and may have serious consequences, but are not moral in nature. If a client without children chooses to stay with an abusive husband, I feel I have no right to make a judgment, for she is not abusing anyone else besides herself. I can feel and express concern for her, and I can work with her to determine why she needs to be so self-destructive, but it will not be helpful for her for me to get invested, morally or otherwise, in her moving out. By contrast, if she jeopardizes her child's welfare by staying, I have an ethical responsibility, professionally and personally, to help her see her moral duty to the child, a factor she has quite likely failed to consider.

ACKNOWLEDGING THE GOODNESS OF VIRTUE

While it is appropriate for therapists to maintain some degree of objectivity when their clients are struggling with issues of morality, therapists are, in my opinion, too restrained in acknowledging and reinforcing the goodness of their patients. Therapists are, I believe, not sufficiently sensitized to their clients' goodness: their generosity (**altruism**), fair-mindedness (**justice**), **egalitarianism**, or social **responsibility**. While these same qualities would be highly valued by therapists in their friends, family, or public figures, they might be taken for granted or even "pathologized" in treatment (i.e., altruism mistaken for lack of assertiveness or passivity). This is a clinical as well as a moral error, for, as will be shown in this book, increased virtue often means improved mental health. Throughout the book we will give examples of ways in which increased virtue denotes and promotes enhanced interpersonal functioning. If patients become more giving, honest, loving, responsible, and fair-minded, not only will they themselves be happier, but they will be likely to behave in ways that will enrich the lives of their family, loved ones, and community.

In contrast to psychotherapists, pastoral counselors see the recognition and fostering of goodness in their clients as an overt and important part of their role (Clinebell, 1984). Pastoral counseling teacher Clinebell describes eight characteristics of what he calls a "healthy conscience." It is positive and liberated from subservience to legalistic rules and moral codes; it is shaped by participation in a community and in consciousness-raising experiences; it is continually growing, is responsive to crises that challenge, is alert to its own blind spots and to new areas of human need; it is integrated—aware of the wholeness of the human; it is caring and nurturing of others; it is socially responsible, with a global inclusiveness to its caring; it is androgynous (i.e., egalitarian and mutually respectful with regard to gender); and it is concerned with the survival of mankind (Clinebell, 1984, pp. 165–166).

The "healthy conscience" is another way to describe what I mean by goodness. All the qualities of which it is comprised are, in my view, naturally fostered in the process of psychotherapy.

Chapter 2

"VIRTUES" IN PERSONALITY

ASSESSMENT AND PSYCHOTHERAPY

One of the major reflections of, if not reasons for, the separation of morality and psychology is the lack of connection made in clinical psychology between values and personality.

Feather (1982) defines values as a special category of motives, specifically "those motives that involve normative considerations of 'oughtness' and 'desirability' linked to an evaluative dimension of goodness and badness" (p. 87). Intuitively, we would think that values should be a critical variable in the definition of personality; yet most, if not all, personality theories make short shrift of moral values and behavior as aspects of character. Psychology has typically taken the position that values have nothing to do with personality.[1] The prevailing view is expressed by Hunter Lewis (1990) who defines values as personal beliefs about the "good" and the "just" and the "beautiful," and states that

> personal values are beliefs, not personality traits, and *no matter how interconnected beliefs and personality traits may be*, an effort to analyze the former solely in terms of the latter is certain to fail. (p. 8, emphasis added)

[1]A notable exception is Rokeach who has conducted empirical research on values since the 1950s.

16

Therapists seem to have been quite content to live with the ambiguity regarding what, if anything, personality has to do with one's values and behavior related to values. The fourth meaning of "character" in *The American Heritage Dictionary* is "moral or ethical strength; integrity; or fortitude." Nowhere in psychology or psychotherapy does this connotation of character appear; the primary definition—"the combination of qualities that distinguishes one person . . . from another"—is the only usage that can be found in the literature.

The separation of personality from morality and values is reflected in the absence of variables related to morality in the commonly used personality assessment tools. The psychopathic scale of the Minnesota Multiphasic Personality Inventory (MMPI) and two or three social judgment questions on the Wechsler Adult Intelligent Scale (WAIS—the standard IQ test) are the only measurements that might appear on a standard test battery that remotely concern morality.

Not only is the connection among personality, values, and morality in psychology quite fuzzy, but there seems to be considerable confusion in the field as to what exactly morality is. For example, when Kohlberg (1976) spoke of moral development he was talking about fairness or **justice** in a fairly abstract sense. Gilligan (1982) (using females as subjects in her research) proposed an alternative morality based on caring for others, which highlights the values of **altruism** and **responsibility**. Meanwhile, Bok (1978), a psychologically oriented philosopher, suggested that most immorality stems from lying and equated truthfulness (**honesty**) with positive morality as a whole, while psychiatrist Lifton (1976) emphasized an active concern for the survival of the species as the core of morality (**responsibility** on the societal or global level). These discrepancies are barely acknowledged in the literature.

Obviously, the field has labored with a semantic gap in the area of positive morality. The morality of the individual cannot be considered in personality assessment unless the construct of morality is defined in a broad enough way so as to include and unify all the above characteristics. I have drawn a term from philosophy and religion that, despite its pious connotation, serves very nicely in encompassing various forms of goodness. That term is **virtues**.

Virtues, as defined by philosophers Flanagan and Rorty (1990) refer to one's habits and dispositions in relation to others and in relation to one's view of life's overall meaning and purpose. Jordan and Meara (1990) describe virtue ethics as those that shape who one *is* rather than what one *does*, and that pertain to the overall purpose of one's life. Virtue ethics are nurtured pragmatically and with feeling in the context of community, rather than contemplated intellectually in isolation. Virtues manifest themselves in a person's behavior fairly consistently over time, with relatively little cognitive effort or forethought required. A virtue is more of a character trait than an isolated incident of behavior.

In this book we are only concerned with interpersonal virtues, those that involve people's relationships and interactions with other people. We are not concerned with individual virtues such as cleanliness, faith, and hope. I have identified five dimensions of behavior that are basically inclusive of attitudes and behaviors considered by most western cultures to be *virtuous in the interpersonal realm*. These are:

1. *altruism* versus selfishness
2. *responsibility* versus irresponsibility
3. *justice* versus injustice
4. *egalitarianism* versus elitism
5. *honesty* versus dishonesty (meaning lying, cheating, stealing)

Courage has been left out of this typology, because it seems that courage might be needed to pursue any of these virtues intensively. Care and compassion have also been omitted because they seem integrally related to all of the interpersonal virtues.

We will now explore the possible relevance of these virtues to personality assessment and to the process of psychotherapy.

A SCALE FOR THE ASSESSMENT OF VIRTUES

I have presented the concept of virtues as a way of organizing our discussion of goodness. We identified five virtues that have been given attention in the psychological literature: **altruism, responsibility, egalitarianism, justice**, and **honesty**.. Using these categories, what follows is a rough sketch of how positive morality might be clinically assessed. Table 1 can be used as a recording sheet in the assessment of the various virtues.

Criteria for Scoring

What constitutes the presence of a virtue, and what determines the amount or strength of that virtue in an individual? I have loosely adapted Rest's theory of four levels of moral development (Rest, 1986) as criteria for involvement in a virtue. The first level involves interpreting an event or situation as having some moral relevance, in terms of what actions were possible and who would be affected by each course of action. The

Table 1: Scale For Assessment of Virtues

Domain			Virtues		
	Altruism	Responsibility	Egalitarianism	Justice	Honesty
Self					
Intimates					
Friends					
Community					
Society					
Global					

second level involves making a judgment about the moral aspect of this situation. The third level involves making a moral decision about the situation—one in which moral values are put above personal interest. The fourth level involves following through on the action resulting from the decision made.

My scale assesses the degree of an individual's interest and involvement in a certain virtue and her tendencies with respect to that virtue. The assessment can be made of oneself or of another. Take, for example, the virtue of **honesty**. If a person usually does not even consider honesty worth paying attention to, he would receive a 0 on honesty. If he tends to be sensitive to issues related to honesty, but has little feeling about it and does not give it much thought, he would receive a 1 on honesty. If he tends to do some careful thinking about that virtue and/ or have some strong feelings about it, but does not come to any decision about how he might act, he would receive a 2. If he tends to go so far as to make a decision to act in a moral way, in this case, to be honest— even though it is not in his self-interest—we might give him a 3 on honesty. If he is consistently committed emotionally, cognitively, and behaviorally to that particular virtue—in this instance, is consistently honest even in difficult circumstances—we would give him a 4.

Let us look at how one might be rated on the virtue of **altruism**. A zero rating is given when a person would hardly ever notice he has a choice, opportunity, or dilemma arising in that area. For instance, a person who never gave any attention to the question of whether he was generous or stingy and very rarely did anything voluntarily in the service of others, would rate a 0 in altruism.

A person attains the first level of a given virtue when he tends to pay attention to situations that present him with a moral choice with respect to that particular virtue. For instance, when a person rating a 1 in altruism is confronted with a homeless family, she is likely to realize that what is going on might afford someone an opportunity for generous action (''Someone might give that starving family money if they were generous''), but is likely to forget the whole situation quickly.

A rating of 2 could be achieved by a person who tends to notice the moral issue, thinks about and/or has feelings about it, but usually does not make a decision to do anything about it. (''Oh gosh, it's terrible people have to be homeless. I feel so bad for them!'')

A rating of 3 could be achieved by a person who tends to notice, has feelings about the situation, thinks it over, and decides to do something, but frequently does not follow through with his choice. (''I'll donate some money next time I go by.'')

A rating of 4 would be given to a person who could could be counted upon to be consistently and actively involved in helping the homeless.

While it is not being applied in this book, one could rate the virtues negatively as well as positively on a scale of minus 1 to minus 4, according to the degree to which the opposite of each virtue is present, i.e., the degree of stinginess (opposite of altruism); elitism, such racism or sexism (opposite of egalitarianism), and so on.

It would seem that only saints would score high on all the virtues. What is significant diagnostically is not one's cumulative score, but a person's overall virtue pattern. It is interesting to notice which scores are very high and which are notably low on a given profile—and how this constellation relates to one's perception of oneself.

The imbalances on a person's virtue assessment are a fairly accurate portrayal of her priorities in life and suggest a lot about her relationships. For example, a radical social activist who scores 4s and 5s on **justice**, **egalitarianism**, and **altruism** might score a 1 on **honesty** because he lies to his wife and/or steals and cheats in the effort to support his causes. Another person who is a purist with respect to **honesty** might be indifferent to matters having to do with racism (**egalitarianism**) and/or not be particularly likely to give money to charity or to give his time to help his poor neighbor's children (**altruism**).

There is a very important second dimension to this scale. Each virtue must be considered in terms of whether it is operating on the *private* versus the *public* level. As indicated on Table 1, most of the moralities or virtues can exist on a number of levels from very closely personal (''self,'' ''intimate'') to relatively more public arenas, such as ''society'' or ''global.'' Again, it is the discrepancies and imbalances that make a virtues profile interesting, not the overall score. A person can be very concerned with and active in a given moral dimension on a public level and not at all on a private level, or vice versa. He might, for example, be concerned with justice on a family level, exercising discipline fairly with his children, and yet be totally unconcerned about justice on the societal level. Another person might work tirelessly for public policy related to **justice** (e.g., capital punishment or *habeas corpus* issues), and yet be oblivious to injustices committed against blacks in his neighborhood or against individuals who do not conform within his own family. Someone can be very **altruistic** with her friends, but be totally unconcerned and/or ungenerous when it comes to the needs of her community. A person in public office can be highly **responsible** with respect to his constituency, but careless or cruel when it comes to meeting his commitments to spouse or family. A person might be **egalitarian** with respect to seeing to it that his male and female children obtain equal opportunities, yet have little concern for equal employment opportunities in business or public life.

It seems one of the major factors differentiating us from one another may be the degree to which these virtues are present, absent, paramount, or peripheral as traits in our personalities, and how much they operate in our close personal relationships or in larger social contexts. These variables play a part in our image of ourselves as well as in others' image of us, and they may vary with other psychological factors such as self-esteem and depression. In Chapters 8 through 11, the relationships of the virtues and their absence to various clinical syndromes will be presented.

Impressionistic as it may be, this scale provides a vocabulary by which the topic of virtues can be discussed in therapy and in other situations as well. The patient and/or the therapist can assess the patient's virtue pattern at the beginning of therapy, and then see how these might have changed over the course of treatment. Some of the distinctly low or high spots on the profile might become targets of treatment. For example, many people labeled "codependents" or "enablers" are too involved in intimate **altruism** and not enough with social **responsibility** (see the anecdote about Jane later in this chapter and the section on the "too-good enabler" in Chapter 10). Using this chart, the patient's overly emphasized altruism would be duly recognized as a strength, rather than turned against him as an indication of his masochism. Appropriately respecting the enabler for his generosity to those close to him, the therapist can then encourage him to build up his altruism in the public domain, as well as working on the virtues of **justice**, **honesty**, and **egalitarianism** on the private and public levels.

The scale can be used projectively as well. Discrepancies between the therapist and the client with respect to their assessment of the client's level in a certain virtue or on the profile in general might reveal significant distortions in the client's self-image. An assessment of the therapist's virtue level by the client might yield interesting transference material as well as revealing interpersonal feedback for the therapist.

Quantification of the virtues and their dimensions is really not necessary for the scale to be useful. The virtues scale is first and foremost a springboard for a dialogue about goodness. Just reviewing the distinctions among the virtues and between the private and public domains is enough to assist the patient and the therapist in discussing the area of values in a way that is not judgmental or threatening.

It is the contention of this book that effective psychotherapy changes the client's virtues profile for the better—increasing virtues that are neglected and evening out the imbalances among the virtues and their level of operation in the private and public domains.

CHANGES IN VIRTUES THROUGH PSYCHOTHERAPY

The following anecdotes will familiarize the reader with how the virtues can be considered in the context of assessment and treatment. These stories depict the positive moral changes made by three patients in the course of their therapy.

The first is the self-report of a woman who was in group and individual therapy with me for several years. The interview in which she made these remarks was conducted a few weeks after her therapy was completed. During her treatment she did not know I was writing a book on morality. The second anecdote involves Bart, whose commitment to pacifism was deepened during two highly charged group therapy sessions at the beginning of the Persian Gulf war. The third story is that of Jane, whose presenting problem was the immorality of her husband, and whose therapy involved a number of significant changes in her own virtues profile.

Pauline's Report

After her therapy was completed, I asked Pauline if I could interview her for a book I was writing, explaining that I could not tell her what the book was about until after we talked. She readily agreed. At our meeting I simply asked her, "What impact, if any, do you feel that your therapy has had on your morality?" With absolutely no prompting,

Pauline mentions how she grew with respect to all five of the previously discussed virtues during her treatment.

In terms of morality as defined from expectations from my church, parents, and society, I would not say anything much changed as a result of psychotherapy. I still buy into most of that. A lot of my views on sexual morality are still pretty much the same. I still wouldn't have an affair with the married guy I talked about in group, even though some people felt it might be good for me.

As a result of therapy, though, I had to rethink morality, and I was constantly looking at what I believed. I kept trying to move from being judgmental to being more flexible. What happened, though, over and over and over again, especially in group, was that I had to look at my initial reaction which was "That's wrong!" or "This is how it has to be!" I remember I was very judgmental with Sandy [who was gay]. What I was angry at him for I would still be angry about today [having unprotected sex], but I did not realize how little I knew about homosexuality and how moralistic I was being—how he was not going to hear anything from me, because of where I was coming from. He was the first gay person I ever really got to know, and I ended up learning a lot (**egalitarianism**).

It was so helpful dealing with Marsha and her abortion in the group, when I had to be there for Georgette [Pauline's young daughter]. I had been pretty judgmental about abortion. If I had not worked through my feelings about it in group, I would have turned that already sad situation into a disaster. As it was, I was really there for her and, more than anything else in the last few years, it turned our relationship around for the better.

Going along with making snap judgments about others, I couldn't see when I was wrong. When I think back I remember how somebody practically had to hit me over the head before I could see what I was doing, particularly with stuff with Martin [her teenage son]. I remember when he was drinking beer and shooting at cans with a shotgun in the backyard. It took the group the whole session to get through to me how serious this was (**responsibility**). It almost had to be physical, invasive somehow! [Pauline's family of origin had been extremely physically violent. I don't think she was conscious of this when she made the previous statement.] Consequently, learning was pretty painful. Gradually, it is much easier for me to hear what people are saying.

I couldn't stand up for myself when people were abusive to me. I remember in group when you made Dan role-play Martin and talk abusively to me until I could hold up my hand, stop smiling, and say firmly,

''Stop!'' Well, it must have taken me half an hour to be able to do it. I couldn't really feel that it was not all right for him to be doing that to me (**justice**, accountability).

If not to grow is immoral, then I have become more moral through therapy. I was very stagnant until I entered therapy [approximately age 40]. I now feel a youthfulness of spirit and want to experience new things.

I have learned in the last few years what my purpose is on the planet. This may sound egotistical, but I know the world is better for my doing the work that I do [health care administrator]. People are influenced by me in positive ways. It is so different than before when I did the same work, but not for the same reasons. Before I was doing it so that I could get my needs met—for fame and fortune and appreciation from people. I was getting gratification that I couldn't get at home or anywhere. I still get attached to people at work, but I am not looking for stuff from them. It's much less selfish (**altruism**), even though I feel wonderful about it. I feel like my God said to me, ''Back then when you were doing all this stuff, I was not pleased. You were doing good things, but for the wrong reasons. Now I'm pleased.''

I have not told you this, but I have decided that in the next ten years I am going to move to the public sector and work in public health. I would like to be a part of building policy to solve problems such as AIDS prevention (**altruism**—global). I may work abroad somewhere for something like the World Health Organization, not driving a truck, but contributing my skills. I am planning my finances so as to be able to do this. I am also preparing my kids, trying to foster their independence so that they will be all right without me when I move on. I used to want them to be dependent on me. Now I really want them to be healthy and independent (**altruism**—intimate).

I had to become more **honest**, more willing to accept the consequences of being honest. I am more honest with peers, colleagues, employees. I am much more honest with myself as well as with people who are hurting me, like I said.

I am much more truly spiritual now than I was ten years ago, even though back then I was much more involved in the church *per se*, serving on committees, and so on. Somehow, I think this has to do with therapy. Maybe the more we look inside ourselves, the more we find a connection with God.

Pauline experienced an increase in all of the virtues in the personal and in the public domains, and she attributes this change to psychotherapy. Two other factors may be playing a part as well. It could be argued that the way Pauline thinks about herself and her life is a consequence of having reached a new developmental stage. She is in her late forties, a time when Erikson (1963) says we may extend our efforts toward generativity beyond immediate family and community. Having lived long enough to glimpse despair, internally and in the world, we try to counteract its pull by aspiring toward wisdom and integrity.

Had Pauline not been in therapy, she might have found the guidance she needed through her faith, friends, and support groups in her community to help her move to the next psychosocial stage. Another factor that may have contributed to Pauline's moral growth may have been the faith she acquired in the course of having to face and conquer adversity. During her years of therapy she endured a combination of losses through death, physical illnesses, legal and economic disasters, which would test the strength of any human being. Just knowing she had come through all that intact gave her a sense of gratitude and appreciation of life that, I am sure, bolstered her moral self.

For the most part, however, I think we can credit Pauline's extraordinary work in therapy for her enhanced goodness. One aspect of therapy that Pauline did not mention, but I am sure contributed to the positive moral changes was the unerring support she received from the therapy group. Rarely has a group been called upon to help a member through so many disasters. The caring and **altruism** she was shown by the group was a source of solace to her when others in her life had abandoned her. Being the recipient of such devotion was a new and, I believe, heartening experience to Pauline, who had always felt she had to be invincible and not need others.

In addition to all the interpersonal virtues, we see that, in her years of therapy, she also obtained a greater sense of purpose in life, increased flexibility and spontaneity, a higher degree of empathy, and a deeper sense of spirituality.

The War as Projective

The next story depicts two highly charged encounters between two therapy group members in which the male client, Bart, is confronted with some contradictions between his proclaimed values and his actual interpersonal behavior.

Before we delve into the story of Bart, I would like to make a comment about what I learned about psychotherapy and morality during the Persian Gulf War. While much of this book describes the reframing of issues from the personal to the public level, this story illustrates how it is possible to take moral issues in the world and use our reactions to them as data about our personal internal conflicts, moral and otherwise.

When the war finally broke out, it was on everyone's minds, therapist and client alike. In my work with my clients during that tumultuous month, I made a strong effort to hear what was being said about the war on two levels. First, I tried to respect the explicit moral opinions of members who expressed them. Second, I tried to hear each individual's statements as his or her own personal projection of core conflicts onto the war situation.

In the anecdote below, you will notice how much of their own personal material group members brought to the group experience of the beginning of the war. Recognizing this phenomenon presented me with a bit of an ethical dilemma. Was it trivializing the war to turn it into "grist for the mill" for individual group members? I decided that such exploration could only make the experience more meaningful for the members, and in fact it was a wonderful opportunity for us all to learn about the power of projection and projective identification. And after all, what else is violent conflict about on any level—personal, community or national—but the process of displacement, splitting and projective identification (see Chapter 7)?

The Violent Pacifist

It was Wednesday, January 17, 1991, at 8 p.m. and the U.N. Coalition had begun its intensive bombing of Iraq. After most of the group had gathered—Bart was late—Leanne told us that her brother had been called to serve as a medic. "I wish I could contribute myself," said Leanne.

"Have you told your brother how worried you are?" asked Deborah.

"No, I feel that will make it serious. He'll feel he might die," said Leanne.

"So he won't worry about that if you don't bring it up," said Deborah fatuously.

"That's Leanne's family pathology," I said. "Fear of being serious. Get serious and you die." (We all were familiar with Leanne's use of humor as a defense in the group.)

The group began talking about fears of terrorism, the environmental risks, Israel being bombed, and the fear of losing people who might be drafted. Fear of and anger at Saddam Hussein was, of course, a major theme, articulated most strongly by Frank and Joe, who saw him as the only culprit in the struggle. Their anger was palpable, while sadness and regret preoccupied Janet and Deborah.

Janet sighed, "How can people torture each other?"

Deborah said, "I feel pain for everybody on all sides. I ended up praying. I've never done that. It's bigger than I am, and it hurts."

Ted, an isolated depressed 59-year-old librarian, remarked, "I've been sort of identifying with the people in authority—Bush and Baker, feeling how much **responsibility** they must feel, and I wish them well."

I thought, though did not say, that there seemed to be two distinctly different perspectives being put forth that were gender-linked. The women, particularly Deborah and Janet, were inclusive in their thinking without taking sides. Deborah particularly seemed to feel joined with, if not responsible for everyone. Leanne was more concerned with her relationship with her brother than she was about the right and wrong of the war, and felt a responsibility to help out, even though it was not clear that she believed in the cause (**altruism**). The women's statements would resonate with Carol Gilligan's theory (discussed more in Chapter 6) that women tend to construct morality in terms of relationships and nurturing, holding the virtue of **responsibility** to loved ones and to the vulnerable as a higher priority than more abstract issues of **justice**, which are typically given greater emphasis by males. In general, the men saw the situation in terms of "good guys" and "bad guys" and right and wrong. Ted was no exception, but was more measured in his approach, identifying with the autonomous decision-making process undertaken by the "right side's" leaders. While, as we shall see in Chapter 6, Lawrence Kohlberg (1975) would have identified Ted's as a highly sophisticated moral position, it seemed a little too intellectual to the group and to the co-therapists at the time.

About 20 minutes into the session, the door flew open and in burst Bart—an eminent 37-year-old scientist who looked more like an MTV rock performer—wearing a little wool scarf, hair flying, breathless. Hearing the tail end of Leanne's presentation, he shouted, *"The whole thing is a crock of shit!* I know I shouldn't belittle the group for going along with this war, but I fear for my little brother who is draft age. There is no reason why a civilized country should be slaughtering innocent people! I'm going to Washington this weekend, and I plan to burn a flag and get arrested. And I'm wearing this scarf the whole war."

My co-therapist, George, said, "Whoa, Bart, how do you know everyone supports the war? You haven't heard anyone say anything yet."

"I'm sorry, but I don't want to be considered as part of the America that condones this. I'm still fucked up from Vietnam. I stayed stateside, but it was still a huge trauma. If there's a draft and my little brother wants to go to Canada to avoid the war, I'm helping him. Leanne, if I were you, I'd get all my money and tell my brother to split. This is a crock of shit and you're buying into it and so is your brother!"

Leanne was taken aback. Her first reaction was to get very angry. "Wait a minute, Bart! I feel like you want to fight with me. ('Are we going to have a war right here in the group?' she implied.) You're attacking my patriotism and my family's as well. What right. . . ."

"Could you tell us more about your experience with the war in Vietnam, Bart?" I asked.

Bart answered, "I wanted to be a conscientious objector, but my father [an abusive alcoholic] wouldn't let me. He said, 'No son of mine is going to be no goddamn wimp,' and he ripped up the papers and threw them in my face. He then called me a 'scum' and a 'rat' and a goddamn draft card burner. I had to be over 18 to be a C.O. without his permission, even though I was old enough to get drafted and go to Nam and get killed. I can never forgive myself that I didn't stand up to him more. I got a good lottery number and didn't have to go anyway."

"So you want to make sure your brother doesn't have to face what you did. You'll help him," noted Frank, another member.

Deborah said, "I can really relate to this. I protested against the war, and my mother [also an abusive alcoholic] was very upset. She said she would never love a daughter who wore overalls in public."

Struggling once again with the warped values of their alcoholic parents, at least two if not more of the group members were reminded of their right to decide for themselves what they believed was right and wrong.

At the end of this interaction I said, "Bart, I'm glad you brought this up. I hope that you will begin to take your pacifism more seriously."

The group thought I was trying to be funny, but I wasn't.

"No, I mean it. You are very bellicose in your pacifism. We need you, particularly in your profession as scientist, to contribute to making the world a less violent place, by helping people understand the unity of the planet. I don't think you can help us much until you sort out your beliefs as a pacifist from your resentment toward your father."

The group knew that Bart's father had treated him with unmitigated cruelty. He had beat Bart and criticized him unmercifully throughout his childhood. The father had died shortly after the conscientious objector incident took place. Bart's father's last words to his son before he died in the hospital were, "Get out of my face."

The next week, the group was temporarily waylaid from the war by some good news from Janet about being able to adopt a baby.

Soon, however, Joan asked Bart, "Did you go to Washington?"

"It's next week, but I'm going," said Bart.

Leanne said, "My brother is going to Turkey. I saw some footage of P.O.W.'s on the TV and I got so scared.

"Ours or theirs?" inserted Bart rudely.

"Now wait a minute, Bart," said Leanne. "This may be a long war. We're going to need some rules. I feel I'm respecting your position, but you seem to be positive you are more morally correct than I."

"I know I am. I hate the administration."

Deborah and I both said, "Sounds like everyone has to agree with you 100%."

Bart said, "I *won't listen*. It's too important."

Janet then said, "I feel like you're angry at us."

Bart protested, "I feel like I'm being attacked for not being patriotic."

Deborah said, "Bart, I'm not sure if you're burning the flag or burning your father. It's 'you scum, you rat' toward us now. It's here all over again!"

Bart backed off, stunned at the realization that he was behaving just as his father had toward him. "God! . . . I'm sorry," he said. He leaned back in his chair. "Gee this is so complicated. I really care for Leanne. I don't want to hurt her."

At this point Leanne began to get teary, "Bart, if it helps you to be angry like this, it's okay. I really do know you care about me."

"I still feel bad that I lashed out," said Bart. "I have so much guilt and fear about how much anger I still have at my dad. I still feel ashamed of the way I let him treat me. And I realize, I said I would work for peace, and I haven't done a thing for 15 or 20 years!"

"Exactly," I said. "That's why it's great you did this work in here—both for you and for the rest of society. It would be a shame to waste any more time not being a pacifist when that is such an important part of who you are."

At the end of the session, Bart went over to Leanne and hugged her, saying sincerely, "Leanne, I really hope your brother is okay."

This anecdote illustrates how unresolved shame and rage can contaminate one's moral position. Twenty years after his father's death, Bart's unresolved fury at him had stalemated him in his passionate desire to become an active pacifist. Through the group encounter, Bart began to separate his worthier moral strivings from his "hurt child's" desire to wreak revenge on his dead father. He began to work on his feelings about his father in the group as they emerged in the transference with the male therapist, George, and with his fellow member Ted; meanwhile, he began volunteer work with a group of scientists involved in designing civilian projects in the Middle East.

At least four of the five virtues were fostered in Bart by this experience. The group encounters provided an opportunity for Bart to relocate in himself the **altruistic** pacifist who had wanted to be a conscientious objector at 18. He became more sure than ever that war, for him, was an unconscionable wrong (**justice**). The confrontation forced him to be more **honest** with himself. Finally, Bart became more **responsible** in his pacifism, realizing that it begins in his personal relationships, such as with Leanne. He realized that being verbally abusive and intolerant with her was inconsistent with a pacifist stance.

From Moral Confusion to Values Clarification in the Therapy of a Couple

Although Joe was a pillar of his community, a store manager everyone could rely on, he had "cheated on" his wife Jane with various women for 30 of their 35 years of marriage. When Jane discovered this, she was beside herself with anger and hurt, but told no one. Seven years later, upon once again catching him in a liaison, she sought therapy to try to gain enough confidence to leave Joe. The therapist asked to see Joe for one or two sessions with Jane so as to get a clearer picture of the problems in their relationship, and Joe agreed to come in, but was not, at that point, interested in further therapy. After a few couples sessions, Jane was encouraged to join a therapy group.

Jane was filled with outrage at what she called Joe's "immorality." Everyone in Jane's therapy group agreed with Jane that Joe was a very "dishonest" fellow, and they could easily understand how deeply his behavior upset her. They also noted, however, that Jane had never told anyone in the family about it, and wondered why, if she thought he was so wrong, she felt it necessary to protect him.

More surprising than this, however, was what was revealed to the group by Jane about her own morals and values. While it was clear that Jane would voluntarily be boiled in oil before she would have an affair, she accepted in herself many other behaviors that others might find morally reprehensible. For example, the group learned that spying on Joe had become almost a passion with Jane. In fact, Jane had always spied on all five of her children, inspecting drawers, reading diaries, and surreptitiously following them in her car. When questioned on the "rightness" of that, it was clear Jane saw nothing wrong in it at all. While Joe's **honesty** was of great concern to her, she was oblivious as to how dishonest she was herself. "Joe may be a *sneak*," one of her fellow group members said, "but you Jane—you're a *snoop!*"

Similarly, Jane did not seem to find lying and stealing very offensive, even when she herself was the victim. Jane and Joe's 13-year-old daughter, Mona, stole money several times from her parents, and when Joe wanted to impose a stiff punishment, Jane would invariably talk him out of it. When Mona routinely lied about her whereabouts after coming home late, Jane did not get particularly angry, nor was she willing to punish Mona on these occasions either. On the other hand, when Mona was found alone with her boyfriend in her bedroom, Jane was livid.

Other areas of responsibility within the family seemed to elude Jane's attention and concern. Her 33-year-old son, Frank, was living at home, not paying rent, not working, and buying and smoking marijuana regularly. Jane kept avoiding the subject of Frank both with her group and with Joe. The group, the therapist, and Joe all felt the young man must be given an ultimatum regarding working and contributing to the family or moving out, but Jane did not recognize her "enabling" behavior or its consequences. Even though she was pretty sure that the young man was smoking pot in the presence of his impressionable younger sister Mona, she showed none of the moral outrage about this that she had shown regarding Joe's affairs.

In terms of her **responsibility** to the world outside her family, Jane also seemed oblivious. When Joe's aged father insisted on driving the car even though he was legally blind, it took her group a while to convince her that she had a responsibility to take away his keys and/or call the police on him, if by some chance he should manage to get behind the wheel.

As well-mannered as Jane was, she had few moral compunctions when it came to violence. When Joe, who had refrained from his affairs for a year, tried to resume a liaison with a married woman, he was swiftly apprehended by Jane who had been "tailing" him in her car. Jane physically assaulted the other woman in a public parking lot, an action for which she suffered not the slightest remorse.

Jane was the only child of an extremely domineering mother, to whom she was still dutifully subservient. Jane's father, who died when Jane was in her thirties, was severely alcoholic and very passive. Jane perceived her father as being completely under the mother's thumb, but she also thought he might have had an affair at some point in his marriage. In Jane's family "right" was what Mother wanted, and "wrong" was what displeased her. Late in Jane's father's life, he implored her to encourage Jane's mother to resume having sex with him. Jane, mortified at the request, refused.

Jane's moral confusion stemmed from a total lack of guidance in her childhood. Overprotected, while also being used as a servant, Jane was not encouraged to seek an education, formal or otherwise. As in the case of many therapy patients, there were never any discussions in Jane's family of origin about how to manage some of the moral dilemmas that arise in child or adult life. Morality was discussed only in terms of sex, with Jane's mother lecturing Jane that any woman who had sex outside of marriage was automatically a prostitute. Unlike their own parents, Jane and Joe tried to educate their older children about the responsibilities of sex—Mona missed out on this because she was too young at the time—but other aspects of moral education were transmitted haphazardly. Some guidance on matters relating to **altruism** and **responsibility** on the personal level seemed to have been provided by Jane whereas teaching the values of **honesty**, **egalitarianism**, and **justice** and virtue on the public level fell to Joe.

It seemed that therapy for Jane involved, at least in part, her learning to see herself not just as a victim of Joe's indiscretions, but as an adult who heretofore had been morally myopic, but who had the capacity to develop a keener moral vision and to make better moral decisions. In terms of our virtues model, she needed to work on fairness (**justice**), **responsibility**—public and private—and aspects of **honesty** such as refraining from lying and snooping. She was already very **altruistic**, a real strength, which manifested itself via her obvious caring and concern for people in the group and which won her much affection and appreciation.

It was important, as it is with any patient, to help Jane approach these deficiencies with the confidence that she could make substantial improvements, and to avoid making her feel ashamed. The biggest source of resistance to behaving in a moral way is shame, for if a person is ashamed, he will punish himself by not doing anything that might enhance his self-esteem or improve others' opinion of him. The therapist pointed out to Jane that many people, like Jane, have not been taught much about values and morality as children, but that there is no reason that this cannot be learned in adulthood. In fact, this an area where we all could benefit from an expansion of our awareness.

In Jane's case, the group was used to help Jane see beyond her moral blind spots. The sessions in which Jane was confronted by the group were always lively and resulted in Jane making immediate positive changes in three morality areas, becoming more **honest**, more fair-minded (**justice**), and more **responsible**. This is consistent with Haan's research findings (Haan, 1978, 1985) that discussions of real-life ethical dilemmas, conducted in a safe environment where all opinions are respected, generate intense interest and considerable moral learning on the part of participants.

A typical "moral session" with Jane will now be related:

JANE: I'm mad at Frank. He's smoking marijuana again.
GROUP: Oh, gee, that's too bad.
GROUP MEMBER (GM)#1: How do you know?
JANE: (*proudly*) I checked his stash.
GROUP: Huh?
JANE: Oh yes! Every morning when he's out walking the dog, I go in to his drawer and see how much is left in the jar in his top drawer.

(Several GMs laugh. GM #2 and #3 look upset.)

GM #2: Wait! I thought you told him he had to get all of the drugs out of the house or he could not stay.
JANE: No, I didn't tell him that yet.
GM #3: Does he know you are looking through his stuff?
JANE: (*smiling*) No.
THERAPIST: How do you feel about that, #3?
GM #3: That really makes me uncomfortable. That's just the kind of thing my mother did to me when I was a kid. Looking through my stuff without permission.
GM #4: What bothers me is that he lies to you, but you lie to him, too.
GM #1: (*sadly*) That's right. There's no trust.
GM #5: Right! And no rules. I try like hell to set rules with my kids and stick by them. My parents did that. They were lousy in some areas, but they were good on rules.
THERAPIST: Jane, you are quite quiet. Are you surprised by the group's reaction?
JANE: Yeah, they're saying just what Joe says.
SEVERAL GMs: Really? What do you mean?
JANE: He says I shouldn't snoop around like this. But then I say, how are we going to know whether he's smoking grass or not?
THERAPIST: What does he answer?
JANE: I think he just gives up when I say that.
THERAPIST: Jane has a dilemma here. What does the group think about that? If Jane gives up spying on Frank, how will she know if he's doing drugs?
GM #2: I think you should just ask him straight out.
JANE: What if he lies?

(*A few seconds of silence.*)

GM #3: Well, that will be crummy if he does. But at least if you stop lying and sneaking you will feel better about yourself.

GM #2: Another thing—you haven't done what you said you would do which was to tell him straight out that there will be no drugs in your house—Frank's, Mona's, friends'—nobody's. I think you are reduced to snooping because you haven't done your part yet—confronting Frank.

GM #4: If Frank is going to lie, make him have no choice but to do it right to your face. There's more chance he'll feel guilty that way. He doesn't feel guilty now, because he knows you are sneaky. He can just say, "Well, I may be hiding this dope, but she's a hypocrite—she acts like a thief sneaking into my room."

THERAPIST: What about Joe in all of this?

GM #5: He should be right there by your side when you make this ultimatum. He's been letting you do the dirty work. And I mean "dirty work."

In this session Jane began to consider a number of things she had not thought of before: that she was guilty of some of the very behaviors that troubled her in Frank; that it might be more realistic to change her own behavior than to try to change Frank's; that in correcting her own morally inconsistent behavior, she would feel better about herself, and would therefore offer a decent role model for her son and daughter.

Ironically, of the two spouses, we found that Joe, though delinquent in the area of **responsibility** and **honesty** with Jane, clearly scored higher than Jane on the other virtues. His contextual application of these values from private to public was wider than hers as well. Joe is concerned about **egalitarianism** and **justice** in his community and beyond. He was fair-handed within his family and in his community by voting, paying his taxes, and conducting his business with integrity and propriety. He was neither sexist or racist. Joe was well-known in the community for his **altruism, honesty**, and dependability.

As Jane became more confident, Joe, partly sparked by the realization that Jane might now actually be able to leave him, but also by some genuine remorse, decided to entered couples therapy with Jane. He seemed to feel positively about Jane and appropriately guilty for his affairs. He said he wanted help for himself and the marriage in order to avoid future temptation.

The proclivity toward extramarital liaisons in Joe's family did not begin with Joe. Joe's father did not just have affairs but was, before and after his wife's death, quite promiscuous. He had even molested two of his grandchildren, including Joe and Jane's oldest daughter on one occasion. To Jane and Joe's credit, when told by their daughter of this incident, they immediately confronted the grandfather, and threatened to never let him see their children again if they heard of him doing it to any child ever again. Once again, when sexual misbehavior was the problem, Jane had no problem swinging into action.

It would not be stretching matters to assume that Joe's sexual acting out was generated by the part of him that identified with his morally reprehensible father, but the therapist decided not to focus too much on this in the couples therapy. Joe had already committed himself to working on the marriage, and Jane wanted him back, so there seemed to be little point in dwelling on his past misdeeds. Instead, the therapist attempted to clear up some of the moral confusion in their family as a whole by drawing on Joe's strengths in the nonsexual moral arena. The therapist thought this might draw him out of the "culprit" role and restore some of his dignity in the eyes of his family. Since Jane had protected him by not telling the children about his infidelities, this was not an impossible goal.

It was clear from the early discussions in couples therapy that Joe had been frustrated for years by his wife's spying and snooping, and also by the fact that she had absolutely no concept of rules or discipline in relation to raising their children. She undermined every rule they made together, and virtually every infraction committed by the children went unpunished. Thwarted in his somewhat crude but well-meaning attempts to establish some sort of moral order in their household, he felt emasculated and disempowered. His response to these feelings, which he could not express, was to resort to the very behavior he had always found most repugnant in his father. While it provided sexual and narcissistic gratification, his affairs only served to expand within him a sense of shame that had been germinating since childhood. As he felt more shame, he engaged in the behavior more. As we shall discuss more in Chapter 8, the best way to punish oneself for what one is ashamed of is to do more of it, so that the shame, the worst of all punishments, will be worsened.

The therapy for Joe involved helping him become established as a moral leader rather than "sinner" in his household. First, Joe had to make a commitment to cease all infidelity and to stick with it. He was able to keep this pledge in part because the therapist gave him other moral responsibilities that only he could fulfill, given Jane's moral limitations. A major intervention by the therapist was to give Joe permission to make and enforce rules in their house. The therapist asked Joe if he thought there should be a rule in the house against snooping.

"Yes, but it's useless to make such a rule because Jane would break it," said Joe.

"Maybe she would, but does that give you an excuse for not standing up for what you think is right in your own house?'' queried the therapist. ''If there are no rules, than Jane cannot ever learn to hold the right person accountable when a rule is broken.''

Joe proudly announced at the next session that he had declared snooping off limits and everyone in the family, including Jane, had readily agreed to comply (**justice**). This was the beginning of a change of power and authority that seemed to work well for everyone, including Jane who gradually lost the resentment and mistrust she had been carrying toward her husband for decades.

Joe's psychopathology was strongly linked to his ''demoralization.'' Being moral meant a lot to this man, and his philandering was quite contrary to his own value system. In therapy, he was encouraged not just to refrain from behavior that his wife considered immoral, but to be proactively moral. With the therapist's help, Joe was then able to take moral leadership in other areas of family functioning. This helped his self-esteem enormously and regained him his wife's admiration and appreciation.

Meanwhile, in the course of group and couples therapy, Jane began to cultivate in herself a morality that had never really developed beyond the earliest rudimentary stages. She learned that snooping compromised her own sense of self-worth and eroded Joe's trust in her, almost as much as his affairs had damaged her trust in him (**honesty**). This realization motivated her to refrain from all such behavior. She became much clearer about her **responsibilities** as a parent, learning to deal firmly and honestly with both Frank and Mona, holding them, as well as herself and Joe, accountable for their actions (**justice**). Clear rules were made and punishments were set forth ahead of time and enforced when the rules were broken. Jane and Joe worked hard to learn how to stop enabling Frank and to let him learn to take responsibility for himself.

Jane even broadened her concerns beyond the highly personal arena she had hitherto focused upon, realizing that as a citizen of her community she had some responsibility to protect public safety when she had it in her power to do so, as in keeping the blind father-in-law off the road. She began to respect and assist Joe in his good works in the community instead of seeing them as threatening diversions of his attention from her (**altruism**).

Section Two

THE HISTORY OF GOODNESS

Chapter 3

AMORAL BIASES IN PSYCHOLOGY

AND PSYCHOTHERAPY

A traditional principle of psychotherapy has been that psychotherapy is a "science" and, therefore, that morality has nothing to do with it. The medical doctor practicing psychiatry is expected to think and function as a scientist. The psychologist "scientific practitioner," even when practicing clinically, is expected to adhere first and foremost to the rigors of scientific methodology and technique. Even social workers are mandated to use principles derived from the social *sciences* in their work with people. While all three of these professions carry codes of ethics to guide *practice*, the morality of the *patient* is not a target of change in the therapy, largely because it is not considered a valid topic for "scientific" consideration.

Despite this bias, some people have refused to believe that psychotherapy is a science or that mental illnesses are medical disorders. In the 1960s, Thomas Szasz (1961) offered strident critiques of the medicalization of mental illness, claiming that psychiatric diagnoses are demeaning labels without any scientific validity and that most psychiatric treatments, particularly drug treatments, are thinly disguised forms of social control. He pointed out that mental illness has to do with people's moral beliefs. A given diagnosis and the attending treatment, Szasz suggested, functions as a social sanction, a condemnation of the morality of the particular behaviors commonly associated with that diagnosis.

The underlying "scientific" thrust of traditional psychology and of psychotherapy, therefore, is in the direction of *amorality*. The amoral bias has at least four thick roots in Western intellectual history: the assumption of alienation, positivism, Darwinism, and individualism. These four biases greatly influence how human problems are viewed in therapy and direct therapists' and clients' attention away from goodness. If these biases can be actively ferreted out and questioned as part of treatment, however, opportunities for the recognition and enactment of the five virtues emerge.

THE ASSUMPTION OF ALIENATION

Tarnas (1990) identified three pivotal Western theories, two astronomical and one philosophical, which radically redefined our conceptualization of what a human being is and which account in part for the gradual removal of human morality as the target of scientific inquiry. He names these ideas the *"trinity of alienation."* According to Tarnas, the upshot of these three intellectual revolutions, which occurred over the course of four centuries, was to relegate the individual human to a small and inconsequential position in the cosmos and to promulgate the idea that there is little in the universe connecting human beings to one another.

The following paragraphs written in italics are paraphrased from a speech given by Tarnas entitled "The Western Mind on the Threshold" (1990). The comments in regular print are my interpretations of how Tarnas' "trinity" has contributed to basic biases in the theory and practice of therapy.

Copernicus

"The human soul has not felt at home in the modern universe," since before Copernicus (1473–1543) discovered the rotation of the planets around the sun and wiped out mankind's notion of himself as the center of everything. No longer "the central focus of cosmic meaning," the human became a "peripheral being in a vast centerless cosmos." Meaninglessness had made its debut in the modern world, and humankind's relevance in the overall scheme of things was in doubt. Freud once commented to the effect that Copernicus took the first big bite out of man's love of himself, the erosion of which was almost completed four centuries later by Darwin, who reduced humankind to a mere link in an interminable genetic chain.

Concomitant with the Copernican discovery of our cosmic insignificance, the Renaissance was beginning to flower. Intense interest in the humanities, the arts, and architecture during this time reflected great enthusiasm and admiration for humankind's intelligence, creativity, and political power. Perhaps the birth of our awareness of our insignificance spurred a compensating drive to grasp and realize our potential. Nonetheless, Copernicus' discovery that the earth was just one planet among many in our solar system and that our solar system was one of many in the universe must have contributed to the moral relativism of the modern and postmodern age. After all, if humankind's existence is not significant in the overall scheme of things, why should our conduct on earth be viewed as being of particular import? This attitude filters into psychotherapy, where relativism with respect to morality and values seems to be the rule more than the exception (Bellah et al., 1985).

Therapy patients may be particularly sensitive to this sense of existential insignificance. While they may unconsciously try to compensate for this lost and alienated feeling with narcissistic defenses, many patients are suffering from a hyper-awareness of the magnitude of life and their inability to make an impact on, much less control the world around them. "What, then, are the logical and moral implications of this realization?" the client wonders aloud to the therapist. "Is it hopeless? Should I kill myself? Should I run away? Does it matter what I do?"

I think that for a therapist or a client to ignore these concerns or to consider them irrelevant to therapy is to give in to the bias that people and existence are indeed insignificant. Such avoidance suggests to the patient that what he finds important does not matter to the therapist and, by extension, that he does not matter to the therapist or, perhaps, to anyone else either. When the therapist does engage with the client in these matters, letting him know that he, too, struggles with the same feelings of powerlessness and insignificance from time to time, the patient realizes he is not alone. Only the truth of the experience of connectedness can counteract the scientific truth of separateness.

Descartes

Descartes (1596–1650), French philosopher and mathematician, was the author of the famous statement "Cogito ergo sum," or "I think, therefore, I am." Descartes conceptualized a mind-body split, emphasizing the superiority of "mind," which is radically different from the inert "matter" of the body and the rest of the world. Descartes articulated "the experience of the autonomous modern self—separate from an objective external impersonal world which it seeks to master."

While there was an inherent power in the intellectual skill of Descartes' Renaissance man, he is conceptualized as alone in his awareness, unconnected to his unconscious, to his body, and to some extent, to his fellow man. The strong emergence of portraiture as an art form in

Europe during the sixteenth century (in contrast to the heavily populated paintings and wall sculptures of the previous century) illustrates the emphasis on the separateness of the individual that was building during this century. Portraiture also emphasized the head as opposed to the body, illustrating the Cartesian valuing of the mind over the body (thought over sensation) and the separateness of mind and body.

By Descartes' logic, life and aliveness is in the individual mind, whereas "other people," as well as the body, are part of the inanimate world. This is the genesis of the psychologically stultifying concept of the "other" as "object," a term that filtered into psychoanalysis two and a half centuries later.

Descartes rendering of the "objective" world as lifeless may have had alienating consequences for the rest of us, but it opened up many opportunities for scientists. The implication of Descartes' theory was that virtually everything but "the mind" could be empirically studied and verified. The mechanistic study of "facts" in a world devoid of spirit or mystery became the bedrock of the scientific tradition known as positivism, which will be discussed shortly. The facts to be studied by academic psychology became pieces of animal and human behavior, well-suited for observability and measurability. Meanwhile, vital aspects of humankind like thinking and feeling, not to mention spirituality and morality, were denied respectability as subjects for scientific consideration.

Thanks to Descartes, the universe, once enlivened with spiritual presences and moral directives, which could be revealed through myth, art, and ritual, could now be viewed as inert and devoid of any moral answers that would be considered valid by rational man.

The objectification of people, acts, and relationships may have contributed to the pervasive utilitarianism in the Western view of morality today. We tend to see life as a series of trade-offs of benefits and costs. This comes through in our therapy when we encourage patients to make decisions based on their ultimate usefulness for themselves rather than applying any moral standard (Bellah et al., 1985).

The separation of mind and body, the repudiation of spiritualism and ritual, the emphasis on the individual, the objectification of humans, and the utilitarian world view are all part of the Cartesian legacy, passed down in full measure to the practice of psychotherapy centuries later.

Kant

Kant (1724–1804) further dignified the human mind while continuing to alienate humans from their world and each other. For Kant the world that is known is constituted by the mind. The human mind cannot know the world as it is itself. If the only reality is the mind's own experience, then reality is always an interpretation. Humans will never achieve the goal of understanding the independent reality, because we cannot mirror a world with which our connection is so indirect and mediated. We are isolated from the universe in that everything the mind defines is determined by its own subjective character.

Perhaps this glorification of humankind's intellectual powers was a defensive reaction against the sudden recognition of our relative insignificance in the universe suggested by the Copernican revolution. In any case, Descartes and Kant painted a picture of humankind as individually and autonomously trapped in our own heads.

By tying morality to *a priori* philosophical principles, Kant would seem to have been making morality more absolute—less relative rather than more—but this is not the case. In fact, Kant considered any and all moral rules to be of a lower order than, or dependent upon, the principles of the system of thinking that created them. Change the system of thought, and you change the rules. Morality had become an artifact of logic.

There was, however, a window in Kant's relativistic thinking, which allowed for a richer morality at a future time. According to Kant's own logic, the mechanistic explanation of phenomena is in us, not in the world. We are not stuck with this paradigm if we do not want to be; we are capable of devising new schema with which to organize human experience and morality.

The assumption of a rationalist morality—that moral thinking is equivalent to rational thinking has greatly limited our conceptualization of what might be included under the rubric of morality. As it is, we are not sure what can be thought of as moral besides **justice** and **egalitarianism**, which lend themselves fairly well to rational analysis. Subjective and ephemeral human interactions like love, friendship, nurturing, and the other three virtues of **altruism**, **responsibility**, and **honesty** are not as well-suited for rational analysis; yet, they are powerful forces and should be understood for their moral as well as other psychological ramifications.

Some therapies are quite in harmony with the rationalist, Kantian view of reality. Cognitive therapy, for example, seeks to change the belief systems of the patient, from which, it is claimed, most of their problems derive. Family systems theory, drawing on theories of Bateson, Watzlawick, and others also give high priority to changing the underlying frame of reference or mode of thinking about a problem as a vehicle to solving the problem. Approaches that are harmonious with Kant tend, however, to be cut-and-dried—devoid of mystery, feelings, and art. There is nothing wrong with being rational and systematic in thinking about and doing psychotherapy; however, when the heart is taken out of the process the feelings of alienation in the patient, which are often the source of his problems to begin with, are exacerbated.

The Effect of the Alienating Trinity

"The cosmological estrangement initiated by Copernicus, and the ontological estrangement of modern consciousness initiated by Descartes were completed by the epistemological estrangement initiated by Kant . . . a three-fold prison of alienation."

Kant's recognition of the subjective nature of mind in relation to the world has been steadily built upon in the nineteenth and twentieth century by philosophers (Nietzsche), scientists (Heisenberg, Kuhn), linguists (deconstructionism), political and economic thinkers (Marx, Foucault), and sociologists (Weber). For all of these thinkers, every bit of knowledge is contextual, meaning is rendered by the mind, and the world beyond the mind cannot be contacted without being saturated by the mind's own nature. Freud also believed that, to a very great extent, what we experience is projection. Freud focused an even brighter spotlight on the mind as supreme, enlarging its scope with his discovery of the unconscious.

As a society we are like the schizophrenic child caught in a double-bind by the schizophrenogenic mother (Bateson, 1979). We have a vital dependency on the world, as does the child on its mother. We are encouraged to find spiritual and moral meaning while being taught that not only is nothing knowable or absolute but the universe is nullifying and soulless anyway. The logical conclusion we come to is, "Why bother?" Like the schizophrenic child enmeshed with his mother, we are trapped in the society that inflicts this cruel paradox and cannot, as Bateson would say, "leave the field."

As a result of the powerful ideas of the "trinity of alienation," the individual came to be seen by science, the culture, and finally by psychology and psychotherapy, as alone in, but apart from, the physical universe, and having no real connection to other individuals, save what could be mediated through the process of thought. We see, then, how such tremendous emphasis and value came to be placed on individual, rational thought and on logical discourse as the most, if not the only, valuable mode of relating and exchanging knowledge.

THE TYRANNY OF POSITIVISM

The "scientism" that many see and decry in recent psychology was thus with it from the start. . . . From the earliest days of the experimental pioneers, man's stipulation that psychology be adequate to science outweighed his commitment that it be adequate to man.

—Koch, 1959–1963, vol. 3, p. 783

To consider morality as a subject for study in psychology has been antithetical to the epistemology and methodology of positivism, which has dominated scientific psychology since its inception at the end of the nineteenth century.

Taking its legacy from the philosophies of Plato and Descartes, positivism was officially defined in the nineteenth century by French philosopher Comte as "logical positivism." Logical positivism asserted the primacy of (empirical) observation in assessing the truth of statements of fact and held that metaphysical and subjective arguments not based on observable data are meaningless. In the positivist framework, meaningful statements either exist *a priori* or are derived synthetically by means of scientific experimentation conducted by deductive methods (paraphrased from *The American Heritage Dictionary*, 1981).

Some topics of psychological study, such as physiological psychology and animal behavior have lent themselves very well to positivist methods. The positivist framework has typically been less useful, however, when psychology has attempted to explain the vast panorama of phenomena, which are basically invisible and/or nonquantifiable. Most of the stuff of psychotherapy has to do with ineffable aspects of experience, which do not easily lend themselves to empirical investigation.

Two of our most established psychotherapies, behavioral and psychoanalytic, were derived from theories whose architects considered themselves dyed-in-the-wool positivists. It is important to understand the positivist underpinnings of these theories and therapies in order to grasp why and how morality could not in any way have been encompassed in them.

Behaviorist Positivism

Early behaviorism represents the apex of logical positivism in psychology. The paragraph quoted below from Watson's revolutionary manifesto of behaviorism, delivered in 1913, represents the epitome of positivist thinking. It became doctrine in American psychology for much of this century.

> Psychology as the behaviorist views it is a purely objective experimental branch of natural science. Its theoretical goal is the prediction and control of behavior. Introspection forms no essential part of its methods, nor is the scientific value of its data dependent upon the readiness with which they lend themselves to interpretation in terms of consciousness. The behaviorist, in his effort to get a unitary scheme of animal response, recognizes no dividing line between man and brute. (Watson, 1936, p. 276)

Watson drew a very narrow parameter for the study of psychology, eliminating introspection, meaning, and consciousness. These limitations have prevailed to a great extent even to this day, with near tragic consequences. As the author of a six-volume history of the science of psychology, Koch (1959–1963) laments that it is hard to respect a science of human behavior that eliminates the study of so much of what makes us human. Many have felt as Kimble (1989) does: "Who can possibly care about a psychology that is silent on such topics as thinking, motivation, and volition?" (p. 493).

The positivist scientific approach in behaviorism has a number of troubling moral implications for psychotherapy. The positivist framework assumes no free will on the part of "subjects" or "patients." It is the goal of psychology to "predict" and "control" human behavior. Carried to the extreme this assumption that human behavior can be predicted and controlled by the psychologist, and *not* by the free will of the subject, implies that the psychologist is, if not omnipotent, a lot closer to it than other mortals. Such a line of thought has a serious potential for, and indeed has already resulted in, abuse.

Watson said he could cure and teach anything by means of classical conditioning (1930). Since, in Watson's view, only a psychologist understands and manipulates the process of conditioning, does that not make the psychologist the most powerful person in the world? The fact that Watson's boast proved hollow and only a small sector of human problems succumbed to classical conditioning, does not allay concerns that such grandiose self-attributions seemed entirely justifiable to Watson and to others within positivist psychology.

Skinner's view of the psychologist's power made Watson seem self-effacing. In *Beyond Freedom and Dignity* (1971), Skinner suggested that the psychologist become the mastermind and leader of what he viewed as a utopian world, fully organized according to the principles of operant conditioning. After discovering reinforcement and experimenting with it for a few decades, Skinner had concluded that operant conditioning was *the* answer to all the human dilemmas that religion, philosophy, and the humanities had ever attempted to explain.

Given behaviorism's underlying assumptions—that man is the same as brute, that the study of consciousness is impossible and unnecessary, and that there is no free will—it is not surprising that behaviorists would not develop a therapy that would enhance goodness or address moral problems. Although later behaviorists, such as Dollard and Miller (1950), Bandura (1978) and the cognitive behaviorists, at least began to allow for introspection and cognition in psychotherapy, the positivist bias still prevails in this sector of psychotherapy, perpetuating its essentially amoral direction.

Freudian Positivism

More than two decades before Watson's manifesto, Freud had launched psychoanalysis in Austria with the firm conviction that he was inventing a new and distinctive hard science in the positivist tradition (Sulloway, 1983). Freud's first training in research was at Physiological Institute, an institution steeped in the heavily empiricist von Helmholtz doctrine. Freud predicted that future researchers, if not he himself, would find physical substrates for all the "psychological" discoveries made in the course of his clinical work (Gay, 1988). Drives, psychic structures, and complexes, he was sure, would all be found to have empirically verifiable neurological counterparts.

Freud's was a very biological brand of positivism (Sulloway, 1983). He conceptualized people as bodies, more alike than different. Despite his lyrical and metaphysical descriptions of the psyche, Freud firmly believed its functions were a manifestation of the physical brain. Freud continually rationalized a lack of empirical data for his theories on the basis that future research would find them (Gay, 1988). When he came upon a human phenomenon that was particularly difficult to explain—free will, for example—he always presupposed it had a logical empirical basis, which had not yet been explained by scientific inquiry. What seemed to be spontaneous behavior, he was sure, had "intertwined causal threads that are too remote in origin, large in number and complex in their interaction to be readily sorted out" (Gay, 1988). By circular reasoning, Freud used positivist science's failure to give any clue into matters of subjectivity and experience as proof that scientific inquiry would some day find the answers.

Thankfully, despite his determination to make psychoanalysis a pure science, his own imagination rescued Freud from becoming trapped in the dryness and inconsistencies of logical empiricism. His writing bursts with feeling, whimsy, and empathy, and he explores boldly a myriad of dark, mysterious, and totally unquantifiable aspects of the human experience.

Freud's biological positivism was totally consistent with Western medicine of the nineteenth and twentieth centuries. Most of Freud's analyst followers were M.D.'s and thought very much along the same biological lines. Even though the medical model has been inadequate to the task of explaining human complexities and morality, it has held sway as the dominant theoretical basis for the development of psychiatry and clinical psychotherapy since Freud.

The stranglehold that positivism has had on the science of psychology and the grip that the positivist-based medical model has had on psychotherapy have together rendered morality illegitimate as a topic for psychological research and/or for discussion in psychotherapy. This enormous blind spot in both domains has left many puzzles unresolved and many questions—such as, "What is goodness?"—not only unanswered, but unasked. This gap in our knowledge, besides being enormous, is also highly significant, for it is just this kind of question that needs to be answered in order to insure the survival of the planet. As Smith (1991) says, "we have put our faith in empiricism and it has been shaken."

Chapter 4

MORE AMORAL BIASES:

DARWINISM AND INDIVIDUALISM

The following questions loosely incorporate a spectrum of beliefs about the relative innateness of goodness and of self-serving, or egoistic, motivation.

1. Do you believe that human beings are inherently endowed with an altruistic instinct and act cruelly only as a consequence of mistreatment or neglect?

2. Do you believe that human beings are born selfish and always operate from their own self-interest or in the interest of their kin, even when it appears they are being altruistic?

3. Do you believe both of the above are correct?

4. Do you believe that the human being is born completely neutral and that both goodness and evil are engendered entirely through experience?

One's answers to the above questions are a matter of degree and can be placed on a continuum. If one sees *just* altruism as innate and selfishness as acquired strictly through experience, then one's belief falls on the far left of the continuum. If one believes that humans are *born just egoistic* and cultivate apparently altruistic behavior only to further or preserve self-interest, then one's belief lies on the far right of the spectrum. The beliefs of someone who sees both altruistic and egoistic motivation as both innate and cultivated or modified by life experience fall on the middle of the spectrum. A "yes" to question 4 does not fall on the spectrum at all.

If you believe 1, 2, or 3, your beliefs are well supported by the theory of evolution. When it comes to the application of Darwinian thinking to human beings, known as social Darwinism, approximately half the field believes altruism has no intrinsic survival value; I call this *egoistic* Darwinism. The other half believes that it does; I call this *altruistic* Darwinism. Both of these are strong traditions in Western thought, and Western psychology and psychotherapy reflects both of these biases even though they are quite contradictory.

EGOISTIC DARWINISM

Two centuries before Darwin, Hobbes wrote, "Such gentler virtues as justice, equity, mercy and, in sum, *doing to others as we would be done to*, without the terror of some power to cause them to be observed are contrary to our natural passions" (Hunt, 1990, p. 44).

Darwin published *Origin of the Species* in 1859 at the height of the industrial revolution in Europe. He posited "survival of the species" as the central organizing principle and motivational force in nature as a whole, an idea that carried staggeringly important implications for morality.

Far more than Darwin himself, Darwin's student Spencer is responsible for the egoistic Darwinian perspective that became the prevalent form of social Darwinism in the 1870s in England and that was popular in America. Spencer's ideas were born out of the industrial revolution, *laissez-faire* economics, and physics, as well as the biological theory of evolution. On every front, growth, expansion, and differentiation were taking place. Industrialism, British and German imperialism, and American pioneerism in the West were all in full swing by the late nineteenth century and competition was brisk in the marketplace. Adventurism and exuberant expansionism were highly valued, and some clear "winners" were emerging on the international and economic scenes (Bismark, Queen Victoria, and the economic magnates in the United States). By the same token, huge groups of people were becoming "losers," exploited and ravaged by these winners, such as children (child labor), the American Indians, and colonized peoples in Africa and Latin America.

Implicit in Spencer's egoistic Darwinism is the assumption that goodness and "fitness," in terms of survival value, are equivalent. Social control should not be imposed by governments, for it will interfere too much with the natural selection process. Left to their own devices, humans' competing needs, desires, and impulses will balance each other out. The drive for self-preservation will dictate compliance on the part of weaker groups with stronger groups; the desire to secure allies and cohorts in the struggle against other groups or countries will prompt occasional acts of benevolence on the part of the more powerful groups toward the weaker.

Egoistic Darwinism promotes some positive values, which we tend to attribute to the so-called "middle class," such as hard work, ambition, family responsibility, frugality, and self-sufficiency (Hofstadter, 1944). These less brutal instruments of individual self-interest are thought to have emerged through the evolutionary net because they satisfy our inherent need to compete without the result of everyone being obliterated in the process. In this framework, values are essentially sacrifices that are made for the sake of ultimate expedience. Since competition is the game of life in the egoistic Darwinist view, all human interactions must be viewed in terms of their cost-benefit ratio. Bellah et al. (1985) have commented that this cost-benefit approach to life permeates our society and was the inherent ethos of the highly individualistic psychotherapies of the 1970s and 1980s.

Egoistic Darwinism has frequently been appropriated to lend "scientific" credibility to the perspective of those who suggest that governments need not intervene to make things fair and equitable and is used as a justification for imperialism and social irresponsibility (Hofstadter, 1944). Kohn (1990) suggests that there is a "reactionary political agenda lurking within sociobiology" (p. 24); Eisenberg (1972) puts it even more strongly, "Pessimism about man [and his basic motives] serves to maintain the status quo. It is a luxury for the affluent, a sop to the guilt of the politically inactive, a comfort to those who continue to enjoy the amenities of privilege" (p. 124).

While egoistic Darwinist assumptions have supported *laissez-faire* politics and economics in some quarters, these same ideas have caused others to conclude that immorality must be curtailed by active government control. As Thomas Huxley, a Victorian Darwinian biologist, stated,

The "cosmic process," i.e. the life of the Universe, and the "ethical process," i.e. the moral life, are diametrically opposed to each other. . . . The cosmic process, crimsoned with blood, is a denial of all moral principles. . . ." (Weiss, 1965, p. 87)

Two pillars of psychology, Freud and the behaviorists, both fall on the far egoistic end of the egoist-altruist continuum.

Mitchell (1988) stated

Freud regards what is distinctively human and special in mankind
as a tenuous overlay upon a rapacious, bestial core, which is only
with great difficulty brought under the control of civilized motives.
(p. 74)

Freud's view of the development of the individual, Mitchell says,
including the development of thought, is an exact "analogue of the
structure of Darwin's theory of the evolution of the human species. . . .
Phylogeny is recapitulated not only in ontogeny, but in the very process
of thought itself" (p. 73). Following the procedures of anthropological
and archaeological excavation, Freud's psychoanalysis uncovers the
most recent and more developed thought first and works it way down
to deeper and more primitive earlier material. On the individual level,
Freud's id corresponds to the primitive precursors of the human on
the species level; it serves as the repository of man's phylogenetic and
historical evolution.

Freudian psychology holds that individual human motivation is
spurred by biologically based innate drives, sexuality, and aggression
(and after 1920, the death instinct), which have no purpose other than
to insure the survival of the species. Freud conceptualized morality,
indeed civilization itself, as an unwelcome necessity, which evolved for
the purposes of containing the inherent destructiveness of humankind,
"like a garrison in a conquered city" (Freud, 1930) (see Chapter 7).

Behaviorist B. F. Skinner stated, "In the scientific view . . . a person's behavior is determined by a genetic endowment traceable to the
evolutionary history of the species and by environmental circumstances
to which as an individual he has been exposed" (1971, p. 105). Like
Freudian theory, behaviorism allows for no built-in altruistic instinct
and, in fact, implies a built-in selfish motivation. It will be recalled
that Watson's manifesto specifically equated "man" and "brute," each
striving for supremacy in the battle for natural selection. While environmental conditioning shapes the individual, the selection of what shall
be shaped and in which direction is determined by science's basic law
of nature, namely, that the fittest shall survive.

The theory of evolution, as we all know, shook the foundations of
organized religion. As the infamous Scopes trial demonstrated, Darwinism challenged a basic Creationist tenet in the Judeo-Christian tradition
and challenged mankind's need for a religious explanation of human
existence. At the same time, however, the theory of evolution happens

to resonate with some of the more deeply entrenched values of Christianity, and this may have contributed to its acceptance (Hofstadter, 1944). Egoistic Darwinism does not totally contradict the Catholic notion of Original Sin. The Freudian conceptualization of guilt as a reaction formation against the sexual and aggressive drives (see Chapter 7) is really not that different from guilt as conceptualized in Catholicism. Both Catholicism and psychoanalysis involve confession, but in Catholicism, absolution comes from the priest, whereas in psychoanalysis forgiveness comes from within the patient, with the analyst trying to assist the patient in working through his guilt internally. The individualistic values promoted by egoistic Darwinism—hard work, ambition, creative entrepreneurship, and family and group loyalty are considered highly virtuous by Calvinists and appreciated to a fair extent by most other Protestant sects as well.

ALTRUISTIC DARWINISM

As with egoistic Darwinism, altruistic Darwinism had pre-Darwinist philosophical roots. David Hume (*Treatise of Human Nature*, 1739), Adam Smith (*A Theory of Moral Sentiments*, 1759), and Schopenhauer (*On the Basis of Morality*, 1841) all argued for the existence of sympathy and altruism as a basic motivator of human behavior.

Darwin himself believed in the intrinsic goodness of humankind, saying that altruism could aid the members of a species in their struggle for survival (Darwin, 1871). He stated that "'the noblest part of our nature' . . . is itself securely founded in the social instincts" (Hofstadter, 1944, p. 91). He wrote that the origins of moral tendencies could be traced back to the lower animals, that "remote primitives practiced division of labor, and that man's social habits have been of enormous importance in his survival" (Hofstadter, pp. 91–92). Darwin was distressed when his writings were used to justify immoral behavior in the name of natural law. Protesting a newspaper article in which he was quoted as saying that "might makes right," Darwin stated that he did not wish to interpreted as meaning that "Napoleon is right, and every cheating tradesman is also right" (Hofstadter, 1944, p. 85).

The altruistic Darwinist perspective does not believe that the goal of evolution is survival at any cost. As John Dewey (1922) conceptualized it, human evolution moves in the direction of progress—the collective mastery of challenges. In his writings, Dewey pointed out the survival value for the species not just of altruism, but also of the capacity for compromise and problem-solving.

HOW TO ACCOUNT FOR GOODNESS

As will be discussed later in our section on moral action (Chapter 5), it has been fairly well substantiated that prosocial behavior—action in the service of another without anticipation of reward or punishment (Macaulay & Berkowitz, 1970)—does exist, whether it is maladaptive, as the egoistic Darwinists claim, or adaptive as the altruistic Darwinists suggest.

The argument about whether altruism is maladaptive or adaptive relates directly to the question of whether it is built-in or whether it is acquired through social learning. If altruism could be firmly established to be adaptive, then according to evolutionary theory, it would have to be seen as biologically based and cultivated through natural selection. If altruism were found to be maladaptive, on the other hand, evolutionists would have to assume that it was not built-in, but rather secondarily cultivated through social interaction.

In social psychology, William McDougall (1908) argued strongly for sympathy or empathy to be considered a basic instinct, but his theory was resoundingly trounced by the behaviorists of his era. J. Philippe Rushton tried to prove that altruism might be inherited, and hence built-in, by comparing approximately 280 pairs of identical twins with the same number of pairs of fraternal twins on the degree of similarity within the pairs on the variable of altruism. The degree of similarity was 50% higher in the identical twins than it was in the fraternal twins, suggesting a strong genetic altruism factor (Hunt, 1990).

The findings of Hoffman (1989) and Radke-Yarrow and Zahn-Wexler (1984), discussed in Chapter 5, that empathy is evidenced in very early infancy, would suggest that altruism is basically innate. Newborns cry when they hear another infant crying, even when they do not respond to other noises of similar loudness. Hoffman (1989) describes this as the beginning of global empathy, which is a general state of agitation in response to another's distress without any self-other differentiation. Several studies have substantiated the "negative faces hypothesis" (Wispe, 1991)—that people have an inherent sensitivity to displays of negative emotions by others. In these studies, subjects tended to involuntarily mimic the movement of cohorts shown to be in pain (Fultz, 1992).

Egoistic Darwinists account for the persistence of altruism in the species by the "free rider" theory. Loosely described, this theory suggests that altruistic genes are propagated only because they happen to exist in conjunction with other qualities within the same individual or in members of his genetic group, and that these other qualities, *not* the altruistic attributes, have saliency in the fight for survival. One scientific psychologist of this persuasion is Herbert Simon (in Adler, 1991). Simon believes that altruism is not an adaptive trait. He says that what we call altruism is actually "docility," which is *not* adaptive, but tends to look that way because it is frequently paired with good social learning skills, which *are* highly adaptive. The benefits of being a good social learner, Simon says, far outweigh the losses of being altruistic (docile). People (or monkeys) who are docile and survive do so because they happen also to be adept at social learning and accept society's instructions well. Altruism without good social skills, he claims, is nothing but irrationality—a poor tool for survival.

Sociobiologist Edward O. Wilson of Harvard, an altruistic Darwinist, questions Simon's claim that altruism is really docility camouflaged by good social learning skills (in Adler, 1991). He points out that docility coupled with good learning skills would render one highly prone to being taught to do stupid things, which would impair, not enhance, survival. Altruistic people are not inherently docile, Wilson claims, for if they were, they would have died out by now. It is altruism itself that is adaptive, Wilson insists.

In favor of the egoistic Darwinist argument, however, Hunt (1990) cites recent mathematical analyses and computer simulations that, by compressing millennia into minutes, have shown that groups containing altruists have a survival edge over groups without altruists in the short run, but that, eventually, altruists are wiped out by internal competition from the selfish members.

Two Darwinian theories, supported by scientific research, provide support for the existence of altruism. The first is *reciprocal altruism*, the notion that altruistic behaviors of various species and groups survive because they intermesh to the mutual benefit of both. For example, the grouper allows the wrasse (a tiny fish) to swim inside its mouth where it cleans certain ectoparasites from the grouper's mouth and eats them. Altruistic Darwinians explain the perpetuation of altruistic behavior on the basis that it serves to generate a beneficial response from another source.

The second principle supporting altruism is *kin selection*. Edward O. Wilson (1975) suggests that the tendency to protect the species by favoring and protecting one's relatives has been passed along through the course of evolution. The trait favoring kin selection carries with it the tendency toward cooperative and altruistic behaviors toward those considered "kin." J. Philippe Rushton stretches the concept of kin selection beyond literal kin. He espouses the theory that we somehow "detect" genes similar to our own—even in people not known to be relatives— and act altruistically toward those who bear them in order to preserve our species (Rushton et al., 1984).

IS ALTRUISM JUST EGOISM IN DISGUISE?

Until recently, most psychology research has presupposed an egoistic basis to altruistic human behavior. Hoffman's original explanation of prosocialism (1975), for example, conceptualized it in a classical conditioning framework—as a learned response designed to dispel the unpleasant affect one experiences when one sees or hears another in distress.

A major task for those arguing that there is such a thing as pure altruism has been to establish the existence of free will. The reason why this is crucial is that if nothing we do can be considered voluntary, then goodness and restraint from immorality cannot be seen as voluntary, in which case they are, by definition, not moral. Free will is necessary for morality and goodness.

Charles Peirce, a nineteenth-century U.S. scientist, paved the way for a psychological theory of free will by arguing that it is unscientific to pretend that there is not some element of spontaneity in nature (Hofstadter, 1944). William James, who received a solid education at Harvard in science in the early Darwinian years of the 1860s and 70s, but retained and cultivated a mystical interest as well, propounded the existence of an innate free will in drastic opposition to Spencer: ". . . there belongs to mind, from its birth upward, a spontaneity, a vote" (James, 1920). Innate free will, he reasoned, would be necessary for adaptation to new circumstances and thus for survival.

To substantiate the existence of free will and, hence, morality, Williams James argued for the evolutionary significance of the built-in moral inclinations or "sentiments" described by Hume two centuries ago. Again pitting himself against Spencer, James argued that sentiment and emotion were of the utmost importance in the perpetuation of the species. He believed emotions were the seat of morality. John Dewey (1922) also emphasized the significance for survival of the human intellect, emotion, and impulse, all of which he assumed were built-in at birth. Much later, another Harvard psychologist, Kagan (1984), pointed out that certain feeling states may be a "non-relativistic platform upon which a set of universal, or principled, moral standards can be built" (p. 123). Glantz and Pearce (1989) suggested that each of our emotions, even the negative ones, may have served a positive evolutionary purpose and, therefore, by definition, a moral purpose over the millennia.

Guilt and gratitude made us pay our debts. Sympathy and empathy induced us to give—and thereby helped each one of us to build up a fund of gratitude in others. Moral outrage led us to censure and punish those who did not live up to their responsibilities.

Envy helped us to make sure that sharing was customary and no one accumulated too much. (p. 34)

In the philosophical arena, Blum (1987) and Wallach and Wallach (1990) have each argued that the egoism-altruism distinction might be invalid anyway, given Hoffman and his followers' discoveries about their identical beginnings. The existence of empathy in early infancy suggests that egoism and altruism, at least at the beginning of life, are not in conflict at all but are, in fact, one and the same. Wallach and Wallach say that, even later in life, goodness and desire often unite provided there is autonomy.

In a thorough review of all the prosocialism literature, however, Wispe determined that altruism is really altruism and not egoism in disguise (1991)—they are separate phenomena. Daniel Batson (1990) created a model to test for the existence of a purely altruistic motivation in human behavior. He found that studies that offered egoistic explanations for behavior and altruistic explanations together were significantly more predictive of human behavior than models that just offered egoistic explanations. His work also showed, however, that we are considerably *more* altruistic when self-interest plays a part.

DARWINISM AND PSYCHOTHERAPY

The egoistic Darwinist framework, which lies at the basis of Freudian analysis, sees the core of the patient as selfish and always potentially aggressive—in other words, bestial. The best moral outcome we can achieve as a patient in Freudian analysis is to better manage the beast (the id) within us, by making the unconscious conscious. Neurosis is caused by attempts on the part of the psyche to inhibit unmanageable primitive urges by means of defenses that are often burdensome and self-limiting. Analysis helps us liberate these mute and destructive biological forces by transforming and translating them into conscious mental representations, dream imagery, transference material, which can then be verbalized to the analyst without injury to the analyst or to the patient.

Although she does not speak of it in these terms, Alice Miller (1984a) considers the egoistic Darwinist view as represented by Freudian drive theory to have destructive consequences for patients who undergo Freudian analysis. This view of the child, she says, perpetuates a fundamental error already present in the thinking of many, if not all, dysfunctional families. Many analytic patients get worse rather than better, because the analysis reinforces the message they already received from their parents that they are inherently selfish or even monstrous. The

Freudian message that children are born egoistic and selfish allows victims of parental abuse to blame themselves for their pain rather than
their parents, which keeps them from having to face their parents' cruelty or neglect. Children of abusive parents often try desperately to
preserve their idealized images of their parents, even in the face of
massive evidence to the contrary, because, as Fairbairn put it, "It is better to be a sinner in a world ruled by a god than a saint in a world ruled
by a devil" (1952, pp. 65–66).

Another problem with the egoistic Darwinism is that it fosters a
relativistic view of the world, which sees human interactions in terms
of cost-benefit ratio for the individual. Bellah et al. (1985) have pointed
out that this view is strongly held among therapists. The underlying
value of egoistic Darwinism, which has trickled down into psychotherapy, is that selfishness is inevitable and, therefore, acceptable, as long
as it is tempered by a realistic appraisal of pragmatic concerns and limitations. Since ultimately, one will "lose" if one is not willing to compromise, human interaction is seen to be in the service of "getting the best
deal possible." This is the perspective held by Fran's mother in the case
anecdote given later in this section.

Bellah et al.'s complaint is that therapists tend to equate goodness
with what the patient finds desirable. They often agree to help patients
achieve their wishes and wants without discussing the values underlying these pursuits. A patient may want help becoming more ambitious
or achieving more wealth. Does the therapist accept this desire at face
value, or, does he assume that the patient wants something deeper and
more meaningful in his relationships with others—either something that
he has despaired of acquiring or that he feels would be more possible to
attain if he had more money and power? The therapists of the 1980s,
Bellah et al. claim, shared the superficial values of their clients and felt
that the purpose of therapy was to help get what you want out of life.
"Life [as] a lovely banquet to be negotiated" (Wallach & Wallach, 1990)
was then, and may be still, the therapeutic ethos; you may have to give
up a few things and adjust your attitudes a bit, but it's all out there for
the taking, love included. The assumption seems to have been that this
is what we humans are exclusively about—meeting our own needs and
wants. The satisfactions afforded by giving to others and of belonging
to a community seemed to be of secondary importance to the therapists
and clients interviewed by the Bellah team.

Alfred Adler (1927) wrote that the desire for a social life, for community, was built-in. He noted that babies exhibit immediately the

> inborn social feeling . . . in his early search for tenderness, which
> leads him to seek the proximity of adults. The child's love is always

directed towards others, not, as Freud would say, upon his own body. . . . Only under the stress of the most severe psychopathological degeneration does the social feeling which has become firmly based in the soul of every child at this tie, forsake him. (p. 46)

Karen Horney wrote that humans are endowed with the propensity to self-realization, which will not be fully developed "unless he relates himself to others with a spirit of mutuality" (1950, p. 15). She discusses the "evolutionary constructive forces inherent in man" (p. 15). Fromm (1964) wrote of the capacity of [man's] nature for goodness and productiveness, but agreed with the Old Testament view that man has an innate capacity for evil.

Like their mentor, Horney, third force psychologists such as Allport and Maslow similarly saw a positive evolutionary force, which strongly implied a component of humane behavior toward one's fellow man (Maslow, 1971). Weiss, a psychoanalyst writing in the 1950s, said he saw no reason why evolution should be construed as weeding out goodness. He saw evolution as

a positive and creative development toward unity and wholeness as opposed to the split between the man and the beast "dualistic, or absolute standards of morality are [both] incompatible with a holistic and dynamic view of human nature. Man is an integrated individual; man is part of the whole of humanity and of the larger whole of nature. He is endowed with the potentiality and the need for healthy growth, creative self-realization and constructive cooperation with others. (1965, p. 71)

It will be made clear in Chapter 7 that psychoanalytic thinkers of the object relations schools have seen altruism and egoism as united, mediated through the natural dynamics of attachment and love in the infant-caretaker relationship. While altruism itself might not be innate, the infant's need to bond is. Because of the child's constitutional need to connect with a life-sustaining other, she embarks during her first moments of life on a journey of relationships, which soon become characterized, in increasingly complex ways, by loving and hating, giving and taking, helping and hurting, gratitude and envy, and all the other emotional springboards of moral development.

Psychoanalysts of the self psychology persuasion see the need for self-esteem as a primary motivator of behavior (Kohut, 1971). The innateness of the drive to acquire recognition from other human beings has been substantiated in research by Stern (1985), in which infants only hours old were seen to engage in behaviors that "pull for" responsiveness and mirroring by adults. Though the drive for mirroring is egoistically motivated, it may stimulate empathic and altruistic behavior in the self and the other as a vehicle for obtaining approval, but also as a way of connecting.

If you are a therapist, do you espouse the egoistic Darwinist model of the world? If so, then you should consider discouraging altruistic practices on the part of your patients on the basis that they could endanger him or his kin. You should point out to your patients that "nice guys finish last." If you agree with Simon that altruism is by definition irrational, then to reinforce it would be to foster "craziness" in your patients.

Even when therapists themselves are not egoistic Darwinians, (I hope, not too many are), it is important for them to realize the moral consequences of a egoistic Darwinist world view when they encounter it in their patients. The patient with such a perspective will view the world in terms of winning and losing, and would see success and goodness as virtually equivalent. "Might makes right" may be his or her motto. This person might feel almost morally compelled to succeed and particularly ashamed if he fails. The egoistic Darwinist patient may be quite concerned with his therapist's status in the profession and in the community, and will only choose and respect a therapist whom he perceives as being a "winner." In terms of clinical syndromes, egoistic Darwinism may go along with, or feed, narcissism, paranoia, or sociopathy.

In the following two anecdotes, Mabel and Fran each take a step in separating, philosophically and emotionally, from their families of origin, both of which are strongly egoistic Darwinist in their life view.

Case of Mabel

Mabel is a 40-year-old single professional woman who has been a client in therapy for many years. Her family epitomizes the egoistic Darwinian framework. In the following anecdote, Mabel is urged by her therapist to confront some of the assumptions inherent in her family's pessimistic view of humankind.

Mabel's family consists of her mother, an elderly widow, who for the past 40 years has ventured out of the house about four times a year; her developmentally disabled older sister, who never leaves the house; and her brother, 36, who has graduated from college but does not work. The sister has not visited a dentist or a doctor since she was a little girl, and has very poor hygienic habits. All social services that Mabel has tried to bring to bear have been adamantly refused by the rest of the family. While Mabel pays her mother for rent, food, and a good proportion of the other bills, her brother and sister contribute nothing.

While everyone outside of her home likes and respects Mabel, she feels totally unappreciated by her family, who frequently taunt her in her efforts to better herself. Mabel, having scrupulously saved her money, was seriously pursuing the option of buying a house and moving out. The family had reacted to this with their usual derision, probably believing she would never do it. Because Mabel is so responsible and pleasant, friends had recently begun inviting her to "house-sit" for them, something that Mabel had enjoyed because it gave her a "dry run" at living alone. When she told the family of an offer she received to stay in a nice house in a nearby town for a month, she received the following comments, which she wrote down for her therapist.

"You should charge them."

"You should use all their things."

"Hmmmph, I'll bet they have money" (insinuating, Mabel thought, that it was acquired by not-so-honest means).

"They're using you."

"You're taking a chance, too. A burglar could break in while you're there."

The reason Mabel took such notice of these comments is that they related to a conversation she had had with her therapist a few days earlier about guilt. Mabel had mentioned that, while she was no longer afraid of living alone, she was staying home out of guilt. Reflecting on Mabel's Catholic background, the therapist asked her if she believed in original sin. She said, yes, people are born selfish, and the only reason people do good things for others is for hidden selfish reasons such as avoiding guilt.

Her family's comments about the house-sitting once again called Mabel's attention to the fact that goodness for its own sake did not exist in the rest of her family's mind. She recognized how much she herself operated from this belief, assuming that her own generous and responsible behavior would disappear unless compelled by guilt. She looked doubtful as the therapist cited several examples of Mabel's own behavior over the years that did not seem to fit under the category of guilt-avoidance, particularly actions on behalf of her friends for whom she readily felt empathy and cheerfully helped when they were in need.

The therapist also brought up an angle on the guilt matter that Mabel had not thought of. "There are a number of things one might feel guilty about in your situation other than the wish to leave home," the therapist mused.

"What do you mean?" queried Mabel.

"Well, there are a couple of potentially moral issues here. One involves your responsibilities to your family, but another involves your responsibilities to the rest of the world. I gather you have always considered the more personal responsibilities of higher value. Now, granted, you would not feel comfortable deserting them, for you have committed yourself to their financial well-being and to some personal involvement as well. But, one might say that meeting their needs is not your only responsibility. You have administrative and communication skills that would be of great use to causes which might be just as worthy. Your friends and community need you, too, yet they receive little of your time. Is it moral not to offer your gifts where they might be actually appreciated and therefore better utilized?"

Mabel left the session cheerfully so the therapist did not know she had touched a nerve until a few days later when she received the following letter.

> What you said last session was the cruelest thing you ever said to me. I would be totally justified in never returning to therapy with you.
>
> But just in case I do want to come back, please hold my Tuesday appointment.
>
> Sincerely,
> Mabel

When Mabel appeared promptly the following Tuesday, the therapist said, "So, Mabel, what in the world did I say that made you so upset?"

"I don't know," said Mabel. "But it was terrible, whatever it was. Funny, though, I'm not angry anymore."

"You don't know!" said the therapist astonished.

"Not really. But you see, something happened in the meantime that changed my feelings about it all.

"My first cousin, my mother's niece, a woman in her forties, died this week of cancer. She was a very, very nice woman, with two young children and a nice husband who really loved her. When I told my mother, she said, 'Hmmph, I knew she shouldn't have had her kids so late. That's probably what killed her.'

"I went out and bought a card and made all of them [her family] sign it, and mailed it. Then I made plans to attend the funeral. I asked my mother if she wanted to go, but of course she said no. She bitched at me for going. 'Why do you want to go to that? You don't have to go. We sent them a card.' ''

"I felt very angry and sad," Mabel continued. "I realized I was going to the funeral not out of guilt, but out of affection for my cousin and her family. They are good people. They don't just do things out of guilt or to serve themselves. And neither do I. And you know what else? I really want to move away from home now. I don't want to be like them anymore."

Whether or not Mabel ultimately moved out is of less importance than the fact that she was able to take a step back from her family's negative egoistic Darwinian perspective. Even though she was angry and frightened at first, Mabel was able to "take in" the therapist's message that she could make her own choices about what was moral. She began to see how the family projected its own selfishness and insularity onto the world, and to recognize that she had had plenty of first-hand experience with human goodness, despite her mother's claims that there is no such thing. Soon after this, Mabel began volunteer work in her community where she and everyone else quickly gleaned how great a contribution she could make.

In the process of questioning her family's egoistic Darwinism and in clarifying her own beliefs on the matter of inherent good versus evil, Mabel clearly demonstrated an increase in her level of public **altruism** and **responsibility**, while sharpening her sense of **justice** and **egalitarianism**. Extending her altruistic efforts to friends and to her community, where it was welcomed, greatly enhanced Mabel's self-esteem, while having a more secure sense of right and wrong helped her to stand up more forcefully to her family's criticisms and manipulations.

She Gave Away Her Brains

Fran, age 50, was a superb teacher of some renown in her city. She sought therapy for the first time with a therapist with whom she had had some peripheral contact when the therapist was working as a teacher 20 years earlier.

The therapist was glad to see Fran after all these years, but immediately noticed that she looked terrible. Her skin was blotchy from crying, her face puffy, and she had gained a lot of weight. Since Fran had mentioned on the phone that she had had a hysterectomy, the therapist assumed that her state of disarray was a consequence of cancer and recovery, but this was not what Fran wished to discuss.

"I want to quit my job," said Fran. "In fact, I've been trying to quit for the last 10 years. I have a love-hate relationship with teaching. I feel so desperate. I'm so depressed about it, and my husband, who was supportive about the cancer and all, has no patience with me. I mope around. I don't correct my papers." Fran went on to explain about the difficult conditions under which she had been working, with kids coming to school high, and with poor preparation in the lower grades.

"Burn-out?" the therapist queried.

"I guess so," but then Fran went on to say that she was currently taking classes to become certified in early education and work with the gifted. It turned out she would be ready to take a job in this area in the fall, and this was February. She was also taking a course relating the arts and math and was going to attempt some curriculum work in that area. Since Fran had such a great reputation, all of these dreams were probably going to come true, so it was puzzling to the therapist that she was so desperate about having to teach for just four more months at her current school.

"I don't get anything back from teaching anymore."

"But you will when you change jobs, won't you?"

"Mmmmm. Well, I want to work in a think tank with creative people."

"Well, isn't that what you will be doing in your curriculum development work?" the therapist asked, even more confused.

"I just want to work in a think tank, maybe in a corporation or something."

The therapist decided to get off the teaching subject for the time being, and explored her feelings about the cancer and the recovery. Fran decided to take a couple of weeks off, exercise, rest, get her hormones and thyroid checked, and if she did not feel better, go for a consultation for psychotropic medications.

The second session, Fran looked a little better, having begun her leave of absence. The therapist took a detailed history, and learned that Fran was an only child of an enmeshed couple and that her critical and domineering mother had been a source of aggravation and pain to Fran all her life. Fran said she had great difficulty being assertive with her mother, as did her father. Not thinking this was particularly unusual, the therapist remarked that sometimes "mother issues" are stimulated when a woman goes through a radical body change. This produced little reaction. When Fran talked about her mother, she talked very meekly with a silly little smile on her face.

The third session, Fran was back to being extremely depressed about teaching. It was clear that it was not just the difficult present job that she wanted to leave, but education in general. Yet, every time she said, "I want to leave teaching" tears would come to her eyes. Inwardly, the therapist was upset that Fran might actually leave the profession, which needed her so badly. The therapist's own guilt for having left teaching was operating, combined with a keen sense of loss that the therapist knew Fran's quitting would represent for so many students and parents in the future.

The therapist said it seemed odd that Fran was making all these creative plans in education, if what she wanted to do was to get out of it. We went back to talking about her mother, and a fuller picture of this rather unpleasant woman emerged.

"This woman is so selfish that absolutely no one likes her. She told us when she dies not to give the furniture to the Salvation Army but to chop it all up and burn it. She said she didn't want anyone to get it for free or for cheap. She thinks I was stupid to marry my husband because he's Italian. She hates Italians even more than blacks.

"She always hated my teaching. She always thought I could do better, make more money and have a lot of power. 'You're smart in school and dumb in life,' is something she still says to me. I have a high IQ and was in Mensa and everything and she thought I should be a doctor."

I asked Fran to speak as her mother would to her.

"You're giving away your brains!" Fran bellowed as mother.

"Could you respond to your mother?" the therapist asked, suggesting she move to a different seat.

Fran switched seats and stared blankly, tears rushing to her eyes. "I can't talk to her. I still can't talk to her. After all these years." She was in despair.

"I'm not sure anyone can talk to your mother, Fran," the therapist said. "I think you need to talk to yourself, to the part of you that thinks the way she does, that you're getting ripped off, because you have chosen a profession in which you serve others."

"Fran," the therapist continued. "Do you know anyone anywhere who does what you do better than you do?"

"I guess not," she said. "But I don't feel like I'm getting anything back."

"There's mother again," the therapist said. "In teaching, as in social work, the ministry, medicine, there can be long periods where we don't get much back. Right now, it feels like a dry well, but soon it will be more fun and creative. Even if it weren't going to get better, though, is your gift yours to throw away?"

Here the therapist was no longer speaking from a guilty need to have Fran stay in teaching, but was on firm ground. "I think that I have a gift for psychotherapy, and I believe I would do it for free, gladly, if I had to."

Before Fran could answer, the therapist said urgently, "What was the name of that teacher who died?" the therapist was thinking of a man at Fran's school whom the therapist had met a few times, who many friends had said was a tireless teacher. One needed only to meet this man to feel the wonder and confidence he fostered in his students. He had been a mentor of Fran's in the 1970s. The therapist had heard that he had recently died of cancer at age 55.

"Jack!" she gasped, clearly amazed that the therapist had thought of him.

"Yes. What do you suppose was his epitaph?" the therapist asked.

Fran burst into tears. "'He built people!'" she exclaimed. "Many people say I am a lot like him," she added quietly.

"I'm sure that's true," the therapist said.

Later, Fran commented, "Gosh, what I have is so valuable, and yet I could think of taking it and destroying it . . . to be a wonderful daughter to my mother . . . I guess I am countering some of the rottenness my mother dumps on the world by doing some good."

The next week, Fran had decided to go back to teaching. She seemed very happy in her resolve, but suddenly, the night before returning to work, she became depressed again. In her therapy session, the therapist explored what had set her back. Fran reported an unsatisfying phone conversation with a friend at work. The friend had said Fran "was crazy for not taking as much paid leave as she could get."

"Uh-oh, Fran," the therapist said, smiling. "Here you go again. 'Smart in school, stupid in life, and giving away your brains.'" Fran laughed and laughed. "No, Mom," she said. "I'm good at what I do, and it is worth doing."

Fran finished out the school year with enthusiasm. The next summer she decided she did not want to change schools after all, but rather was happy to continue "giving away her brains" at her current location, where she was badly needed and much appreciated.

INDIVIDUALISM

In the late 1980s hit Broadway play, *The Heidi Chronicles*, Wendy Wasserstein tracks the journey of a well-educated, sweet, and unimaginative woman from her prep school years in the late 1960s through the 70s and into the 80s. At the end of the play, having had her heart broken several times each decade by the same narcissistic man, Heidi opts for having a baby by artificial insemination and raising it alone, while she works at home as an editor. The last scene finds her cradling her baby, proud that she has at last achieved what she could not find in the context of her people-pleasing life up until now: *absolute autonomy*.

At the beginning of the play, Heidi seems like she is about to get a bit involved in the world, as she gets dragged to some anti-war protests by her boyfriend, but by the second act she has already grown out of any need to change the world. Her intellectual and moral sensibilities offended by the competitive acquisitive life of the late seventies and eighties, she continues to pine after the same selfish boyfriend, now married, and becomes increasingly depressed. A sensible, up-to-date woman, she enters therapy and works hard on her self-esteem, so she can learn not to be dependent on anybody and, therefore, not have to adopt their crass manners and selfish values.

The value of individualism, so taken for granted in our time, is drummed in heavily throughout *The Heidi Chronicles*, while the notion of community is mocked. Groups of any kind are shown to be bad business. They bring out the worst in everybody, except for incorruptible Heidi, who feels "bummed out" with and left out of every group she tries to join. The war protesters are depicted as chaotic and narcissistic, her work cohorts are cut-throat, while the consciousness-raising group Heidi joins consists of female caricatures ("butch," "bitch" and sickly-sweet earthmother).

A corollary to the anti-communitarian message in the play is the idea that morality is a totally personal thing. Heidi and her gay friend seem morally triumphant when, at the end of the play, they remove themselves from a decadent society—while still enjoying its material resources, of course—and from the world of relationships as well. Why try to change the world, when you can live guilt- and hassle-free, with a few people around who agree with you on just about everything?

If you are a therapist, you might want to consider the following question: If Heidi, at the end of the play, had just completed therapy with you, would you be proud?

The individualist bias is not universal; it is culturally and historically determined. The moralities of various cultures fall into three categories: individually-based, also called *"rights-based"*; *"duty-based,"* which is lodged in a hierarchical system that provides privilege for the powerful and protection for the weak; and *"honor-based,"* which arises when a group bands together for mutual avoidance of shame and protection of honor (Shweder et al., 1987). Western morality is heavily rights-based, with emphasis on the rights of the individual. While the honor-based model is more prevalent in Arab countries, we are certainly not exempt

from it here in the United States, where "macho" values often supersede egalitarianism or concern for the welfare of others. For the most
part, however, the individualistic, rights-based ethos pervades our culture, including our systems of psychotherapy.

In the seventeenth and eighteenth century respectively, two philosophers represented two distinct strands of Western individualism. John
Locke (1632–1704), whose ideas influenced the formation of the United
States government, saw the individual as prior to society; society only
comes into existence through the voluntary contract of individuals, all
of whom are trying to maximize their own self-interest. This utilitarian
view of human interaction has filtered into psychotherapy (Bellah et al.,
1985, 1991).

French philosopher Jean Rousseau (1712–1778) also saw the individual as prior to society, but he pictured a very different kind of individual, one who had a natural inclination to be with and relate to others.
Rousseau believed that if people are just left alone, they naturally create
harmonious and mutually beneficial arrangements with one another.
For Rousseau, the root of evil in society is meddling with the individual's tendency toward goodness. We can see the legacy of Rousseau's
romantic ideals in the humanistic psychotherapies of Fromm and Maslow and subsequent clinicians such as Fritz Perls, founder of Gestalt
therapy, who placed the highest possible premium on individualism,
particularly autonomy. Perls' famous edict "You do your thing; I'll do
mine; and if we happen to meet . . ." epitomizes the individualistic
ethos as it later became applied to humanistic psychotherapies in the
1960s.

The discoveries of Darwin supported both of these contrasting individualistic philosophies. Egoistic Darwinism echoed Locke's theories,
while altruistic Darwinism dovetailed nicely with Rousseau's philosophy.

As we have seen, beginning in the early Renaissance, a succession
of astronomical and other scientific discoveries up to and including Darwin's theory of evolution, seriously challenged man's sense of specialness in the universe. Darwinism threw into question the Judeo-Christian
assumption about mankind as a species apart, presenting scientific evidence that humans were just another link on the long chain of life.
These insights were combined with an increasing sense of the vast numbers and different types of people in the world; a recognition of the
potential of technology to accomplish as much or more than humans in
many areas, brought into question the power of humans as such.

Gaylin (1990) suggests that the kind of exaggerated individualism we see in Western society today arose in the nineteenth century as a narcissistic compensation for increasing feelings of powerlessness, lack of specialness, and anonymity fostered by the industrial revolution. In a world where few people could be special, the quest for individual identity and distinctiveness was intently pursued through competition for the acquisition of individual wealth and power. Few Western voices opposed individualism as a primary value in the nineteenth century, with the notable exception of Marx, whose solution to the problem of the growing dehumanization of the worker was less individualism and greater joining together for the benefit of all. Individualist values were bolstered in the twentieth century when the horrific abuse of power by the totalitarian collectivist governments of fascism and communism greatly intensified the desire to preserve individual rights in those societies fortunate enough to preserve their freedom.

Bellah et al. (1985) interviewed 200 people from "middle America" to learn "what resources Americans have for making sense of their lives, how they think about themselves and their society, and how their ideas relate to their actions" (p. ix). They wanted to get at the nature of public and private life in America. The team concluded that modern culture is a "culture of separation" (p. 277) in which an overemphasis on autonomy and individual rights has led to fragmentation of the society. There is little sense of community, or even commonality, in people's private lives. In the intellectual realm, every independent scientific discipline has its own language and method, destroying any sense of coherence in our perception of life and nature.

Wallach and Wallach (1990) call the morality that results from the separationist, individualist bias "minimalist morality." What we have today, the Wallachs say, is a sort of hands-off morality, which coincides with the libertarian assumption that the greatest good we as humans can achieve resides in our capacity to do no harm, to respect the physical and psychological space of others. This value is reflected in our laws, few if any of which command us to do good, but rather restrain us from doing harm (Hunt, 1990). Liberty under the law means the freedom not to have to contribute to society or help our neighbor, or to try to be "good people."

The most serious consequence of individualism in society is alienation. In *The Pursuit of Loneliness* (1976), Philip Slater suggested that the priority placed on individualism has motivated people to flee from what they really want, which is community, engagement, and dependence. As Mona Affinito (1990) says, "The focus on individual rights and responsibilities has been a major route to good mental and moral health"

but "carried to the extreme of neglecting connectedness and commitment to others, however, it leaves loneliness and isolation in its wake"
(p. 3).

The most notable individualistic feature of psychotherapy, up until
the advent of self-help groups, has been how private it is. While confidentiality is important for practical reasons, the exclusivity of therapy is
not necessarily advantageous to the patient. As Veroff et al. (1981) stated
about psychoanalysis:

> Psychoanalysis is the only form of psychic healing that attempts to
> cure people by detaching them from society and relationships. All
> other forms—shamanism, faith healing, prayer—bring the commu-
> nity into the healing process, indeed use the interdependence of
> patient and others as the central mechanism of the healing process.
> (pp. 6–7)

The second feature of psychotherapy that makes it so individualistic
is the prevalence of "intrapsychic supremacy" (Levine & Perkins, 1987).
While they modified the individualism of Freud somewhat by emphasizing the preoedipal parent-child relationship, later psychoanalytic theorists preserved considerable intrapsychic focus, continuing to emphasize "self-organization at the expense of attachment" (Mitchell, 1988,
p. 78). It is easy to see how intrapsychic dominance evolved in the
context of the medical model of psychiatry and psychotherapy. Doctors
have always looked at and treated one body and one brain at a time.
Surgeons do not have to think about how two people's livers interact,
and heart specialists do not treat a community of hearts. (An intriguing
idea, perhaps, but not one that has been pursued to my knowledge.)
Likewise, medically trained psychiatrists have not tended to think of
people in the aggregate, but have focused on and treated the disease
in the individual at the expense of attending to mental illness in the society (Szasz, 1961). To the extent that psychoanalysis and behavioral medicine has been practiced by physicians and other medical personnel, the emphasis on curing the individual "body-mind" seems
understandable.

The third individualistic feature of psychotherapy is the assumption
of egoism on the part of the patient and, indeed, of all humans. In the
framework of "egoistic Darwinism" discussed in the previous section,
the survival of the species is assumed to be effected by each individual
struggling for his own survival—at the expense of anyone who gets in
his way. Even altruistic Darwinist clinicians are extremely individualistic

in their perspective. Erich Fromm saw a central concern with the uniqueness of one's self as an important part of mental and moral health.

> Each person's virtue is in his unique individuality. . . . [The] character structure of the mature and integrated personality, the productive character, constitutes the source and the basis of "virtue," and that "vice" in the last analysis, is indifference to one's own self and self-mutilation. . . . man's aim is to be himself and the condition for attaining this goal is that man be for himself. (Fromm, 1947, p. 7)

He expresses suspicion of power-based ethics, which foster self-denial, obedience, and the suppression of individuality. From the altruistic Darwinian perspective, Fromm believed, like Horney and Maslow, that the freedom to achieve self-fulfillment is an automatic route to interpersonal morality.

The fourth and probably strongest individualist value in psychotherapy is autonomy. Analyst Weiss (1965) wrote, "first among the criteria for healthy moral values I place autonomy" (p. 72). Such priorities still prevail; in a study of therapists' moral and religious values, the condition of autonomy, "being a free spirit" was found by Bergin (1991) to be the most strongly supported value by mental health professionals. "Hanging on too long" in any relationship, be it parental or romantic is a sign of pathology, whereas problems that spring from excessive detachment, such as aloofness in relationships or isolationism, are not seen as being nearly as sick as excessive dependency or even the simple unwillingness to separate. While a therapist who cares "too much" for a patient will likely be criticized for breaking boundaries, fostering dependency, or, at the very least, losing perspective, a clinician who may not be able even to establish rapport with his patients may still be highly respected by other professionals for his objectivity.

Reflecting the tradition of Kant who saw the capacity for autonomous thinking as the key point of differentiation between man and beast, all psychodynamic therapies see autonomy as a primary objective of healthy child development and of treatment. The child's task between 18 months and three years is to separate from the mother, say child developmentalists such as Margaret Mahler (1975), or else chronic difficulties with separation may result, including pathological conditions like the borderline personality syndrome (Masterson, 1976). Ego psychologists such as Anna Freud and Hartmann saw "differentiation" and "individuation" as key to adaptive growth.

Individuation, or autonomy, is a major goal of most psychotherapy. Object relations theorists see "good" object relations as the goal of therapy, "good" being defined in terms of the degree of differentiation achieved. According to the self-psychologists, only if one is free of the need for approval from others can one acquire adequate self-esteem (Kohut, 1971). While self-psychology suggests that the client be given unconditional approval as a part of treatment, the goal is for him to internalize the positive messages from the therapist and wean himself away from this source of validation without having to replace it with another. Even family therapists, who use a systems, as opposed to an intrapsychic model, tend to see leaving home as indispensable for the recovery of the troubled youngster and his family.

The value placed on autonomy in psychotherapy may have been exaggerated to the detriment of society. The Bellah team (1985) found that the therapists they interviewed guided their clients toward a "me-first, me-only" kind of thinking and action. Family therapists differed only in that they thought in terms of "my family" as opposed to just "me." The therapists saw no wider purpose in their role beyond helping clients get past the pain in their lives. If they encouraged clients in community activities or altruistic endeavors at all, it was purely for purposes of boosting individuals' self-esteem. Few of the therapists interviewed gave any indication that the "recovered" patient, reinvigorated through therapy, has any responsibility to contribute to her community. The fruits of a client's therapeutic labor are to be enjoyed solely by herself and a few significant others.

The assumption that autonomy is sufficient or even necessary for mental health needs to be questioned by the therapy profession. While it is true that self-other confusion contaminates the quality of object relationships, taking for granted that a high degree of independence must occur before successful relationships can begin may unnecessarily exacerbate a patients' isolation. The possibility, argued convincingly by Sullivan (1953), that a person cannot begin to learn how to be in an intimate relationship unless he first learns how to be a "chum" and a community member, should be more carefully considered by therapists who are overly wedded to individualistic models of psychology and psychotherapy. Sullivan promoted a "social recovery" for schizophrenics (1962) via the creation of a community of empathic personnel with the patience and training to teach patients the mores of communities outside the institutions.

Philosopher Martin Buber stated that one must love one's neighbor before one can love oneself (1966). This is completely the reverse of what most therapists suggest to their clients. It is not often suggested that learning to become more interdependent with a wide circle of people who are joined together in mutually satisfying emotional ways might be just as important for mental health as repairing one's individual psyche and/or one's most private relationships. While clients regularly complain in therapy about feelings of loneliness, there has not been much emphasis in therapy on the problem of isolation as a cause of mental illness, nor on the relationship of belonging and community to problems of individual psychopathology.

One psychologist has resoundingly disputed individualist models of personality and mental health. Seymour Sarason actually equates individual mental health with what he calls the "psychological sense of community," which he defines as

the sense that one was part of a readily available, mutually supportive network of relationships upon which one could readily depend, and as a result of which one did not experience sustained feelings of loneliness that impel one to actions or to adopting a style of living masking anxiety and setting the stage for later and more destructive anguish. (1974, p. 1)

All along, Alcoholics Anonymous and some of the group therapies have quietly held the banner for models of treatment that help individuals by helping them connect rather than separate from other people. Group therapists and members of therapy groups and AA know without question the healing power of connectedness and see community as essential to the development of good self-esteem as well as relief from depression and anxiety. Some psychodynamic group models use the healing processes of the group-as-a-whole to help members.

In my opinion, Heidi's therapy was not a success. At the very least, her termination from treatment was premature. As Kitwood (1990) said,

A person who remains in "therapeutic egoism" whether as "unblocked manager" or as "assertive woman" is little more than a needy greedy infant; but with greater resources than an infant for gratifying desire and greater skill in manipulation of others. (p. 109)

It is clear that emptiness and depression lies ahead for Heidi if she maintains her isolated and self-serving life-style. In my opinion, if Heidi were really better, she would be expanding herself in the area of the five virtues. Instead, at the end of the play she has her baby and her friend and that's all, and she has limited herself to **responsibility** and **altruism** in the context of these two very personal relationships. The other three virtues and the public domains on Heidi's virtues chart would all show very low numbers.

Heidi's retreat from the toxic relationships of the past is only one step in what should be a much larger project. Having divested herself of some of her negative introjects, Heidi will have to be honest with herself about the part she played in all these bad experiences and relationships. She will have to own her own rageful parts, which she has been able to project onto others, who have been all too willing, albeit unconsciously, to fill these roles in her script (through projective identification). She will realize that she, also, has been unfair (**justice**) and judgmental (**egalitarianism**).

THE PRICE OF THE FOUR BIASES: GOODNESS

Each of the four amoral biases can and often does obscure from the therapist's view various aspects of goodness in her clients, which might otherwise be revealed in the therapy.

The assumption that people are *alienated in the universe* may diminish the therapist's appreciation of the greater lovingness the individual may have acquired in life and through the therapy relationship.

The *positivist* bias may channel the therapist's priorities into valuing therapeutic outcomes that are supposedly more empirical and quantifiable, rather than recognizing and appreciating clients' expression of their virtues.

The *Darwinian* bias, whether egoistic or altruistic, can lead therapists to minimize the value of patients' prosocial behavior. If the therapist is an egoistic Darwinist, she will be likely to cynically interpret altruism as undercover egoism; and if she is an altruistic Darwinist, she will probably diminish altruism's worth by seeing it as endemic to the species as opposed to voluntary.

The *individualist* bias is likely to cause the therapist to highlight the recovered patient's increased independence rather than recognizing the importance of improved relatedness, sense of community, **responsibility** to the larger world, openness to people who are different (**egalitarianism**), and enhanced sense of **honesty** and **justice**.

Chapter 5

MORAL SENSITIVITY AND

MORAL ACTION

The American Heritage Dictionary defines moral as "of or concerned with the judgment of the goodness or badness of human action and character, pertaining to the discernment of good and evil." The next three chapters will summarize some theories from social, developmental, educational and psychoanalytic psychology about how this capacity to distinguish right from wrong develops and what motivates people to act prosocially (on behalf of others). Attention will be paid to how moral development may take place through psychotherapy.

REST'S MODEL OF MORAL DEVELOPMENT

Rest (1986) has developed a four-component model, which is a helpful vehicle for organizing psychology's disparate contributions to understanding moral development. The model constructs what has to happen for a person to behave morally. This is not a linear model; the processes are not stages, rather, they are interactive.

Component 1 is *moral sensitivity*—the ability to perceive moral problems, moral contingencies, and choices of moral action, and to notice who will be affected by these choices and in what ways.

Component 2 is the process of moral judgment, evaluating which course is morally preferable. This process of *moral reasoning*, studied extensively by Piaget, Kohlberg, and others, has often been mistaken as comprising all there is to the psychology of morality.

75

Component 3 is deciding and committing to what one believes is the best moral choice; this involves giving priority to moral values over other personal values and making a decision to do what one thinks is right. This process is a function of *moral attitude*. Psychoanalytic perspectives are helpful in explaining how a predisposition toward morality develops in the context of personality.

Component 4 is the implementation of *moral action*—persevering and following through on the moral decision. Besides motivation, moral action demands the will and the ability to overcome obstacles that may arise to block the moral effort. Moral action is also dependent upon situational factors.

Components 1 (moral sensitivity) and 4 (moral action) will be dealt with in this chapter; Component 2 (moral reasoning) will be discussed in Chapter 6; and Component 3 (moral attitude) will be the topic of Chapter 7. As in previous chapters, material from psychotherapy cases will be used to illustrate the concepts presented.

MORAL SENSITIVITY

Moral sensitivity means receptivity, perceptiveness, and responsiveness to the moral right or wrong of a situation. Moral sensitivity is the spontaneous altruistic responsiveness that can be seen in the youngest child (Blum, 1987) or the oldest adult. It is a source of goodness, for it springs from concern for others.

The focus of this section will be on sensitivity to the presence of immorality. To be morally sensitive, one must be able to recognize the moral implications of a situation spontaneously. Though it happens in a flash, this perception is an extremely complex process, which involves affect, cognitive reasoning, and interpersonal skills. One must be able to read social cues, interpret social situations, experience empathy, and recognize and identify and interpret one's own gut feelings in response to these stimuli. While individual personality factors come into play in moral sensitivity, situational factors are crucial, as is social learning.

Because psychology has been so influenced by Kantian philosophy, with its high valuing of reasoning and abstract logic, it has tended to conceive of morality as a totally rational process. The phenomenon of moral sensitivity seems to have escaped psychology's scrutiny because it is not logical; rather, it is based on spontaneity and emotional, not cognitive, processes. The omission of moral sensitivity in psychology's understanding of morality has been a glaring one, for, as we shall explain, moral sensitivity is the spark for both moral judgment and moral action.

Insensitivity to the occurrence of immorality is a common feature of people who seek psychotherapy. Moral insensitivity goes along with other kinds of insensitivity: to feelings, to beauty, to destruction of the environment, to creative possibilities in a person or a situation. Insensitivity is, we know, usually born of pain and trauma, although sometimes there are constitutional factors operating as well. The best defense against pain is to make oneself numb, and numbing becomes a habit, so that even the recognition of basic goodness and evil becomes blunted.

An important task of therapy is to sharpen moral sensitivity, for, without it, the patient has no way of evaluating his own behavior and that of others. In a therapy group, a young woman, Joyce, was describing her mother's successful attempt to ruin a recent holiday for her children, in-laws, and grandchildren, because she was angry at her husband for losing his job. I turned to Regina, another member whose mother was prone to similar behavior, and who seemed to be listening intently.

"Regina, do you think Joyce's mother was wrong to do what she did?" I asked suddenly.

"*Wrong?*" Regina repeated. "What do you mean, 'wrong'?"

"Would you act that way, Regina?" another member asked.

"I don't know. I wasn't there," she replied, befuddled.

Joyce exclaimed, "I used to think just like you! I excused my mother for everything. No, Regina, you would never do what my mother did, no matter how upset you were. My mother was *wrong*—selfish, irresponsible, unfair, mean. I can see that now, and when she does act that way, I have to tell her, although I'm scared to death every time."

It is only when the numbing defense is relinquished and the pain of the abuse has been felt that a client can begin to count on her instincts to signal her when an immorality has been committed in her presence. Like Joyce, Regina had built up enormous defenses against recognizing that her mother, who had continually proclaimed herself as good, was actually a cold-hearted woman interested only in getting her own way. The therapy group provided a safe environment where Regina and Joyce could gradually allow the "psychological ice-floes to melt" (Kitwood, 1990, p. 197) and feel the pain of having grown up with their unloving mothers. A year later Regina had a much keener moral sensitivity, picking up on issues of right and wrong as they emerged in the group and elsewhere. She even confronted her mother when she was cruel or manipulative. This was not accomplished without extreme pain.

In this section, four aspects of moral sensitivity will be described: paying attention, moral outrage, connectedness, and empathy.

Paying Attention

In a transcript at the end of this book, Marie, whose mother recently died of cancer, reports that she frequently visits Hospice to remind her self to "pay attention" to "those moments" that she has been given to share with those she loves, for they may soon be gone. It is clear in the anecdote that Marie considers "paying attention" to be her moral responsibility.

A study by Csikszentmihalyi and Rochberg-Halton (1981) found that families where high levels of attention are given to each member had members who were more sympathetic, helpful, caring and support-ive, affiliate, loyal, warm, friendly, sociable, cooperative, less denying, less defensive, and less unsure of their worth than families where the quality and quantity of attention was spotty or low. Psychotherapy, particularly group therapy, provides a considerable amount of quality attention to the client as well as affording the client an opportunity to "get out of herself" and attend to others (Mullan, 1987, 1991).

Bellah et al. (1991) ascribe considerable moral significance to the phenomenon of paying attention, seeing it as a vital factor in an egalitar-ian community or society. They say that democracy means paying atten-tion. By attention, the authors are referring to "an openness to experi-ence, a willingness to widen the lens of apperception when that is appropriate" (p. 256). Widening this spectrum of awareness requires increased honesty and leads to a greater understanding of the needs of others and of the collective human environment, opening up greater possibilities for **altruism**, **justice**, and **responsibility**.

In earlier writings, Bellah et al. (1985) were highly critical of the moral insensitivity of psychotherapists, seeing them as materialistic and socially unconcerned. Ironically, however, their description of "paying attention" seems to me to be exactly what psychotherapy does for and engenders in clients. Just as moral sensitivity is the *sine qua non* of moral development, paying attention is the first step to moral sensitivity. Once one is alert to and aware of others, one can then begin to perceive moral issues when they arise.

Giving Up Lying

A necessary part of perceiving moral issues is the willingness to give up lying to oneself and to others—"to become more open to experience, to live more truthfully, with less distortion" (Kitwood, 1990, p. 199). This involves giving up the defenses that have preserved emotional anesthe-sia and is the central challenge for every therapy patient. I have often told my therapy groups that the purpose of the group and the major rule of the group are the same: "to learn to tell the truth." As they become involved in the group, they become increasingly aware of how hard, and how important, this is.

Many clients harbor one central lie. Confronting and refuting this central lie, whether it occurs in therapy or outside, creates a major crisis, which, if they can get beyond it, is what finally allows these people to grow, emotionally and morally. Many who cannot face their "lie" will terminate therapy prematurely. One rageful woman begged her individual therapist to get her a family therapist so that her family "could confront Tom [her husband] with *his* anger." The therapist reluctantly agreed, and indeed, what happened was just what the therapist feared. The family confronted the *mother* with how *her* rage made them feel. The mother abruptly terminated treatment, taking the family with her.

Jack, an alcoholic in recovery, whose father had literally whipped and tortured him as a child, had never confronted his father. Instead, Jack called his father on the phone every Sunday to chat. Although his descriptions of the abuse were lurid, Jack could not experience any real feelings about his childhood, let alone any real moral outrage at how he had been treated. His affect was deadened and he used humor to defuse all attempts on the part of the therapist or his group to get close to him. Finally, desperate to get through to him, the therapist decided to address Jack's moral insensitivity head on. She pointed out to Jack the number of lies he was telling each time he talked to his father. The patient showed no reaction, responding with his usual combination of intellectualization and humor.

By means of a letter, which Jack slipped under her door the next day, the therapist learned that Jack had indeed felt moral outrage after the session—not toward his father, but toward the therapist. He complained that the therapist had betrayed him by "accusing him of being a pathological liar," and declared his intention to terminate treatment. The therapist called him to come in and talk about the misunderstanding, which he agreed to do. She apologized for having caused the patient such pain, assuring him she had not meant to do so. This was true—she had meant to challenge him a bit, but had apparently overdone it, leaving him feeling overwhelmed, shamed, and helpless without any of his usual defenses. Jack assertively and angrily chastised her for her injustice toward him but accepted her apology. Because of their long and basically positive relationship, the therapist managed to persuade Jack to stay in treatment, but any attempts to interpret his reaction to her as a transference of his feelings toward his father fell on deaf ears.

While the therapist at first regretted her intervention, she also felt that, oddly, her objective had been accomplished. Jack was clearly incensed on a moral level, even though his real father was getting off scot free, and the transference father was getting all the fury. What is more, he had told her about his feelings instead of hiding them, with no laughs, and with a lot of feeling on his face and in his voice.

The incident also points out that to perpetuate the "false self" one usually has to lie to others. For years, Jack hid his anger from his father, encouraging his father to believe he had nothing to feel guilty about. The anecdote is a good example of the fact that confrontation of lies told to protect the false self will generally cause quite a stir in treatment, for better or for worse.

Moral Outrage

Beyond possessing the capacity to discern that a moral issue exists and label it, to be truly morally sensitive, one must have the capacity for moral outrage.

Zerka Moreno (1986) describes a kind of "ethical anger," which "is of a passionate nature, a new experience meant to challenge and arouse" (p. 151). In order to feel this ethical anger, one has to be relatively spontaneous. J. L. Moreno, husband of Zerka and founder of psychodramatic group therapy, stressed that spontaneity, unlike impulsiveness, generates a creative, *adequate*, and *appropriate* response to a situation (Moreno, 1946).

Spontaneity is neither purely cognitive nor purely affective but involves both processes working together. Spontaneity generates new behavior as well as new thoughts and feelings. Spontaneous moral outrage generates action that "upsets actions of persons who offend values we hold dear and which are evident to us" (Moreno, 1986, p. 151). Hannah Arendt (1963) and Robert Lifton (1986) have both pointed out that an almost total lack of spontaneity, creativity, and imagination was one of the most prevalent characteristics of Nazis who participated directly in the atrocities of the Holocaust. It was this observation that caused Arendt to speculate on the essential "banality of evil."

Many patients are so unspontaneous that they cannot even feel their own pain when they are abused, much less feel moral outrage. Others feel the pain but cannot feel anger at the person responsible; they blame the victim, often themselves, instead. In other words, they are capable of some degree of moral sensitivity, but it does not reach the threshold of moral outrage.

As most therapists have learned, the child who is the victim of abuse may, without adequate psychotherapy, become an abuser. When a victim is not allowed to discuss what has been done to her, she suppresses her rage until it is unleashed by and against her own child or someone else who is vulnerable. Alice Miller (1984a,b) believes that the feeling and adequate expression of moral outrage (although she does not call it that) is an essential part of effective psychotherapy. She is highly critical of what she calls the "poisonous pedagogy" of psychoanalysis and other therapies, which have at their root certain notions that serve to excuse abusers and to force patients to take the blame for the abuse. She suggests that Freud's conceptualization of the child as bestial and needing to be civilized by its upbringing serves to validate, or even encourage, the abuse of children by adults under the auspices of "discipline."

Blunted moral outrage is a prominent feature in many new patients presenting for therapy. They tell the therapist horrendous stories about their parents, followed by a smile and a shrug or a comment such as "My father did the best he could"; or "It's in the past and I've forgiven her." A therapy that bypasses the patient's well hidden but legitimate outrage at the wrongs committed against her in childhood, Miller states, is not only useless but harmful.

When abuse has occurred, recognition of that abuse and confrontation of the perpetrator is always the victim's best option, if the perpetrator is strong and receptive enough to listen without retaliation, and if the victim can manage his rage well enough not to physically hurt or verbally "kill off" the perpetrator. When these conditions are not present, or when the abuser is deceased, the patient must settle for feeling and expressing the moral outrage in therapy and for learning to hold the abuser accountable, rather than blame himself. As we saw in the case of Jack, it can be therapeutic for a patient's moral outrage to be aroused and expressed in the transference. Such encounters do not need to be intentionally provoked by the therapist. As self psychology emphasizes, the inevitable failures of empathy on the part of the therapist or therapy group member are more than sufficient to ignite the old hurts and resentments that the patient needs to express.

Sometimes we are confronted with a patient who seems to be unable to feel outrage for what he himself has done. I am not talking here about the psychopath, who consistently denies moral responsibility; rather, I am referring to the otherwise principled person who has done something truly inhumane or irresponsible toward others, but does not seem to feel guilty.

A gay man, whom I had been seeing in group and individual therapy for several years, had been diagnosed HIV positive. In an individual session he stunned me by casually saying that he had gone to the park the previous weekend and had sexual contact with a number of different men.

"What?" I almost shrieked. *"Unprotected?"*

"Um, well, yes," he replied, hanging his head in shame.

I mistakenly believed he understood my point and felt badly for barking at him, until I heard his next sentence: "I know I am supposed to be working on self-esteem in therapy," he said.

"The hell with self-esteem—Rick, that's *murder!*" I cried.

Not too subtle, I admit, but I felt then and still do that the situation did not call for mincing words. My outrage began to penetrate Rick's denial, and he shuddered vehemently thinking about the damage he may have caused. He must have needed another dose of moral outrage, however, for he brought the matter up in the very same way in group the next night, obtaining the exact same reaction from the group members that he had received from me. They loudly and firmly insisted that he stop his promiscuous behavior immediately and urged that he face the terror and rage that he had been acting out instead of feeling. Rick ceased all promiscuous behavior from that point on.

Moral outrage or the lack thereof plays a part in guilt, shame, accountability, and forgiveness, all of which are discussed extensively in Chapter 8.

Feeling Connected

Another factor in the presence or absence of moral sensitivity in a given person or a given situation is the relative connectedness or distance of persons to/from themselves, as well as to one another, and to the acts being committed. Lifton (1986) points out a number of psychological mechanisms that seemed to be correlated with the astounding lack of moral sensitivity of the Nazi perpetrators, and they all had to do with *distancing*.

The first was *derealization*, diminishing the horror of acts by making them less real. In the case of the Nazi doctors, their role in the genocide was, as Lifton puts it, "medicalized." Responsibility was removed from the individual doctors and grotesquely framed as an appropriate expression of the technical and scientific principles of medicine. Derealization was accomplished with the assistance of considerable distortion of facts such as minimizing the numbers of people being killed, and by relabeling—i.e., applying benign and antiseptic names for hideous projects (such as calling Auschwitz a "civil enterprise").

Other distancing mechanisms were *disavowal* and *denial of responsibility*, both of which were easy to do in the hierarchical Nazi society where there was always a superior upon whom one could deflect blame and responsibility should the stirrings of conscience become painful.

The most prevalent mechanism among the Nazi doctors, Lifton discovered, was an intrapsychic process that he calls "doubling," a highly effective method of distancing because it is largely unconscious. Doubling is a process by which the doctor or official seemed to have developed a totally other self to do the evil acts, a self that was connected enough to the original self to remember and value the original self's humane acts, but split-off enough that the latter only barely remembered the atrocities of the former. The "prohibitive" conscience, the part that was concerned with right versus wrong, was retained by the original self, while the values of loyalty, hard work, and idealization of the "Fatherland" and its enterprises were extended to the second self. The part that still felt love and concern for family or for vulnerable others also still resided in the original self. Lifton sees "doubling" as a subconscious truce between two highly conflictual external demands that were made of the Nazi doctor by the party—to participate in ungodly atrocities on the one hand and, at the same time, to feel and appear not only professional, but virtuous.

Lifton's book should, in my opinion, be mandatory reading for psychotherapists in training, not to mention physicians of all types. It shows us the extent to which the supposedly "helpful" enterprises of science, medicine, and psychotherapy can be marshalled for purposes of evil. It serves as a startling reminder of how corruptible we are and how thin the line between virtue and evil can be.

Distancing is a valuable tool of therapy, used to help us gain objectivity, but, like any other tool, it can be misused. Distancing *inevitably* numbs moral sensitivity; we can only control the degree to which this occurs. As Lifton's work shows us, excessive distancing can quickly lead to major failures of empathy, rationalizations of therapeutic error, scapegoating of patients, and even patient abuse.

Empathy

Another indispensable part of moral sensitivity is *empathy*. Social learning theorist and researcher Martin Hoffman (1975, 1989) has discovered that the affective components of moral sensitivity probably precede the cognitive. He has identified that infants begin to feel discomfort in the presence of another person who is uncomfortable within days or weeks of birth. This is an affective response, which requires practically no cognitive development. Gradually, this response interacts with developing cognitive processes to form increasingly more complex forms of empathy. With the beginnings of self-object differentiation, the child knows that he himself is not hurting but is able to feel badly (sympathy) for the other. At two or three years, the child is able to perceive not only that the other (and not the self) is hurt, but that what might be comforting for the self might be different from what might be comforting for the other. Thus, the child might bring flowers to mother when she sees her as sad, whereas, at an earlier stage, she might have offered mother her own doll to cheer her. By late childhood the child has a sense that other people have their own life histories. At this point the child might feel empathy about another person's general life situation, for example if the parent seems very overworked. Even in the presence of cues to the contrary, the child may empathically deduce another's pain; for example, he might feel sorry for a retarded child, even though he sees the child playing happily on the playground (Rest, 1986).

In therapy we see many dramatic examples of how anxiety or narcissism can reduce or blunt empathy. Often, the empathic responses we do see are quite regressed, much like those displayed by Hoffman's infants, rather than articulated in thoughts and words. Recently my group sat mute after a member had told them of a threatening blood pressure condition she had recently had diagnosed. I asked what people were feeling. Many members reported considerable discomfort, characterized by disquieting body sensations and an awakening of fears about their own health. They said they did not initially report these feelings because "it would not help" the physically ill member. She informed them that, while their silence had made her feel as if they were not interested, it was comforting to hear that they identified with her fear. I told them that what they had been feeling was a form of empathy (albeit primitive, a fact I did not mention). After this interchange they were considerably more forthcoming in expressing their empathy when members spoke of painful or frightening situations.

Moral Sensitivity in the Therapist

If the client is going to learn moral sensitivity in therapy, he probably needs a therapist who has this capacity herself. Sensitivity to the presence of a moral issue would seem to be a very important skill for a therapist, and I would hope most therapists possess it. Unfortunately, however, this may not be the case. A study by Lindsey found impairment in almost half of two samples of licensed psychologists and psychology students with respect to the perception of very obvious ethical issues in a taped therapist-client interview (Bergin, 1988). A quarter of both samples did not perceive the inherent ethical problem even when prompted to listen for it. These disturbing results combined with similar outcomes in other studies have implications for the ethical training of psychotherapists (Welfel, 1992).

If therapists are "tuned out" when it comes to moral issues, we must wonder whether patients are also. Perhaps, when it comes to deciding whether or not to discuss moral concerns or goodness, patients are simply taking their cue from their therapists. Perhaps they are getting the message from therapists that therapy is not the appropriate place to air such topics.

It is my contention that moral sensitivity is a fundamental requirement in a competent therapist. A therapist who is not morally sensitive does not have a chance of helping the patient learn to assess moral *accountability*, a mandatory component of successful treatment for people who have been abused and/or neglected in childhood (Harper & Hoopes, 1990; Miller, 1984b).

Addressing Moral Insensitivity in Therapy

Frequently therapy clients will recount startling incidents of abuse without any apparent awareness that there might be a moral component to them. The sadist will frankly describe his behavior as if it is perfectly justified; the masochist will weakly protest the behavior of the sadist, while simultaneously excusing it on bogus psychological grounds ("He was just frustrated").

How does the therapist address this blocking of moral issues without shaming the patient?

A major part of a therapist's job is trying to understand the patient's defenses. Is the person avoiding the moral issue or is she oblivious to it? If the latter is the case, the person may be unconsciously defending against potentially overwhelming feelings of guilt, shame, or anxiety. Chapters 8 through 11 present considerable information about how clients with different diagnoses experience and perceive moral dilemmas through the filter of their respective psychopathologies, and how, given the particular level of defense of a patient, therapeutic intervention can include addressing the moral dimension of the patient's problem.

Therapeutic judgments about the patient's level of defense should help the therapist in deciding *how, not whether*, to address moral issues. Sweeping the moral aspect of a situation under the rug is not, as we stated in the introduction, a viable therapeutic option. Respecting the patient's defenses is vital, but cannot be used as an excuse for letting goodness or malevolence remain unnoticed. The challenge for the therapist is to help the patient, given his particular psychological and emotional capabilities, to understand and to deal with the moral elements of an issue as fully as possible.

A woman and her grown daughter each sought therapy with a different therapist, because of their dissatisfaction with one another. The mother, an extremely wealthy woman, had always made a point of telling her daughter that she could expect a large inheritance when the mother died. At the time of seeking treatment, the mother was furious at the daughter for becoming engaged to a man of whom she, the mother, did not approve, and the daughter was furious at the mother for not approving of her choice of fiancé. Soon after they began treatment, the mother announced to her therapist that she had met with her lawyer for the purpose of cutting her daughter out of her will. She stated this matter-of-factly, with no trace of guilt. The therapist thought, but initially did not state, that the mother's action was not only punitive but represented a breach of promise to the daughter. The therapist recoiled at the mother's willingness to sacrifice her own integrity and even her relationship with her daughter in order to preserve control over her child.

Meanwhile the daughter presented the situation to *her* therapist in a very similar fashion as did the mother. She was full of angry and hurt feelings about her mother's overall "selfishness," responding petulantly, as if her mother had refused to give her a candy bar instead of abrogating a deep personal commitment. Because she could not grasp the moral significance of the mother's action, the daughter was likely to forgive the mother prematurely, paving the way for another "power play" by the mother the next time the daughter asserted her own needs against the mother's wishes. The daughter's therapist also saw the mother's actions as unethical.

In therapy, moral issues can be labeled as such, thereby opening up a whole new realm of experience. This can be done in a way that does not shame the patient or invite her to blame others. For example, in the above situation, either the mother's or the daughter's therapist might say, "At this point you are both so angry at each other that you are not making clear to each other or to me whose rights have been violated and in what way. It feels like actual injustices have been committed—unintentionally, perhaps, but injustices nonetheless. In any case, we have not identified clearly what these injustices are and how they might be rectified. Let us look at the bigger picture of who has obligations to whom in a case like this."

The therapist is asking the client to begin to take **responsibility** for the **justice** of her own situation. She does this by asking the client to take a step back and to look at the whole situation more objectively, to take the position of the judge rather than advocate for her own self-interest.

Both parties are having difficulty distinguishing between wrong as in "it feels bad" and "wrong" in the moral sense. To help her make this distinction, the mother's therapist can question the mother regarding the basis for her belief that one adult is entitled to punish another for a choice of spouse. Secondly, the therapist may pose the question for the mother as to whether the abrogation of a fairly serious contract is justified purely because one does not like what the other is doing.

Meanwhile, the daughter could also be questioned by her therapist about the "right" and "wrong" of the mother's decision, for she is just as confused about this as her mother. She thinks what her mother has done is "wrong" *not* because it is immoral to break a contract, but because she feels she is entitled to the money. Each of the women defines right and wrong in terms of what will most clearly benefit her.

To sensitize the daughter to the moral issues at hand, her therapist might say, "What do you mean, you *deserve* the inheritance? Is the purpose of an inheritance to acknowledge the *deserving-ness* of the recipient? Is an inheritance bestowed as a reward, or as an act of unconditional love?" Such questions will, at the very least, get the young woman thinking as opposed to relying on her emotions to deal with this complex situation. More than an intellectual exercise, however, the introduction of principles of goodness such as **responsibility** and **fairness** sometimes provide options for positively reframing situations that otherwise would be bogged down in personal desires and animosities.

It is amazing how liberating it can be for struggling family members to pluck an intra-family conflict out of the unreasoned and emotional enmeshment of family squabbling and to examine it in the light of ethical reason. When this is done, the question moves from *who* is right, to *what* is right, which is usually not located solely in one person or on one side of an argument. Both parties in a dispute can work together to figure out what is the *right* course for *both parties*.

Whether the disputing parties are seen in therapy together or separately, once the level of the argument has been raised to a legitimate moral (not moralistic) plane, the petty individual desires, insults, and demands will often recede. When moral issues are straightforwardly identified in therapy, patients seem naturally to take on more intelligent and productive modes of thinking and interaction, characterized by give-and-take and a surprising absence of blame and defensiveness. If the result of the therapist's attempt to raise the discussion to a moral level is that the patient feels shamed or blamed, then the intervention has been ill-timed, ill-worded, or the therapist has overestimated the capacity of the client to tolerate confrontation. This does not mean that it was a mistake to call attention to the moral aspects of a situation, but that more effort will be required on the part of the therapist to make the process of seeing moral choices less threatening for the patient.

MORAL ACTION

As will be discussed more in Chapter 6, research has demonstrated what we already know intuitively—that people do not consistently behave the way they think they will in moral situations. Much of moral action seems, as Kitwood (1990) points out, to be natural and reflexive, initiated, as Gilligan (1982) stressed, in the context of a caring relationship

> . . . countless small and unreflective actions towards each other, and the patterns of living and relating which each human being gradually creates. . . . Perhaps it is that each person acquires a repertoire of actions, through observation, imitation, practice and so on, and has these available for the contingencies of everyday life. (Kitwood, 1990, p. 149)

If moral reasoning plays but a small role in moral behavior, what factors play a bigger part? Clearly, "character" is important; the question of how the propensity for goodness, or moral attitude, grows in the developing personality will be discussed at length in Chapter 7. This section will deal with other factors that promote moral action.

An important context for the development of moral action is the roles we play. Many virtues are acquired in the context of being called upon to play a particular role in relation to others. For example, one learns much about **altruism** and **responsibility** in the course of being a parent, while, as an employee, one might learn about the use and abuse of power (**egalitarianism** and **justice**). Indeed, all roles, whether experienced positively or negatively result in a certain amount of moral learning. We learn moral behavior from daily life experiences, from the teaching and modeling of adults, from the media, from friends, and from numerous other sources.

A major propellant for moral action is key life experiences (Vandenberg, 1991). As Kitwood (1990) says, "responsibility, commitment, success, failure, suffering, betrayal, contradiction, the fulfillment and the abandonment of hopes; gradually . . . [coming] to terms with the meaning of a human life, together with the prospect of approaching death" (p. 150) are all challenges that can reorganize our moral priorities. Crises such as the loss of a significant other, the occurrence of a disaster such as a fire or a hurricane, being called to war, losing one's job—all of these can rearrange moral thinking and affect moral behavior in ways that are far from logical.

VARIABLES THAT AFFECT PROSOCIAL BEHAVIOR

Eisenberg and Mussen (1989) have investigated the roots of what they term prosocial behavior, which is defined as voluntary actions to help another. Prosocial behavior can be *egoistically* or *altruistically* motivated. Prosocial behavior can only be considered altruistic if there is no perceived gain for the self. According to Eisenberg and Mussen (1989), in order to act in accordance with learned or internalized norms of prosocial action, one must be able, in the situation at hand, to perceive the other's needs, interpret them accurately, recognize that the other person can be helped, and feel competent to provide the help that is needed. Additionally, the risk entailed in helping must not be prohibitive.

Eisenberg and Mussen categorize the factors that can be considered to contribute to prosocial behavior, many of which are dealt with extensively in this book:

1. *biological*, including individual genetic factors, such as temperament, and species-wide tendencies, such as the tendency to be altruistic to one's kin
2. *group membership*, meaning familial, community, and other groups
3. *socialization experiences*
4. *cognitive processes*, including the level of cognitive development (discussed under under moral reasoning in Chapter 6)
5. *emotional responsiveness* to others, including guilt and empathy (discussed under ''moral sensitivity'' in this chapter and under ''guilt'' in Chapter 8)
6. *individual characteristics*, such as gender and age, and personality characteristics, such as assertiveness and sociability (I would add capacity for care and compassion and self-esteem, discussed in Chapter 7)
7. *situational determinants*. This last factor is the only one that received the attention of researchers.

Situational Variables Affecting
Prosocial Behavior

Eisenberg and Mussen (1989) say that situational variables that affect prosocial behavior fall into two categories: (1) strikingly unique events that radically alter an individual's personality; and (2) temporary external conditions (such as suddenly encountering a bloody, injured child) and singular (or seldom repeated) experiences or transient moods and emotions.

The effect of life-changing experiences on morality is hard to study because they tend to be rather rare and unpredictable occurrences. Clearly, however, major life events—loss, birth, marriage, divorce, success, failures, illness, and emotional, physical, and economic disasters—are of great moral relevance, for they often involve a radical change in one's perception of everything, including moral priorities (Vandenberg, 1991). Indeed, therapy itself can be a life-changing experience.

Eisenberg and Mussen's second category of events that affect moral behavior, *temporary external or internal conditions*, have lent itself far better to systematic study. The factors include:

1. *Mood—positive or negative.* It was found that negative affect decreases prosocial behavior for young children and increases it for adults. The theory that explains this is that helping behavior makes one feel good about oneself and, therefore, once a child happens to stumble on prosocialism as a vehicle for feeling better, it will continue to be used toward that end. Helpfulness decreases in adults, however, if the negative mood is characterized by excessive attention to the self.

2. *Incentives.* Obviously, prosocial behavior that is not altruistic (i.e., behavior that is motivated by internal or external rewards, or by a desire to escape a negative experience or feeling) is highly influenced by the presence of positive and negative incentives for or against acting prosocially. The potential for reciprocity on the part of the recipient functions as a negative or positive incentive.

3. *Characteristics of the beneficiary* also have a significant effect on prosocial behavior.

   The beneficiary's relationship to the potential prosocial agent is important; as the agent's age increases, there is a decrease in the importance given to familiarity of the beneficiary as a factor in choosing prosocial actions.

   Gender and demographic characteristics of the beneficiary seem to make a considerable difference, with some depressing differences found among young children, older children, and adults when it comes to how much they restrain from helping when the recipient is of a different race.

   Children become increasingly less apt to help children of a

different race as they get older, and the trend extends into adulthood. This is sobering evidence that discrimination is learned. With respect to gender, it was found that adolescent and adult males help females more than males, while females are equally likely to help males and females.

The need of the potential recipient is a strong factor motivating prosocial behavior, one that increases with age. The tendency to help the more needy is decreased when the recipient is perceived to be able to help himself and is not attempting to do so.

Not surprisingly, popular children receive more help than do unpopular children; these children tend to be appreciative, friendly, as well as generous and helpful themselves.

4. *Presence of others.* Considerable research is reported by Hunt (1990) and by Staub (1989) on what factors influence ''bystanders'' to help someone in urgent need of assistance. One thing that definitely inhibits helping is fear of looking foolish; conversely, the fear of looking bad if one does *not* help increases helping (Dovidio, 1984; Latane, 1970; Rutkowski, Gruder, & Rober, 1983). A major inhibitor to helping is the feeling of dissociation from the victim, while even the most trivial clues to another's identity can increase a bystander's willingness to help. Additionally, anything that increases feelings of responsibility greatly increases helping (Dovidio, 1984).

Group Therapy as a Context
That Fosters Moral Action

Mullan (1987, 1991) has written that the group structure and ambience brings out in patients ''striking moral characteristics that aid not only their own treatment but the treatment of others as well'' (1991, p. 190). As Papenah said (in Bloch & Crouch, 1985), group therapy brings out the qualities of **egalitarianism**, **altruism**, and **honesty**—three of the five virtues on our chart. Unlike the individual patient, the group member, upon entering the group agrees to share his therapy time with total strangers (**altruism**) and to see their needs as equally important as his own (**egalitarianism**), even though he may be in emotional distress. In joining the group, he commits himself to being truthful (**honesty**), even though this may be embarrassing. Clearly the remaining two virtues, **justice** and **responsibility**, are also fostered. The group patient is called upon to listen to other patient's problems with a view toward being fair (**justice**), not only to the patient, but to the parties he discusses in his presentation. He is also called upon to be **responsible** for maintaining confidentiality and attending regularly even when it is difficult. He learns to take **responsibility** for getting the group's attention, making his needs known, and for the impact of his words and behavior on others in the group.

Social psychology research on factors determining moral behavior substantiate Mullan's and my own contention (Nicholas, 1984) that group therapy inherently promotes moral behavior. Group therapy boasts many of the factors that have been shown to foster prosocial behavior, while also providing plenty of opportunity to practice such action (Nicholas, 1993). The following are some specific ways that group therapy may foster moral action in the group, which may, in turn, lead to increased prosocial behavior outside.

With respect to what we know about "bystander" behavior, group therapy contains many inherent factors that stimulate helping as opposed to holding back. Since helping is valued in therapy groups, helpers will be appreciated by others, overriding the fear of looking foolish, which we previously noted as a disincentive to prosocial behavior. Depending upon the strength of the positive reinforcement and the comparability of situations outside the group, members' helping behaviors might increase in other arenas as well. New prosocial ways of behaving may become integrated into members' self-concepts, a notion supported by Piliavin et al.'s (1984) finding that repeated blood donors "develop a sense of moral obligation to the collectivity [and] incorporate the activity into their self-concept" (p. 481). This is exactly what happens to group members. They begin to think of themselves as helpful people, and they behave in ways consistent with that view.

Situational cues that offset bystander inhibition are only salient if they attract the attention of the bystander. In many situations, self-interest or other distractions override factors that promote prosocial action. For example, distracting noise significantly diminishes helping behavior (Latane, 1970), while ambiguity—about the situation, what one's role is, and who the other person is—greatly diminishes bystanders' willingness to help as well (Cialdini, 1985). In the therapy group there are few distractions and the interaction is often highly focused. If someone needs more group time, comforting, words of caution, or other kinds of group assistance, this need is likely to be recognized by at least one other person, and people who pitch in to help can do so with relatively little interruption.

On the other hand, sometimes the group dynamic is ambiguous and quite unpredictable. Sometimes people do *not* know how to help each other, and perhaps do not even *want* to. As anyone who has led or been in a therapy group knows, such ambiguity can evoke paranoid and sadistic responses, which are the very opposite of moral behavior. Interestingly, however, its very propensity for confusion and chaos also enhances the group's potential as an environment for moral learning (Nicholas, 1984). Research on moral development conducted by social constructionist Haan (1985) has shown that the greatest moral learning takes place in cohesive groups, which are member rather than leader-directed, under conditions of optimum social disequilibrium, where participants' moral mind-sets are challenged, and where they are encouraged to become emotionally as well as intellectually involved in discussion of issues. Client-centered group therapy would seem to frequently attain a state of social disequilibrium, which would produce new moral learnings for all concerned.

The propensity for moral change is particularly high when the content of what a therapy group is discussing has moral ramifications. As I have noted,

> the therapy group finds itself continually grappling with such dilemmas as liberty versus license and individual needs versus the needs of the group, subjects that are talked about quite infrequently in other sectors. In some cases, the group even helps people acquire the thinking and communication skills they failed to develop in their education, and which are vital to the process of forming an intelligent and consistent personal value system. (Nicholas, 1984, p. 142)

Such discussions often stimulate behavioral change as well as reflection, involving an enhancement of one or more of the virtues. After being told one or two times that she is behaving selfishly or after seeing the unselfishness of another, a patient may, intentionally or not, become more altruistic. A patient who is confronted with his own prejudices may learn from others the value of a more egalitarian perspective, while someone who lies habitually may learn through the group's reactions the price he pays for this in his relationships and may work to become more truthful.

The very atmosphere of the group may foster altruism. Samuel and Pearl Oliner studied people who, at great risk to themselves, aided Jews in Europe during the Holocaust (1988). They found that the rescuers tended to come from families characterized by a *climate of warmth, firmness, and emotional guidance.* Given that this is the environment of a good therapy group, it seems worthwhile to explore the possibility that group therapy fosters moral risk-taking in at least some members.

Group therapy provides an opportunity for patients to learn empathy, which, as we have seen, is a crucial aspect of moral sensitivity. Based on his research, social learning theorist Martin Hoffman created a model for the development of prosocial behavior (1989). Hoffman says that when someone observes another in physical or emotional distress, the witness experiences some sort of physiologically based sympathetic affect, a fairly unpleasant sensation. This stimulates the desire first to escape, but if that is not possible, then to try to relieve the internal discomfort by helping. If the witness does attempt to help, attributions are stimulated that become mental representations or "hot cognitions" as Hoffman calls them. In subsequent "moral encounters" these "hot cognitions" may be activated, resulting in more prosocial activity.

If Hoffman's model is correct, then prosocial behavior should be fostered in the group. The group member, uncomfortable as she may be, having contracted to participate in the group, does not generally flee when she is exposed to others in pain. She is given ample opportunity to learn new options for helping, which may broaden her repertory of helpful responses outside the group. She will also develop positive self-attributions about herself as a helpful and responsible individual.

Attribution research (research on how people attribute causality) supports the theory that moral behavior is learned in the group (Hunt, 1990). Batson et al. (1981) found that if a person's sympathetic arousal is called *"empathy"* by others, a person is more likely to help than if he is told he is feeling *"personal distress."* Therapy group leaders may positively or negatively reinforce prosocial behavior by how they label the uneasy silent discomfort experienced in the group when people are feeling bad for a member and not expressing it. The example from Chapter 2, where the group sat mute after a member had told them of a threatening blood pressure condition illustrates this dynamic.

Is Prosocial Behavior Ever Really Altruistic?

As discussed in Chapters 3 and 4, the very existence of behavior that is altruistic without an ulterior motive has been in serious question in psychology until very recently. This reflects a strong amoral bias in psychology, which has a number of intellectual antecedents. For the most part, Western psychology has declared the assumption of an altruistic instinct to be sentimental and frivolous, pointing to the lack of empirical and quantifiable evidence supporting it.

Since the very construct of morally motivated goodness was supposedly invalid, the only way to study morality until recently was to redefine it in terms of its opposite—as a disguised manifestation of selfishness. Most researchers implicitly if not explicitly adopted this model.

Hoffman's (1989) social learning theory of empathy, for example, assumes that empathy, while having some kind of embryonic existence in young infants, is nurtured primarily through the rewards it brings to the empathic agent or "empathizer."

In the late 1980s, however, altruism finally achieved scientific legitimacy. Psychology researcher Daniel Batson (1987, 1990) proposed that there are three types of motivation for altruistic acts. (1) anticipation of reward or punishment; (2) arousal-reducing egoistic motivation; and (3) empathically evoked altruistic motivation. Obviously, only the third motive is purely altruistic. Batson tested models for predicting behavior that included the purely altruistic motive and models that included only the egoistic motives. He found that models that included both egoistic and altruistic motives were significantly more predictive of prosocial behavior than models that included just egoistic motives.

It is interesting to imagine the different directions psychology might have taken had it assumed that people were motivated by altruism. If Western psychology had assumed that an altruistic instinct is latent in everybody, then it would have long since assumed responsibility for discovering contingencies that activate it in the here-and-now, and factors that cultivate a proclivity toward moral behavior in childhood. In other words, psychology might have discovered how moral action could be predicted, controlled, and perhaps even mobilized for the benefit of mankind.

Chapter 6

THE DEVELOPMENT

OF MORAL REASONING

Existing research (summarized later in this chapter) has shown little correlation between how people believe they will act in moral situations and how they actually behave in those situations. One's approach to moral reasoning nonetheless reveals a great deal about who one is. The decisions one makes about how moral dilemmas *should* be handled, even if one does not always follow through on these decisions, reflect one's level of cognitive maturity as well as one's underlying priorities and beliefs about the world.

Swiss psychologist Jean Piaget and American educational psychologist Lawrence Kohlberg have hypothesized that the capacity for moral reasoning develops in a succession of stages that are parallel to Piaget's stages of cognitive development. "Cognitive-developmental" theories of moral reasoning will be synthesized here, along with some of the criticisms that have been leveled at them. The cases of patients in psychotherapy will occasionally be used to illustrate the various developmental stages as they are described.

It has already been suggested that effective psychotherapy often involves patients learning new ways of thinking about the provocative moral dilemmas they bring to treatment. This chapter will suggest that patients' moral reasoning skills may actually be advanced when they are consistently called upon in therapy to think differently about "real live" (as opposed to hypothesized and abstract) moral problems.

PIAGET'S STAGES OF COGNITIVE DEVELOPMENT

Piaget believed that human beings learn through a process of oscillation between assimilation and accommodation (Piaget, 1936/1952). He suggested that the mind organizes experience into general categories, or schemata, and assimilates information in such a way as to fit into these categories. When a critical mass of new data cannot be absorbed into existing schemata, then a new category is formed, a process known as accommodation. Kegan (1982) likens assimilation to the notion of defense in psychoanalytic theory, viewing it as an attempt to resolve without reorganizing, whereas accommodation is seen as true insight, i.e., breaking through to the next level of understanding.

Piaget identified four stages of cognitive development in children, each stage involving successively more sophisticated levels of assimilation and accommodation. The first is the *sensorimotor stage*. Newborns are unable to distinguish between themselves and anything or anybody else, nor can they discriminate between their current experience and that of the past or future. Since they cannot compare experiences, they cannot consciously learn from them.

In the *preoperational stage*, the child's awareness of self and other and of time is more differentiated, but he is still not able to distinguish between how something appears to him and how it actually is. Standing at the top of a tall building, he will say, "The people are ants" as opposed to "The people look like ants" (Piaget, 1948/1965). He cannot grasp that if you pour the liquid from a wide beaker to a tall beaker, that the amount of liquid is the same. (He will say the taller vessel has more liquid.)

In the *concrete operational stage*, roughly corresponding to latency and pre-adolescence in many children, the world has begun to "stabilize" for the child (Kegan, 1982). At this stage the child begins to realize that pouring a given amount of water from one beaker to a differently shaped vessel does not change the amount of water. The child is very enthusiastic about categories and categorizing and believes with great passion that everything has its place in the universe.

As she begins to move into the stage of abstract thinking called *formal operations*, in the early to mid-teenage years, the child begins to be able to perform operations on her operations, to reason about reasoning. She can, therefore, plan and foresee contingencies and consequences.

It is vitally important that therapists understand how children think at each of these stages, because many of the dilemmas patients of any age bring to therapy are "coded" in the earlier levels of cognitive processing. Because we spend most of childhood prior to adolescence in the preoperational and concrete stages, most of our assumptions, "scripts," and theories about *how life is* are formulated in preoperational and concrete terms (Kitwood, 1990). If a therapist used just "formal operations" reasoning in listening to patients discuss their reality, she would have to dismiss most of the patient's ideas as illogical or psychotic. Knowing how the two-year-old, the six-year-old, or the twelve-year-old thinks and views the world, however, helps the therapist understand why things that are not logically linked may be tightly connected in the patient's mind. For the child, two events or perceptions that happen to coincide in time may become inextricably linked, or seen as causing one another, when in fact this is not the case. Another result is that experiences may become inaccurately generalized.

Coincidental events occurring in the life of someone (child or adult) whose thinking is at the preoperational and early concrete stage of operations often become generalized into intransigent pseudo-truths for that person, such as: "Anger kills," which might have emerged from having someone die just after the child has expressed anger toward that person; "Males are strong and decisive; women are weak," which might have emerged from experiences with a strong father and submissive mother; or "My success hurts others," which might have emerged from having one's parent seem depressed when one received an award or a chance for advancement. These notions can become overarching principles for existence that remain fixed in the person's mind and continue to shape their thinking even after they have moved onto the formal operations stage of cognition. Confronting these erroneous and often dysfunctional assumptions is part of the task of therapy.

Racism as a Function of Preoperational Thinking

All racism is generated from the preoperational level of thinking. Negative messages plus one or two bad personal experiences are combined and grossly generalized, congealing to become "fact" about another ethnic group or race. These "half-truths" are then imposed upon other people whose thinking is not advanced enough to resist.

The following discussion took place in a group of white, low-functioning psychiatric patients led by a white male clinical social worker and experienced therapist. It illustrates how racism and preoperational thinking go together, and also how racist attitudes can be therapeutically addressed in the context of treatment.

The group consisted of six people between the ages of 25 and 40, all single, most marginally employed or on disability. They carried diagnoses such as schizophrenic, schizo-affective, and bi-polar disorder. At the opening of this sequence Paul (a patient) asked Lew if he got the new job he was seeking.

"No, I didn't get to the interview," said Lew. "I have to go back. I was just too upset. The day before I was walking down the street wearing my best polo shirt when this car with niggers in it drove by and shot me with those huge water pistols. Those niggers are unbelievable. They're just out to use people, to manipulate you. They're everywhere. I hate niggers. They should be stopped."

"Yeah," agreed Doris. "You're right. There are blacks and there are niggers. Blacks are okay, but niggers are the ones who band together and do not work and get away with everything."

Paul, who has a physical disability that makes him look retarded even though he is relatively intelligent, said, "I work at a hospital and I have the same experience. The niggers are trying to get away with everything."

Morris, the schizophrenic, seemed to be really enjoying this conversation, smiling and agreeing as the racist comments became more blatant.

The therapist, Edward, felt the need to say something at this point, fearing that saying nothing would lead the group to believe he shared what seemed to be their uniformly racist perspective. He said to Lew, "Lew, if you want to work on being a racist as a problem in therapy, I'm available for that, but I need to tell the group that I feel that being racist is based on a lot of things that are not okay."

The discussion continued exactly as if Edward had not spoken at all, with Doris, Lew, and Paul commiserating about how difficult black people made their lives, and the others agreeing by default.

Getting frustrated with the group, Edward said, "Well, there seems to be a consensus in the group that racism is really cool."

Elaine, who had not spoken, said, "No, I don't agree. It's not okay. I don't think people can be pigeon-holed."

Lew protested, "But Elaine, come on, look at them. Niggers are always off having babies so they can get more money. That's why we're in a recession."

Edward said, "Lew, are you aware that more money is spent on farm subsidies than on welfare—to keep farmers from growing their food?" He offered a few other facts of this kind to counter the generalizations made by Lew and the others.

Then Edward said, "You know, maybe there is a way in which racism is cool. You never have to deal with individuals. I am so grateful my father was such a damn racist. Reacting against him, I learned to appreciate people from other backgrounds. I also had a lot of exposure to different people in my town growing up. In fact, it's no accident that at my kid's last party there were Indians, blacks, Egyptians—people of all colors.''

Edward had the group's attention now, particularly with the comment about his father. What they did not appreciate consciously was the paradox involved in Edward's statement: racists—like themselves—by turning people off to their racism, can teach other people—like themselves—to be egalitarian.

Edward then brought the discussion back to the group. ''Paul, what if no one had stopped to see you as you really were and everyone had just kept on calling you retarded.''

''I guess I would have killed myself,'' said Paul.

''Exactly,'' said Ed. ''You were different and that was considered bad and so you were lumped in with retarded people. What prejudice is about is squashing the differences among people.''

Lew was clearly struck by Paul's recognition of the pain of the prejudice directed against him. Lew said thoughtfully, ''You mean, maybe it's better to know individuals and not group people together . . . oh . . . I'm contradicting myself. That's not good.''

''Yes it is, Lew,'' Edward said gently. ''It's very good.''

The conversation continued with each person in the room giving pointed examples of when prejudice had been directed against them because they were mentally ill, female, obese, or whatever.

Through Edward's dialogue with his group, members were able to move the discussion from a highly subjective, reward-punishment, us-against-them, concrete kind of morality to one that ''rose above'' the differences that frightened them, and allowed them to see people as equals (**egalitarianism**). In talking to me about the incident afterward, it was clear that clients' values are very much a part of what Edward sees as targets for change in therapy. Edward, who has had considerable therapy himself, is as forceful in confronting his own racism and sexism as he is that of his clients. It is notable that, while they felt challenged to respond, none of the clients seemed to feel shamed by Edward's confrontation.

Edward was surprised at how easily convinced the members were to renounce their prejudices and identify with the oppressed. As he said, ''It makes you realize that in a way all they need is a little guidance and help in thinking about these matters. They did not get that at home, just as they did not get a lot of what they needed from their parents. We do not hesitate to give our children or our students guidance. Why do we think we should deprive clients of it when it is part of what they really need to have a healthy life?''

Needless to say, the preoperational level of processing of these patients was not changed in the course of one confrontation by their group therapist. Nonetheless, Edward's point is well-taken—without exposure to the wider, more moral view, the clients will certainly not become "disembedded" from racist assumptions. Edward's intervention lifted the level of the discussion beyond the preoperational level of bigotry to a much more constructive plane where some identification with the role of victim begins to occur. If this kind of interaction is repeated over time in Edward's group, some improvement in some of the members' levels of moral judgment might indeed take place.

KEGAN: MEANING-MAKING AS EMERGENCE FROM EMBEDDED THINKING

Kegan (1982) integrated Piaget's theory of assimilation and accommodation with object relations theory to explain the development of meaning-making and psychosocial functioning of the individual over the course of the life cycle. Kegan sees "development" as "a series of internalizations" and notes that "something cannot be internalized until we emerge from our embeddedness in it" (p. 31). The experience of life, for Kegan, involves cycling through mental states of embeddedness, emergence and internalization in our perception of the physical world, relationships, roles, and ideas.

If we are embedded in a relationship, as we inevitably are in the dependent relationship with the parent in infancy, for example, then we have no perspective about this relationship. Instead of us "running" the relationship the relationship "runs" us. This can happen in relationships throughout the life cycle.

Later in the life cycle, by early adolescence, we can become embedded in a role. Being embedded in a role means we are absorbed by it, and it dictates most of our life choices. We are not able to relinquish or appropriate that role as needed, but are, rather, "stuck" in it most of the time. An example might be when we are locked into the role of nurturer, not able to see that we are being taken advantage of or abused, or that there are people available to take care of us once in a while.

We can also be embedded in a philosophy or an institution, letting it govern our decisions and moral practices. A good example of this was the father of Bart, the rageful pacifist whose interaction with the group was presented in Chapter 2. This "Great Santini" type of father was so invested in the "institution" of patriotism and the draft that it superseded all consideration for his son's feelings, let alone respect for his son's point of view about war and the military. In a way, Bart had the same problem. By being so identified with the 1960s "institution" of draft-resisting and flag-burning, he at first could not see how unfair he was being in attacking Leanne when she was so worried about her brother being sent off to war. Another group member, Deborah, made him aware of this when she said "Bart, I'm not sure if you're burning the flag or burning your father. It's 'you scum, you rat' toward us now." This and other feedback from the group helped him step back and become "dis-embedded" from his "institutional" role and to see the moral issue of the war in a context that also recognized the humanity of his fellow group members.

Each time we emerge from embeddedness, Kegan says, there is always some kind of shift wherein what has been experienced as "subject"—identified with the self—moves outside of the self and is experienced as "object." We can examine and talk about the relationship instead of being absorbed by it. We can choose when to play a certain role instead of being constrained to that one and no other. And, as with Bart, we can learn that we can espouse the ideals of a given institution without having to blindly conform to institutional behavior.

Paradoxically, it is only when it is "objectified" in this way that the relationship, the role, the idea or the philosophical position can be internalized in ways that are useful, becoming part of the mix of other experiences, roles, relationships, and ideas rather than dictating our behavior and attitudes and limiting our choices.

While emergence from embeddedness is always occurring on a number of different levels, Kegan says that each of Piaget's stages represents a sort of meta-emergence from a more pervasive state of embeddedness. Each stage, he says, is "the consequence of a given subject-object balance, or evolutionary truce" (1982, p. 39); the process of movement from one stage to the other is "the evolutionary motion of differentiation (or emergence from embeddedness) and reintegration (relation to, rather than embeddedness in, the world)" (p. 39).

KOHLBERG'S THEORY OF MORAL DEVELOPMENT

While we were walking along a busy street together, my niece, age twelve, asked me what the book I was writing was about.

"It's about goodness, and why people choose to be good," I answered.

Walking faster, my niece said, "People decide to be good because they see other people get in trouble for doing the wrong thing, and they don't want to be punished . . . or, they might be good because they want to please people . . . or else, they might just decide to do something right just because it's right."

"That's about the size of it," I said, as we crossed the street.

In the time it took to walk one block, she had summed up Kohlberg's stages of moral development.

Lawrence Kohlberg, a developmental psychologist at Harvard in the 1970s and 80s extended Piaget's theories of moral and cognitive reasoning into a stage theory of moral development.

Kohlberg presented young male subjects with a story containing a moral dilemma.

> The wife of Heinz is near death and the druggist is overcharging tenfold for the medicine that will save her life. Heinz does not have the money. He tries unsuccessfully to borrow it and to obtain the mercy of the druggist. Finally he breaks into the drug store and steals it.

Based on their decisions about what Heinz should do and why and how they justified these decisions, the boys were classified into six stages, described here (Table 2). These stages are the sociomoral correlates of Piaget's cognitive stages. The six stages are clustered into three levels, which are roughly comparable to the gross divisions in cognitive stages.

The *preconventional* level (Level I), which includes Stages 1 and 2, is shaped by preoperational thinking and is guided by a desire to avoid punishment and to satisfy the self. The first stage, Stage 1, heteronomous morality, is a morality that rests solely on fear of punishment. Stage 2 is an individualistic and relativistic morality, based on the understanding that everyone has his/her own self-interest to protect.

The *conventional* level (Level II) is mostly a function of concrete operations and early formal operations and includes Stages 3 and 4. It puts its focus on interpersonal considerations and what is expected by society of its members. Stage 3 morality is guided by others' expectations and a need to conform to what others want in order to gain approval, affection, and respect. Stage 4 morality differentiates society in the aggregate and its needs from those of the individual. Stage 4 morality is based on the demands of one's social system and conscience in relation to society's expectations.

The third level, called *postconventional morality*, is a consequence of attaining the cognitive-developmental formal operations level. It is

Table 2: The Six Moral Stages

Level and Stage	Content of Stage		Social Perspective of Stage
	What Is Right	Reasons for Doing Right	
LEVEL I—PRECONVENTIONAL Stage 1—Heteronomous Morality	To avoid breaking rules backed by punishment, obedience for its own sake, and avoiding physical damage to persons and property.	Avoidance of punishment, and the superior power of authorities.	*Egocentric point of view.* Doesn't consider the interests of others or recognize that they differ from the actor's; doesn't relate two points of view. Actions are considered physically rather than in terms of psychological interests of others. Confusion of authority's perspective with one's own.
Stage 2—Individualism, Instrumental Purpose, and Exchange	Following rules only when it is to someone's immediate interest; acting to meet one's own interests and needs and letting others do the same. Right is also what's fair, what's an equal exchange, a deal, an agreement.	To serve one's own needs or interests in a world where you have to recognize that other people have their interests, too.	*Concrete individualistic perspective.* Aware that everybody has his own interest to pursue and these conflict, so that right is relative (in the concrete individualistic sense).
LEVEL II—CONVENTIONAL Stage 3—Mutual Interpersonal Expectations, Relationships, and Interpersonal Conformity	Living up to what is expected by people close to you or what people generally expect of people in your role as son, brother, friend, etc. "Being good" is important and means having good motives, showing concern about others. It also means keeping mutual relationships, such as trust, loyalty, respect and gratitude.	The need to be a good person in your own eyes and those of others. Your caring for others. Belief in the Golden Rule. Desire to maintain rules and authority which support stereotypical good behavior.	*Perspective of the individual in relationships with other individuals.* Aware of shared feelings, agreements, and expectations which take primacy over individual interests. Relates points of view through the concrete Golden Rule, putting yourself in the other guy's shoes. Does not yet consider generalized system perspective.

Stage	What is Right	Reasons for Doing Right	Social Perspective of Stage
Stage 4—Social System and Conscience	Fulfilling the actual duties to which you have agreed. Laws are to be upheld except in extreme cases where they conflict with other fixed social duties. Right is also contributing to society, the group, or institution.	To keep the institution going as a whole, to avoid the breakdown in the system "if everyone did it," or the imperative of conscience to meet one's defined obligations (Easily confused with Stage 3 belief in rules and authority.)	*Differentiates societal point of view from interpersonal agreement or motives.* Takes the point of view of the system that defines roles and rules. Considers individual relations in terms of place in the system.
LEVEL III—POST-CONVENTIONAL, or PRINCIPLED Stage 5—Social Contract or Utility and Individual Rights	Being aware that people hold a variety of values and opinions, that most values and rules are relative to your group. These relative rules should usually be upheld, however, in the interest of impartiality and because they are the social contract. Some nonrelative values and rights like *life* and *liberty,* however, must be upheld in any society and regardless of majority opinion.	A sense of obligation to law because of one's social contract to make and abide by laws for the welfare of all and for the protection of all people's rights. A feeling of contractual commitment, freely entered upon, to family, friendship, trust, and work obligations. Concern that laws and duties be based on rational calculation of overall utility, "the greatest good for the greatest number."	*Prior-to-society perspective.* Perspective of a rational individual aware of values and rights prior to social attachments and contracts. Integrates perspectives by formal mechanisms of agreement, contract, objective impartiality, and due process. Considers moral and legal points of view; recognizes that they sometimes conflict and finds it difficult to integrate them.
Stage 6—Universal Ethical Principles	Following self-chosen ethical principles. Particular laws or social agreements are usually valid because they rest on such principles. When laws violate these principles, one acts in accordance with the principle. Principles are universal principles of justice: the equality of human rights and respect for the dignity of human beings as individual persons.	The belief as a rational person in the validity of universal moral principles, and a sense of personal commitment to them.	*Perspective of a moral point of view* from which social arrangements derive. Perspective is that of any rational individual recognizing the nature of morality or the fact that persons are ends in themselves and must be treated as such.

guided by the desire to operate according to universal moral principles, which consider the needs of others on a much broader level. At Stage 5, there is a recognition that some values and rights of all people supersede the social contracts of individuals and of institutions. At Stage 6 there is even greater concern on behalf of all people. It is recognized that people are not means to an end, but are "ends in themselves"

The following is a brief description of Kohlberg's six stages. In some cases, therapy clients have been chosen to illustrate the level of moral thinking represented by the stages.

Kohlberg's Six Stages

Stage 1

Jerry, age 42 and a former bookie, was an articulate spokesperson for Stage 1, heteronomous morality. While you might not recognize it from this anecdote, Jerry is quite an intelligent man with a responsible technical job. He is a good father and a loyal and trusted friend to many. He demonstrated no learning disabilities in school and, in fact, even completed some courses at a community college. It is hard to believe, given his generally high level of functioning, how primitive Jerry's moral reasoning is. Not that he is psychopathic or sociopathic—he is very well-behaved and holds high standards of behavior for himself. (Remember, we are just dealing with moral reasoning, not moral action when we are discussing Kohlberg's stages.)

The way Jerry decides whether he is "good" or "bad" (his terms) in his actions is by the nature of the consequences (Jerry's thinking is classically preoperational). The events that follow his decisions or actions are always interpreted as either reward or punishment for what he has done. When it rained on his vacation, Jerry decided it meant he should not have raised the rent on his tenant just before he left home. When he got cancer in 1984, he perceived it as punishment for his gambling and bookmaking, which he had stopped in 1980. Clearly, the overlap between Jerry's moral stage and his narcissism is considerable, which is often the case in Stage 1.

While he no longer gambles nor operates as a bookie, Jerry now sees all of life as a "crap shoot," the stakes of which are rewards and punishments for his behavior. The following incident takes place in group therapy and illustrates Jerry's surprisingly low level of moral reasoning. It also shows how Jerry's fellow group member, Peter, feels he has grown in his own moral reasoning.

JERRY: (*with reference to the gambling*) I let my maker down.

DANA: (*knowing Jerry is Catholic*) If you need God's forgiveness why don't you go to confession and get it over with?

JERRY: That would be hypocrisy. Besides, if I get forgiven and get happy, I'll get cancer. And if I get sick and die, then he [God] will really get me.

ROSA: Gee, Jerry, I'm Catholic, too but even I'm not that bad.

PETER: I used to think that if I ever stepped out of line, whap! Right to hell. I was always *so* good. Then I began to realize that any being capable of being that powerful could hardly give two shits about what Peter Smith did yesterday.

JERRY: Well, I keep seeing this bum in the streets of my town. Every time I lost in gambling, I would see this bum a few hours before. Now, every time something bad happens, which is all the time, I see this bum. It's a sign.

PETER: I no longer think that the bad things that happen are punishment for what I do.

THERAPIST: (*to Peter*) How does that make your life different now?

PETER: I realized that my real punishment was not to love myself. I realize that was my punishment to impose. I'm changing that now.

Stage 2

Stage 2 is a stage in which self-interest is the primary motivation, but compromises can be made in the interests of being realistic, if they will ultimately be beneficial for the self. The individual cannot easily "put himself in the other guy's shoes" and certainly does not consider the needs of the larger system. A wide range of people reason at the Stage 2 level. It is the mind set that is thought to drive the capitalist system, as well as some of the very nationalist and conservative politics that predominated during the 1980s.

The expedient gang leader who has many allies in high places, the shrewd industrialist who will forego environmental concerns if it will make him more money, the self-serving politician who leads his country into war for territorial and monetary gain—all operate at Stage 2, at which wrong is defined as failing to get what you want.

Stage 3

Stage 3 people are highly invested in personal relationships. In Stage 3 people consider morality in terms of what is expected in a given relationship. There is a conscious attempt to adhere to the "Golden Rule," treating others the way one wishes to be treated. Because the person tends to be embedded in relationships, however, she may not be able to see the relationship in the larger context of her life. She will not abuse another, but she may not be able to get out of or distant enough from the relationship to recognize abuse against her self or some of the immoralities she commits to preserve her relationship or protect her loved one.

In the pathological version of Stage 3, we find codependents, masochists, and corruptible politicians, all of whom will put immediately gratifying or necessary relationships ahead of what others might consider to be right or wrong. We saw Stage 3 reasoning in full flower in the case of Jane reported in Chapter 1. Jane's entire morality was conceptualized in terms of what she perceived as being best for her family. It did not occur to her that she had a duty to protect society from her father-in-law's driving, nor that it was wrong to beat up the woman who was having an affair with her husband. As Kegan says, at this stage, if "personal expectation is the source of right-making, . . . a man can be as easily a whore for his children's approval as for that of his political cronies" (1982, p. 59).

Stage 4

At Stage 4 the individual thinks in terms of the needs of the group with which she is identified. There is intense awareness that there need to be laws and rules, and a sense that these should be arrived at by consensus and due process, given the many and conflicting needs that exist in a complicated social system. The sense of justice of a person at this stage is guided by the principle "If everyone did that. . . ." This person tends to see the individual's rights as more or less subsumed by the needs of the group. A person who operates in Stage 4 will be conformist with respect to society's rules or to the rules of whatever institution she identifies with, and may take a moralistic positions with those who diverge from the agenda of this reference group. Bart, the violent pacifist discussed in Chapter 2, and his father are both examples of Stage 4 thinking.

Stage 5

Having achieved formal operations, the Stage 5 person is able to wrestle with divergent moral perspectives and is quite concerned with issues of **justice** and rights. At Stage 5, the individual has a sense that laws should be a function of contracts mutually and freely arrived at by those whom they affect. At Stage 5, the individual is highly mindful of the welfare of others, including people he has never met. He believes in universal guiding principles to which he aspires to be committed. More autonomous than Stage 4 reasoners, he will occasionally perceive and be bothered by the fact that a particular law seems to be inherently unfair to some one individual or to a group.

Ironically, a good example of Stage 5 moral reasoning is another bookie, Dale, age 47, who also does volunteer work with the homeless. Dale does not gamble himself because he is concerned that he will become an addict.

Dale considers himself to be a very moral person. He thinks about morality a lot and has attained a fairly sophisticated level of reasoning:

> I am operating outside of the law, but I've thought about it, and have decided I am not being immoral because I never gyp anyone. I am very, very careful about that. I never coerce people into paying their debts to me. I have let go of thousands that were owed to me because I won't hurt or threaten anybody. Another thing I won't do is encourage an addicted gambler. I'll cut 'em off right away if I spot an addict.
>
> Now I realize that I am not paying taxes on this business. That bothers me—not enough to stop—but it bothers me because if everybody did it the country wouldn't run. I do have other businesses that are legit and I pay taxes on them. But it still bothers me.
>
> So I run my life by balancing things off. If I do something I feel guilty about, I try to balance it. I try to do something good for someone or for some people.

Dale frequently volunteered statements in his therapy about the importance of honesty and responsibility in relationships and in society. He frequently mentioned discussions he had had with friends about a variety of philosophical and ethical issues. For example, he reported an argument he had had with a friend about abortion in which he defended his anti-abortion position with logic and consistency.

Paradoxically, Dale has a son, Joey, who at the time of the therapy was in jail for armed robbery. Dale said,

> It was a stupidly planned attempt, stupidly executed. He has no remorse—none. He says he would have felt a little bad if someone had gotten hurt—otherwise, nothing. It was a game to him, and he lost. But he didn't lose enough. I wish he'd gotten a worse punishment, because he'll be worse when he gets out. He is actu-

ally enjoying the federal prison he is in, because he is making many contacts which will help him "play the game" smarter when he gets out.

(Joey would seem to be a low-level Stage 2 in his moral reasoning.)
I asked Dale if he had any feelings about the son robbing the bank besides it being stupid.

It was wrong, because he endangered lives; he could have hurt someone. It was also wrong to take other people's money, although that doesn't bother me as much, because they'd get it back through the FDIC or whatever. Of course, I would never, never do that, so it does piss me off that he would. That's why I say, "I'm moral; he's amoral."

While his behavior may not be socially acceptable, Dale reflects a sophisticated level of moral reasoning. He is definitely not "institutionally" embedded but is "aware of rights prior to social attachments and contracts" (Kohlberg's Stage 5). He believes that many rules in life are relative, while others like "life" and "liberty" are sacrosanct. He has "the [Stage 5] perspective of a rational individual aware of values and rights prior to social attachments and contracts . . . [He] considers moral and legal points of view; recognizes that they sometimes conflict and finds it difficult to integrate them" (Kohlberg's Stage 5).

Stage 6

The morality of a person at Stage 6 is based on much wider universal principles. There is a commitment to justice, equality and dignity for all human beings. I would extend the meaning of Stage 6 to include concern for survival of the planet itself as well as human beings on it; for the rights and dignity of individual humans will not be fostered or maintained if the planet is wrecked by environmental destruction and disease (Roszak, 1992).

Role-taking and Moral Development

Toward the end of his life in the early 1980s, Kohlberg, while retaining his model for evaluating moral development, realized that the experiences of being in a community and of being part of the process of democracy were crucial for moral learning (Kohlberg & Higgins, 1987). He said, "Feeling a sense of *we*; of collective security; of being in a group, [is] necessary for students to care about fair decision-making and moral dialogue" (p. 110). Kohlberg developed the concept of the democratic school, which he called the "Just Community," in the high school in which he worked in the Bronx, New York. He said the school must be a community where everyone shares in tasks that require positive cooperation and taking one another's point of view. He believed that democracy is not just an end in itself, but a vehicle for education, since "democratically achieved norms are respected and internalized."

In his later years, Kohlberg decided that progression through the stages does not happen automatically with age or traditional education but, rather, is fostered by engaging in a large variety of social experiences, particularly role-playing. Kohlberg stresses the capacity to take roles as fundamental in moral learning. The ability to take roles evolves as one progresses through the cognitive stages; it can even be used as a gauge of moral development level. Central to the Piagetian "formal operations" stage and Kohlberg's postconventional Stages 5 and 6, is the capacity for reciprocal role-taking. Reciprocal role-taking is what is needed to abide by the Golden Rule: "Do unto others as one would have others do unto you." In order for the Golden Rule to even make sense, much less seem compelling, one has to "create a continuing social other" as Kegan says (1982, p. 54). Most children under the age of 11 and many adults as well, cannot do this.

Kegan (1982) read the following story to a class of 11- to 12-year-olds: A boy who is a terrible baseball player is sent to the outfield where he predictably drops an important catch, causing the opposing team to acquire several runs. He is jeered mercilessly for days and weeks. Later in the year, a newer, even worse player performs more clumsily, and the first boy jubilantly joins his former tormentors in teasing and humiliating the other boy. Much to Kegan's horror, all the children but one thought the boy was right to join in the cheering. He was, they said, "entitled to his turn." Kegan explains that, at their developmental level, still in the concrete stage of operations, they could not identify with both boys simultaneously. They could take the role of the other, but not *both others* at the same time.

Even though role-taking capacity naturally increases with development, practice helps. Staub (1971) found that kindergarten children who were given a chance to role-play the part of the distressed other helped the distressed other and demonstrated increased sharing with others. It makes sense that teaching the skill of role-taking should be a crucial part of therapy as well as education. Moreno (1946/1977), founder of psychodrama, based his psychodrama therapy on the process of role-playing and what he called "role-rehearsal." Moreno's psychodramatic method includes the technique of role-reversal, whereby group members play several parts within a single scene, thus acquiring several points of view simultaneously.

Group therapy inherently provides a host of opportunities for taking the role of the other, whether formally as in psychodramatic therapy, or simply through the group process in psychodynamic or interactional groups (Nicholas, 1984).

Criticisms of Kohlberg's Model and Alternative Approaches to Moral Development

Validity Issues

In a thorough review of studies that use Kohlberg's scale and/or a subsequent scale by Rest (the Defining Issues Test), Rest (1986) found that, controlling for age, level of formal education is an overwhelmingly powerful predictor of level of moral development. The education/age factor is 250 times more powerful a predictor of Kohlberg morality stage level than is gender. Formal education is by far the greatest predictor of cognitive stage, when age is controlled for. The validity of Kohlberg's construct of moral stages is thus highly questionable, since the stages seem identical with education and cognitive-development level.

Kohlberg's stages are based on Piaget's stages, which are based on the assumption that rational logic and autonomous thinking are the only crucial aspects of moral development. These values are precisely those held most dear in traditional Western education, which reflects the intellectual priorities of Western culture. Assumptions about the supremacy of logic and autonomy when it comes to defining morality and moral development have been heartily challenged from a number of quarters of psychology in recent years.

One would think that Kohlberg's scale would be biased in favor of people brought up in Western cultures; however, Rest's meta-analysis of studies comparing people across cultures on the Kohlberg scale and controlling for education level, showed a surprising comparability of subjects. The explanation for this is not that the scale is culturally unbiased, but that higher education curricula in most countries are based on the Western values of autonomy and rationalism inherent in the Kohlberg instrument.

My own criticism of Kohlberg's scale is that it does not assess the virtues. It touches on **justice** and **egalitarianism** and interpersonal **responsibility**, but only as they can be expressed within the limits provided by the dilemma. I would like to see a test that evaluates the other aspects of goodness and that measures the outer limits of positive morality—i.e., one that depicts how good people can be.

Lack of Connection between Moral Reasoning and Moral Action

Another criticism of the Kohlberg moral development theory that I, among others, have, is that his stages of moral reasoning are not in any way predictive of moral behavior. People do not consistently behave the way they think they will in moral situations. Some people who think they would not steal the medicine if confronted with Heinz's dilemma might find themselves doing something comparably (or even more) dishonest to save the life of of their child or spouse. By contrast, someone operating at Stage 1 or 2 of moral reasoning, given a situation in which they were called upon to help or make a sacrifice on behalf of another, might be just as likely to be helpful as a more sophisticated moral thinker.

Kohlberg's early research in the 1970s suggested that moral judgment and moral action might converge at the higher levels of moral judgment (Kitwood, 1990). In other words, the higher a person's level of judgment according to the Kohlberg scale, the greater the likelihood was thought to be of his behaving in ways consistent with what he thinks he would do in a given situation. In his review of later research, however, Blasi (1980) found little evidence that this was the case. Sophistication in moral judgment level was found to be somewhat related to behaviors reflecting **honesty** and **altruism**, but no link has been found with the other three virtues: **eglalitarianism**, **responsibility**, and **justice**.

Research has also failed to back up Kohlberg's assumption that the more sophisticated one's moral reasoning, the more likely one will be to resist social pressure at the level of action. Only a very weak link was found between these variables in the studies in Blasi's review.

Social Constructionist Perspective

Some of the most severe criticisms of Kohlberg's model comes from a group of psychologists, sociologists, and educators who identify themselves as *social constructionists*. Social constructionists decry the conceptualization of morality in such individual terms. Instead, they view morality as socially constructed, a "social, emotional dialectic of practical reasoning among people" (Haan, 1985, p. 996). New ideas are shaped cooperatively and despite one person influencing another, the result is a *co-discovery* (Damon & Colby, 1987).

Social constructionist research has demonstrated that presenting a moral dilemma to an individual in isolation, without dialogue with others, does not elicit one's highest level of moral reasoning. Much more sophisticated reasoning is demonstrated by individuals after participating in group discussions about ethical issues (Haan, 1985). The most fruitful discussions for moral education, the social constructionists have found, are those that are leader-*facilitated* rather than directed, in ways that encourage disagreement and personal disclosure. Such discussions create within the individual a sort of creative dissonance, what Haan (1985) calls *social disequilibrium*, which prompts more in-depth thinking about social **justice** and **egalitarianism**. (The other three of our five virtues—**responsibility**, **honesty**, and **altruism**—are not "pulled for" in either Kohlberg's or the social constructionists' moral dilemmas, so we do not know whether the social disequilibrium experience enhances them or not.)

The theory of social disequilibrium provides a strong rationale for group therapy as a moral enterprise. Social disequilibrium is described by Haan as a

> holistic, emotional and interactive experience wherein participants expose themselves to others' complaints and even to the possibility that they themselves may be found morally wanting or even wrong. From the interactional perspective, tolerance for this kind of conflictual interchange is required if development is to occur. (1985, p. 997)

In competently led group therapy, the stress of the group process, combined with the support of the group, tends to dislodge the individual member's outmoded frames of reference and allows them to be replaced with new beliefs and values (Nicholas, 1984). The advancement in moral sensitivity and reasoning achieved by Pauline, Bart, and Jane in Chapter 2 was due in no small part to the dis-equilibrating experience of having their ideas of right and wrong questioned in their therapy groups and being offered alternative moral perspectives.

A major criticism of Kohlberg's model by the social constructionists and others who are wary of the bias of individualism in psychology (see Chapter 4) is that Kohlberg's stages move from a dependency on external pressures at the low end to an overly strong reliance on the self at the upper end. Critics say this does not reflect moral improvement but, rather, a withdrawal from relatedness. As we discussed in our section about "moral sensitivity," a feeling of connectedness is crucial to moral responsiveness. This criticism would be bolstered by our previous example of a Stage 5 client, Dale, the "moral bookie" who, while he is thoughtful about morality, is not particularly socially concerned or involved.

In defense of Kohlberg, Rest (1986), who himself expanded upon Kohlberg's work, explains that Kohlberg's model of moral development is actually a description of how awareness grows in individuals of the existence of a larger social world. Each stage, Rest says, is a progressively more sophisticated set of concepts about the nature of the social good. The theory as a whole is based on the assumption "that with social experience people develop more elaborate conceptions of how to organize cooperation" (p. 10), and that at each level of social cooperation being conceptualized there is a particular sense of fairness. The degree of sureness of moral behavior of the person is, according to Rest, "a function of the degree of fit between the social problem being considered and the concept of cooperation and social organization being used" (p. 11). At Stage 6, the individual has built a moral frame of reference broad enough to encompass a much more complex social organization. He can mentally grasp the needs and rights of a wide range of individuals and groups and, by means of logic, sort through several compelling and seemingly conflicting moral issues in order to set correct moral priorities.

Feminist Perspectives: Gilligan, Her Critics, and Nancy Chodorow

The argument that males and females have different moralities has a long history in Western culture (e.g., the different ethos espoused by gods versus goddesses in the Greek myths) and is reflected in psychoanalysis and psychology. Freud's disparaging view of female morality incensed feminists in his own time and thereafter.

> Women [have a] different level of what is ethically normal. . . . Their superego is never so inexorable, so impersonal, so independent of its emotional origins as we require it to be in men . . . they show less sense of justice than men . . . [and are] more often influenced in their judgments by their feelings of affection or hostility. (1925/1961)

Piaget, who did not make gender distinctions between males and females with respect to other aspects of cognitive development, did claim to have observed a great difference between the genders on moral reasoning. Boys, Piaget said, are much more interested in rules than are girls. Girls have a very pragmatic attitude toward rules, he said, and tend to be only interested in formulating regulations that they perceive will enhance the game (Piaget, 1948/1965).

While Freud and Piaget are criticized by feminists for postulating moral inferiority in females, Kohlberg is reproached for assuming no differences in morality between the genders at all. In 1977, Carol Gilligan, a former student of Kohlberg's, challenged the applicability of Kohlberg's model to females (Gilligan, 1977, 1982) by pointing out that Kohlberg's scale, which Kohlberg used only with male subjects, if applied to females, would show females to be "less moral" than males. Kohlberg's scale, Gilligan argued, rates preoccupation with personal relationships (Stage 3) as less morally evolved than allegiance to an institution (Stage 4) and even less than autonomous, non-aligned, abstract moral reasoning (Stage 5)—even when this "preoccupation" is for the welfare or comfort of another. In listening to young females' responses to Kohlberg's "moral dilemmas," Gilligan found that girls tended to place a higher moral value on meeting one's responsibilities to those in one's care than they did on maintaining logical consistency and adherence to abstract rules of what is fair and just.

Gilligan's alternative to Kohlberg's model suggests that one evolves through stages of concern for an increasingly wide circle of "others" and a building of values that "permit survival . . . of plants and animals and humans, the community, the tribe, the family, the children" (French, 1985, p. 483). The first stage of Gilligan's model is orientation to individual survival; the second is goodness as self-sacrifice, and the third is a morality of nonviolence.

Two criticisms of the two-morality theory have emerged in psychology and feminist theory. First, and foremost, the basic assumptions upon which Gilligan bases her theory have been shown to be invalid. Reviews by Watson (1988) and Rest (1986) of studies on gender differences in moral reasoning revealed that there are no differences between males and females on the Kohlberg test, and a small difference, with females scoring higher on Rest's version, the Defining Issues Test. Kitwood (1990) quotes just one study by Watson (1988) in which highly significant differences emerged between levels of British teachers, with males scoring higher.

Second, the two-morality theory perpetuates some of the same negative stereotypes promulgated by Freud and Piaget. The notion of two moralities, one based on justice and one on caring for others, particularly when a significant gender split is proposed, only serves to raise invidious comparisons between two aspects of morality that should, by rights, be joined together. Apollonians will always favor the more traditional "straight-thinking," "male" ethic of abstract justice over the compassionate but possibly "fuzzy-headed" morality of goodness, while Dionysians will decry the justice morality as dry and heartless and prefer a morality based more on "care."

An undeniably potent factor in Gilligan's theory of morality is that it assumes a strong role for emotion and relationship to others in moral decision-making. If not fueled by love, empathy, and a feeling of connectedness and responsibility to those in one's care, moral reasoning does indeed become dry and abstract, irrelevant to the process of real live human beings trying to live together in peace and harmony. By the same token, however, a morality based purely on personal responsibilities and feelings of relatedness to others is too ill-defined to account for and organize the moral complexities of the larger world. Clearly the two moralities are really two sides of the same moral coin, each incomplete without the other.

While there may not actually be two discrete moralities, one male and one female, it is difficult to argue with Gilligan's observations that males and females seem to differ in their moral priorities. Nancy Chodorow (1978), a feminist sociologist who is also a psychoanalyst, combined considerable empirical research on infant and parent-child behavior with clinical observations, and suggested that, in cultures where mothers do most of the childcare, females are programmed from birth to value nurturing and connectedness and the mothering role. Not only do they identify with their mothers in that capacity, but they are consistently positively reinforced for being caring and negatively reinforced for being independent. Boys, on the other hand, are encouraged not to identify too much with the mother, nor with the perspective of care and nurturance, but rather to strive toward toughness and autonomy from females. Unfortunately, while boys need and crave identification with older males, in cultures where mothers are the primary caretakers, fathers tend to be absent or unavailable; thus, the symbiotic ties with mother linger on into adult life, but in a discomfitting form, with the male consciously and unconsciously devaluing the nurturing he still deeply needs.

The family drama of ambivalence about the "moral mother" plays itself out in society (or vice versa depending on how you look at it). Since the rise of industrial capitalism in the United States, women have been expected to be not only the sole nurturers of the children, but also the sole emotional and moral support of the hard-working husband when he returns from his toil in the big bad world. As the only source of nurturing and love the "moral mother," unaided by father, is "the only game in town" for both her sons and her daughters. She is powerful and difficult to leave.

The "moral mother" is as ambivalent about her role as everyone else. Because she has been deprived of her autonomy, she and her children may never learn to value any parts of her other than the mothering part. Her creativity, intelligence, and competence may be discounted by herself and/or others, and her love may then become tinged with resentment. She may crave appreciation for her sacrifices and create demands on her children that they find uncomfortable or even impossible to meet.

Chodorow suggests that it is this ambivalence toward and on the part of the "moral mother" that accounts for what seems to be a widespread devaluation of caregivers and caring in society. In their struggle to stave off unresolved longings for mother and to dis-identify with her, men have had to diminish the importance of a morality based on love. Women, while clinging to their identity as moral mother, are hurt and angry at the criticism they often receive for their attempts to give care and, at the same time, for not caring enough. All of this has resulted in goodness being put on the back burner by men who see it as threatening to their autonomy, and held in ambivalent regard by women, who sometimes see their own goodness as a source of oppression.

Need for the Narrative Form

Another criticism of the Kohlberg approach to morality is that it is not life-like enough. Morality has to do with how we live our lives on a day-to-day basis—down here on earth, not in an ivory tower. Morality is a function of human passions and concerns, and it springs out of relationships, which are full of complexities and feelings. It is not a dry logical process locked in each individual person's head. As Vandenberg (1991) says

> the roots of morality are to be found, not in logic and scientific reasoning, but in the existential conditions of our lives. People are not just another set of objects to which logical operations are applied. They are co-beings who are in the world with us. (p. 1283)

The reminder that morality is about living with people is echoed by Staub (1989) who speaks of it as "a consequence of trust and connectedness [which] arise from proximal experiences [and] evolve through a history of contact, cooperation and friendly relations" (p. 265).

Based on the premise that morality is about life and relationships, Vitz (1990), as well as Gilligan, suggests that since morality evolves through interpersonal interaction over time, then the major form of communicating moral ideas and learning should be narrative rather than propositional. Stories involve human beings interacting over time in a context, while propositional dilemmas promote individual thought that is logical and objective, but also linear, ahistorical and impersonal.

The narrative invites the listener's or reader's subjective responses, which Vitz and others claim provide more valid information about the responder's moral priorities and motivations than could ever be revealed by his objective thoughts about an abstract moral dilemma occurring in a vacuum. As Vitz says, "what a person will see in a moral situation depends not on moral rules but on what a person cares about" (p. 713). Vitz further points out that the narrative form, in contrast to the propositional form, can describe people's intentions, goals, interests, wishes and desires, all of which play a part in moral decision-making and action. Narrative illuminates not only conscious, but also unconscious motivation. Narrative shows us personality factors and predispositions, which can cast a whole new light on the relative morality of a particular decision even by Kohlberg's own standards. For example, in the case of Heinz's dilemma, we are not told what kind of a man Heinz was before this situation arose—how he thought and felt about life and about his wife. If Heinz were a philanderer prior to his wife's illness and made the gesture of stealing the medicine to atone for his peccadillos rather than because he really believed it the right thing to do, then this would not reflect high-level moral thinking.

Chapter 7

PSYCHOANALYTIC PERSPECTIVES

ON HOW WE BECOME GOOD

What is a "good person"? How does one become "good"?

In the previous two chapters we dealt with three of Rest's four components of moral development: moral sensitivity, moral action, and moral judgment. This chapter explores the development of *moral attitude* in the context of personality.

Two very different perspectives have been generated by psychoanalysis on how a predisposition toward goodness grows in an individual as a consequence of childhood experiences. Freud's explanation for the development of goodness was that it is a totally defensive process. We become altruistic and socially responsible as a result of our efforts to control our powerful biologically built-in yearnings to be greedy, destructive, and promiscuous. The second rationale for goodness stems from object relations theory and holds that being good to others is a natural outgrowth of a different biologically based need—the need to attach and to give and receive love. While they are based on different views of human motivation, these two psychoanalytic concepts of how goodness develops do not really conflict; rather, together, they offer a fairly complete explanation of both prohibitive and prescriptive morality.

120

FREUD'S THEORY ABOUT HOW
WE BECOME *LESS BAD*

Freud's theory of personality was based on the idea that biologically based needs, known as "drives," are the source of human motivation. Like our animal ancestors, Freud said, humans are compelled to assuage their hunger, thirst, and sexual desire, and to fight whomever or whatever might threaten the satisfaction of these cravings. What appears to be voluntary moral action on the part of humans toward one another, Freud says, is ultimately, if indirectly, a defense against "the pleasure principle."

The pleasure principle is based on the Darwinian assumption that the selfish pursuit of instinctual satisfaction is endemic to survival of the species. Freud's view is consistent with the most negative view of evolution, in which no concessions are made to the existence of altruism as a built-in trait (see section on "Egoistic Darwinism", Chapter 4). Freud gave no credence to the possibility that the virtues—**altruism, honesty, responsibility, egalitarianism,** or **justice**—serve any evolutionary purpose in and of themselves.

By 1920, however, Freud began to question the unilateral dominance of the pleasure principle in human motivation. After bearing witness to man's inhumanity to man via the carnage of World War I and the fierce anti-Semitism that was already emergent in Europe, Freud struggled to account for human self-destructiveness, a tendency that seemed to contradict the pleasure principle and the laws of evolution. He posited *thanatos*, the death instinct, as an additional and alternative motivating force to the pleasure principle. *Thanatos* was conceptualized as the unconscious desire to return to an inorganic state (1920/1961). The moral implications of the concept of *thanatos* are discussed in Chapter 6.

Neither Freud's pleasure principle nor the death instinct allows for the development of positive values and virtues. For Freud, pangs of conscience and acts of goodness were all defensive—unconscious attempts, however disguised, to manage aggressiveness (1930/1961), libidinal cravings, and narcissistic urges (1914/1957). All moral precepts, values, and codes of behavior were burdensome internalizations of the restrictions imposed by parents and society, reluctantly accepted in childhood as a way of forestalling the threat of punishment and feelings of guilt. His morality was, therefore, primarily prohibitive, focusing mainly on what is *not* allowed and what we must *not* do, as opposed to prescriptive, giving indications of how to lead a better life.

Freud described three psychic structures that assist us in managing our drives and becoming "civilized" and "moral." They are the *superego*, the *ego ideal*, and *conscience*.

"Moral Structures" in Freudian Theory

Superego

The superego, said Freud, develops with the resolution of the Oedipus complex. When the young child (five to six years old) realizes that he cannot sexually possess the parent of the opposite sex, he relinquishes incestual strivings and begins to settle for an admiring alliance with the parent of the same sex. He begins to identify with the same-sex parent, incorporating that parent's values as well as other attributes and expectations. This is not a particularly pleasurable or spontaneous experience for the youngster, since the whole process is really a reaction formation against the lingering desire to kill that parent and sexually join with the parent of the opposite sex.

For Freud, the superego was a necessary evil. While it fulfilled an important function for the protection of civilization against the greed and destructiveness of the human race, it represented a "tyrannical function of the mind" (Dilman, 1983, p. 121) for the individual. In 1930, Freud wrote:

Civilization obtains the mastery over the dangerous love of aggression in individuals by enfeebling and disarming it and setting up an institution within their mind to keep watch over it, like a garrison in a conquered city. (1930/1961)

The punitive, often primitive workings of the superego are seen by Freud to be the cause of much of mental illness. Because the passions it tries to control are so strong, the superego can fail to manage them (psychosis); engage in "overkill" causing crippling guilt (depression, neurosis); or some combination of both. Since so much of superego functioning is unconscious, Freud explained, neurotic superego problems can generate pathological states of mind, self-destructive behavior, and somatic states, which are hard to explain or to alleviate because they are driven by "a sense of guilt which is finding atonement in the illness and is refusing to give up the penalty of suffering" (1923, p. 228). When guilt is unconscious in this way, the person "does not feel guilty, he simply feels ill" (p. 228).

The Ego Ideal

The second guiding force of morality, according to Freud, is the ego ideal, a structure of the psyche that evolves in response to the child's need to defend against his archaic narcissism. (1914/1957). According to Freud, the infant initially loves and idealizes the self only. Gradually, he begins repressing this love of self and directing the idealization toward another person, usually one or both parents. The values and standards perceived by the infant as being held by this idealized object or objects then become a standard by which the ego measures its worth. Later the ego ideal is broadened to "the common ideal of the family, class or nation" (p. 123). While, early on, the feeling of not having lived up to the standard of the ideal results in a fear of the loss of parental love, it later "is translated into a sense of guilt" toward "an indefinite number of fellows" and a "dread of the community" (p. 123). This fear of censure for not having lived up to the standards of one's society is the only reason Freud gives for why people might develop and adhere to the virtues of **altruism, responsibility,** and **justice.**

The concept of the ego ideal provides a small window for prosocial behavior that the superego does not. The existence of the ego ideal explains why virtuous behavior might occasionally be gratifying for the doer as well as the recipient. As Gaylin (1990) says, Freud's ego ideal is a potentially constructive self-critical force, which modifies the primitive cruelty of the superego by allowing us to set our own standards and judge our behavior according to these potentially more benign criteria. We tend to feel proud and satisfied with ourselves when we succeed in meeting the standards of goodness that we have incorporated from the idealized objects.

On the other hand, the ego ideal, while it can inspire us, can also brutally cut us down to size. It is the ego ideal, according to Freud, that is responsible for dousing us with shame when the standards we have set for ourselves are not met (Lewis, 1971). Sometimes the demands of the ego ideal are as unreasonable and unattainable as any generated by the superego, and when this is the case, an individual can be tortured by feelings of inadequacy. In Freudian theory, it is the desire to avoid shame, rather than the desire to be or do good, that accounts for most virtuous action prompted by the ego ideal.

Conscience

Though the terms conscience and superego are often used interchangeably in his writings, conscience for Freud was basically superego with a

wider range. It is the internalization of society's collective fear of retaliation for murderous thoughts and feelings during the Oedipal period.
Collective Oedipal guilt for having murdered the Oedipal father causes
men to band together "with equal rights and united by the totem prohibitions which were to preserve and expiate the memory of the murder"
(Freud, 1921/1957, p. 205).

Like the superego, conscience operates defensively. Freud stated
that the "dread of castration [in the Oedipal phase] is probably the
kernel round which the subsequent fear of conscience has gathered"
(1921/1957, p. 233). Stirrings of conscience are then perpetuated by the
fear of society's potential to punish wrongdoers; the dread of being left
alone; and the jealous worry that others will get more than we will if
we do not make sacrifices on behalf of the larger social group.

This latter motivation—greed and jealousy in relation to others in
society—forms the only rationale we find in Freud for the institutions of
egalitarianism and **justice**. He stated "social justice means that we deny
ourselves many things so that others may have to do without them as
well or, what is the same thing, may not be able to ask for them. This
demand for equality is the root of social conscience and the sense of
duty" (1921/1957, p. 196).

Caring as Reaction Formation

Freud basically ruled out the existence of goodness for its own sake. For
Freud, all virtue and goodness were at best disguises for egoistic motives, and at worst, subversive influences on prohibitive morality. He
stated that the "origin of every social impulse is an evil impulse" (1921/
1938, p. 861), and "the tender altruistic trait . . . merely compensates
for the opposite attitude of brutal egoism which is at the base of it"
(p. 863).

Caring and love, far from inspiring us to be virtuous, Freud said,
have exactly the opposite effect. "Conscience has no application to anything that is done for the sake of the object; in the blindness of love,
remorselessness is carried to the pitch of crime" (1921/1957, p. 191).

Freudian theory focuses on the child as beast (Mitchell, 1988). This
metaphor reinforces Freud's view of the essential egoism of humankind, a perspective that, even though Freud declared himself to be an
atheist, resonates strongly with the Roman Catholic doctrine of original sin.

Freud was one of the first people to recognize the prevalence of
child abuse in the histories of his psychiatric patients. At first, Freud
took his patients' reports of child sexual abuse at face value and attrib-

uted the presence of psychosomatic and psychological symptoms in these cases to the trauma caused by this abuse. Unfortunately, Freud later reversed himself on this point and decided that the reports of abuse by these patients were largely fantasy, a product of instinctually based incestual wishes. Freud then made matters worse by generalizing these "findings" about clinical patients to the normal population. The result for Freudian theory was the exaggeration of the role of incestual fantasy in personality development. The child, in Freudian psychoanalysis, came to be conceptualized as not just bestial, but lecherous.

Alice Miller (1984a) has objected vehemently to this negative characterization of the child, both in society and in therapy. In her writings she shows that the logical extension of seeing the child as wild, selfish, evil, and promiscuous is to assume that children need to be controlled and harshly disciplined, "tamed," and "put in their place," as opposed to nurtured, valued, validated, and encouraged. This then becomes the rationale that justifies brutality and blaming the victim in psychoanalysis. Miller decries the destructive tendency of analysis to imply that the patient somehow wished for, if not directly invited, the sexual and other physical abuse. She emphasizes repeatedly that attributing a patient's trauma to his own bestial nature as a child not only is devastating to the patient's self-esteem, but is likely to drastically increase the fear, guilt, and powerlessness that is already torturing the patient.

Gaylin claims that "Freud implicitly recognized a moral genetic nature to the human being and a range of emotions in the service of that reality" (1988, p. 51). Perhaps this is true, but when we compare Freud's theory of morality with most subsequent analysts, we find that Freud's theory is considerably more cynical about human nature and offers a more cogent rationale for why we refrain from evil than for why we might develop an attitude that is favorably disposed toward goodness.

Post-Freudian Theories of Goodness

Freud's morality assumed that fear of guilt and punishment is the primary motivator for "not doing bad" and for "doing good." After Freud, personality theorists and clinical writers struggled to find a rationale for values and virtues in personality theory and as sources of motivation.

Neo-analyst Karen Horney believed that we are born moral (meaning loving and caring) and that our morality is affected by influences of home and culture growing up (Mullan, 1988). She did not separate morality from personality, stating that the degree and quality of one's "moral behavior" is a function of one's "total character or personality structure" (Horney, 1950, p. 136). Erich Fromm (1947) made personality and moral values inextricable, saying, "It is impossible to understand man and his emotional and mental disturbances without understanding the nature of value and moral conflicts" (p. 7).

Rank (1954), the existential analysts Binswanger and May, post-existentialists Ernest Becker (1973), Yalom (1980) and, most recently, Vandenberg (1991) have all decried the mechanistic, valueless, will-less view of man implied by Freud's theory, which eliminates vital human concerns such as the fear of death, the meaning of life and suffering, the need for relatedness and belonging, and the fear of aloneness.

Allport (1950), one of the major "third force psychologists" of the fifties and sixties, saw what the individual holds most valuable as a central organizing factor in personality. Allport referred often to "guiding attitudes" (Epstein, 1989). He stated that "to understand a person we have to know what he is trying to accomplish, what he is trying to become, not merely 'how he got the way he is'. . . . It is the long-range intentions that have the power to order habits, thoughts, traits into a unity of function" (p. 148). Another "third-force psychologist," Maslow (1968), conceived of a hierarchy of values to which human beings naturally aspired, ranging from basic needs for shelter and food, to the need for mutually supportive relationships, to the concern for the well-being of others, to the need for self-actualization and spiritual fulfillment.

An interesting theory of goodness, which retains the Freudian model of personality, was proposed by Wilhelm Reich. Reich discussed the "genital character," which he sees as the "ideal of maturity" (1950, p. 165). Having worked through pre-Oedipal and Oedipal conflicts, the genital character naturally displays **responsibility**, dependability, loyalty, seriousness, courage, and integrity, and "goodwill toward others" (**altruism**). He is not greedy (**altruistic**), not envious or jealous (**egalitarian**), is able to forgive, to appreciate, and to give to others (**altruistic**), is **honest**, nonmanipulative, and nonjudgmental (**justice**) (Dilman, 1983; Reich, 1950). It is not clear in Reich's writings how the resolution of the Oedipus complex leads to such a high level of virtue in interpersonal relationships.

Goodness in the Context of Culture: The Ego Psychology Perspective

Ego psychology is a branch of psychoanalytic psychology founded by Heinz Hartmann that emphasizes the adaptation of humans to their environment via the mediation of the ego. From this perspective, individual morality, like every other part of the personality, is seen as developing not just at home with the family, but in the context of culture.

In an article entitled "Ego Morality," Pattison (1968) states, "cultural moral values are part of the necessary structure needed by the growing personality" (p. 193). The values internalized by the individual from his culture are not simply prohibitions but "rather the values and definitions of appropriate behavior by which man governs his behavior" (p. 193). This prescriptive, culturally based "ego morality" is of a wider scope than the ego ideal, which consists of values of parents and other specific idealized persons in the child's life. Pattison concludes that "What ego morality posits is that the individual optimally acts to integrate one's behavior into the commitments to oneself and one's society according to a whole range of social values" (p. 204).

Optimally, Pattison suggests, superego morality, the ego ideal, conscience, and ego morality operate in concert and balance one another. For example, superego prohibitions might help one curtail exaggerated narcissistic aspirations spawned by the ego ideal. On the other hand, as Freud noted, the superego can be highly primitive and neurotically distorted. The positive thrust of the ego ideal and the more tempered and conscious ego morality can act together or separately to offset the superego's self-punitive actions and replace them with more constructive interpersonal endeavors. If the ego ideal has incorporated and identified with parental values that are unrealistic or less than virtuous by society's standards, the more conscious, discriminating ego morality can bring a more objective, self-critical perspective to bear on the situation.

Ego psychologists emphasize that the individual's moral learning does not end at home. Experiences with relationships in school, community, work, and the larger world throughout the life cycle are also crucial. Nonetheless, while the childhood environment is not the only influence, the ego psychology perspective considers it central for the development of ego morality. As Dilman (1983) summarizes,

> praise and blame, encouragement and reward, rebuke and punishment, take place in the course of the development of relationships in which the child meets love, anger, sorrow and gratitude, learns to care for, consider and help others, to give up things for them [**altruism**], to cooperate and in certain cases to look up to and emulate them. He develops expectations with regard to others and learns to respond to their expectations with regard to him [**responsibility**]. He learns to make promises and to rely on those made by others, to trust and be trusted [**honesty**]. He develops a sense of **responsibility** and begins to act on his own behalf in the light of concerns which are now his. (p. 109)

HOW WE LEARN GOODNESS:
THE OBJECT RELATIONS VIEW

Object relations theory pertains to human relationships, how they are experienced by the individual, and how they affect cognition, affect, and behavior. While some object relations theorists recognize the existence of drives and others do not, object relations concepts are lodged in an ego psychology framework, emphasizing ego functioning and adaptation more than the instincts as central aspects of personality development.

Whereas in Freudian terms, morality means knowing what not to do and how not to do it, in the object relations framework, morality is much more positive. In this framework, moral development means an ever increasing capacity to care and to act out of concern for others.[1]

The process of developing this caring attitude starts in infancy. Acquiring values and standards of behavior and learning to tolerate criticism are a central part of the formation of a child's identity and character (Dilman, 1983, p. 109). In the context of a loving relationship, the child learns what Dilman describes as moral emotions, which "develop in the course of early personal interactions—love and the desire to be worthy of it, gratitude and guilt, the wish to make amends, the desire of approval. What rules there are make sense in relation to these emotions and desires" (pp. 109–110). The desire to be loved and accepted, the desire to please the loved one, the ability to respond efficiently to one's own guilt feelings in order to get "back on course" in an important relationship—are all positive moral motivations which are linked. Desire and goodness are not in conflict in this model but rather are in harmony (Wallach & Wallach, 1990), provided the "holding environment" of childhood is adequate.

In contrast to the Freudian perspective, the object relations view is that morality is relational rather than individualistic, and that it is motivated by the desire to give and receive love rather than by a fear of punishment. The object relations model holds that morality is largely voluntary rather than defensive, although the threat of loss of love, care, and approval can be a powerful motivation for acts of goodness.

If the capacity to feel and act upon concern for others is satisfactorily nurtured at home in the early years, it is likely to grow in later years to include an ever widening circle of "others" in the community and the larger world (Sagan, 1988). In this section we will trace some of

---

[1]Not that the object relations theorists spell out a theory of morality—this section is my own distillation of the object relations perspective on morality.

the steps a child must take in order to develop a concern for others and to be able to express and act upon this caring in increasingly wider arenas from the deeply personal to the more anonymous global context.

Secure Early Attachments

Goodness begins at home in infancy. For the child to develop morally, in the object relations framework, he must have satisfactory early attachment experiences from the very beginning of life. In the earliest weeks, he must feel fully taken care of and accepted by his parent figure. He must experience, as Kitwood (1990) says, "a sense of inner abundance . . . [which] ideally would form a child's pre-conscious moral knowledge" (p. 201). The moral agenda at this stage is the building of "basic trust" in others as represented by the parent figure (Erikson, 1963), as well as a generally good set of feelings about the self.

It is these positive feelings of satisfaction and harmony that translate themselves later into a "set of propositions" about the "rights and responsibilities of human living" (Kitwood, 1990, p. 118). These may include the right to self-determination, the right to be validated as a separate person, the right to be loved and cared for and to be able to rely on people, the right to have one's own feelings and thoughts. Needless to say, harsh and inadequate attachment experiences generate the opposite feelings—lack of safety, unmet longings, frustration, and disharmony—which, in turn, generate harsher propositions about the way the world is and a very different set of expectations about one's own and others' behavior.

As Kitwood (1990) says, no one can develop morally without "the security of one or more relationships of outstanding moral quality" (p. 200). If this has not occurred in childhood, then perhaps therapy—group, family, or individual—may fill the gap. The ideal moral and therapeutic environment is attentive, nurturing, and forgiving, and provides the kind of security and love that fosters concern for others in childhood.

Learning to Feel Appropriate
Guilt and Making Reparation

For morality to exist, an individual must be able to feel guilt. According to object relations theorist Melanie Klein (1946), the first step in being able to feel guilt is to relinquish what she calls the "paranoid position" in favor of "the depressive position." In the early months of infancy, when the child is distressed, she concocts rageful fantasies of retribution against the parent whom she feels has caused her discomfort (paranoid position). Later, at about six months, the child develops the capacity to occasionally feel "overcome with dismay when he realizes that the parent with whom he has become enraged and destroyed in his phantasies is the same person he loves dearly [depressive position]" (Dilman, 1983, p. 122).[2]

The capacity to feel depressive guilt is the beginning of a capacity to feel concern for others, which helps the infant learn gradually to control his impulses. It is the beginning of feeling "sorry" (Money-Kyrle, 1955), and it carries with it the desire to make restitution and obtain forgiveness. Klein emphasizes that, while the remorse is fueled by pain at the perceived loss of the object and, therefore, is somewhat self-serving, it is also legitimately altruistic and aesthetic. The child really does feel responsible for having destroyed something he experienced as beautiful and wishes to undo the damage he has done by committing some act of kindness toward the other. When he notices that he has hurt the parent, physically or emotionally, he will actively seek to "save the love object, to repair and restore it" (Klein, 1935, p. 290). This effort to "make the object whole again through love [then] becomes the driving force within the personality" (Greenberg & Mitchell, 1983, p. 126). At this point, it seems to me, the basis of a moral character has been established.

While the potential for feeling guilt and initiating efforts at reparation is constitutionally built-in, it is the parents' interaction with the child that determines whether the child's guilt response develops in a healthy or distorted way. If the parent is nonretaliatory and forgiving, but not masochistic, the child will develop a moral sensitivity that is fairly reliable in subsequent relationships. There are a number of ways a parent can respond to early guilt reactions of the child that can impede the development of the child's moral sensitivity. If the parent typically becomes angry and humiliates the child when she does something aggressive (hitting, food-spitting, yelling), the child may become so fearful of authority that she may not even get to the stage of learning to feel guilty or to apologize. If the parent notices but consistently refuses to accept gestures of "apology" from the child (such as wanting to cuddle or give the parent something), the child may decide that there is no use in even feeling sorry, much less in saying so. If the parent is masochistic

[2]While Klein claimed that paranoia, depression and guilt operate in the first year of life, it is unlikely that these experiences take place in the child's mind exactly the way she describes it, given the limited operations of the sensorimotor stage of cognition. It is not necessary to fix these phenomena at a particular developmental phase, however, to appreciate their fundamental reality in human interaction in people of all ages. Klein is describing modes of feeling and transitions between these modes, which are highly familiar to parents and to therapists, and which have major implications for moral development.

and hides all traces of hurt when the child behaves cruelly or rudely, the child may never learn to read the cues of another's pain and suffering. Some parents find the guilty response of the child gratifying and unwittingly foster it as a way of extracting affection from the child. A child growing up in such a relationship will certainly harbor a lingering confusion about the boundary between guilt and affection.

Many clients find that the first time they really feel their concern for others is recognized and appreciated is in therapy or in their therapy group. Likewise, many undergo their first positive experiences of expressing remorse and receiving forgiveness, or of being the recipient of another's apology and being able to forgive in therapy and particularly in group therapy. Several such instances are described in Chapter 8.

Dis-identification with the Aggressor and the Building of Compassion

In Freudian theory, identification with the powerful Oedipal parent is seen as a defense against the wish to destroy that parent. In identifying with this parent, the child decides to obey society's rules as they are embodied in that parent. This identification includes incorporating the part of the parent that will punish the self (feel guilt) if he strays from what is "right." This is the beginning of identification with the aggressor. Identification with the aggressor was explained by Freud as an extension of identification with the Oedipal parent, part of the process of developing of self-restraint against internal sexual and aggressive drives.

By contrast, object relations theory suggests identification with the aggressor as the basis of immorality, in that it diminishes or rules out concern for others. An aggressor virtually always sees the victim as bad and separate from the self, while the self is seen as good and justified in hurting the other. The minute one becomes consciously or unconsciously identified with the victim, some restraint is likely to enter the picture, and willful immorality against the other will be curtailed.

While Freud thought that healthy growth necessitated an identification with the punitive part of the parent, object relations theorists believe that optimum development requires identifying with the gentle and nurturing parts, and dis-identifying with the cruel and aggressive parts. In the object relations view, good parenting and good psychotherapy both work toward transforming identification with the aggressor into identification with the victim and, further still, into compassion toward and an active interest in helping the victim.

This movement from identification with the aggressor to identification with the victim is the beginning of compassion, a crucial step in the development of positive morality. For goodness to flower, however, identification with the victim is not enough; there needs to be some realization of responsibility for protecting the victim. This requires identification with the compassionate nurturer (Sagan, 1988).

To follow the sequence that takes a person or group from identification with the aggressor to identification with the protector of the victim, one must be able to form positive identifications and avoid, or at least manage and resolve, splitting.

Building Positive Identifications

Freud (1921/1957) differentiated three stages of identification. In early infancy identification means being at one with or merging with the other. As some self-object differentiation occurs, identification takes place through introjection, an entirely unconscious process by which the representation of the other is internalized. One's experience of self and perception of one's identity is determined by these introjects. With further individuation, identification becomes a matter of perceiving shared qualities with another person. The more important the quality thought to be shared, the greater the level of identification with that person (Freud, 1921/1957). Identification is a very powerful force, far stronger than modeling. The child identifies with parental behavior, habits, and values, even while seeming to reject parental authority.

Identification is morally neutral. A child will take on the values of the parent, whatever they are. If the parent values violence as a way to solve problems, that is what the child will learn. If the parent values forgiveness, the child will experience first hand the wonderful relief of being forgiven and will be willing to forgive others. The fact that there is no stopping this identification process, even when the parents' values are inhumane, is a stark reality, which psychology and the culture still have not fully faced. (The profound influence of television as an object of children's identification should be considered as well.) In addition to the problem of wrong values being transmitted to the child at this stage, the unavailability of a parent can result in identifications with negative influences.

Inevitably, identification with parents involves a certain amount of *idealization*—seeing the important other as "all good" and overlooking the bad parts. This serves an important defensive function for a child. Given that no parent really is perfect, then "only by separating out the negative aspects of the . . . parents is it possible to preserve the imago of a benign world" (Sagan, 1988, p. 112). Idealization later extends to older peers and important figures in the child's or adolescent's private world and culture, such as sports figures and musicians. As with identification, idealization is a human need and as such, takes place no matter what the values of the parents or idealized figures are. In other words, idealization, like identification, is morally neutral. If the idealized parent values excitement and money, so will the child. If the idealized parent values honesty and fairness, so will the child.

It is important to note, however, that the quality of identifications are shaped primarily by the nature of the relationship between the child and the person with whom he identifies and the modeling he receives from that person. The way the parent treats the child powerfully overrides the influence of the parent's consciously held values on the child. A child who identifies and idealizes one who treated him with love, consideration, and respect, will probably not be inclined to abuse others, even if the parent has a rather paranoid view of the world. The child will probably grow up feeling pain when other people are hurt and abused, just as his parent felt pain when he was hurt. He will feel a desire to protect the innocent and vulnerable, as the nurturing and compassionate parent-figure took care of him.

Many, if not most, therapy patients do not have a history of strong identifications with positive role models and need positive identifications in order to get better. Therapists and fellow therapy group members are, therefore, likely to become powerful objects of identification for therapy patients. The research of Truax and Carkhuff (1967) suggests that therapist personality variables are powerful determinants of patient outcome in treatment. Since values are part of what is passed on to the patient through the process of identification, the nature of the therapist's values may have a strong impact on a patient's formulation of her own priorities. More importantly, however, just as the moral variables in the parent-child *relationship* are transmitted to the child, so are the values inherent in the therapist-patient relationship absorbed by the patient. If the therapist-client relationship is characterized by mutual **responsibility**, **honesty**, **egalitarianism**, and **justice**, then it is these values that will be intensified within the client through identification. If the therapist or the group member with whom the client identifies is a basically **altruistic** person, the client may identify with this quality and expand it in her relationships outside of the therapy.

The Resolution of Splitting

Splitting, the mental polarization of "objects" (affects, experiences, people, parts of people, ideas) into good and bad, happens naturally in the minds of babies and children and continues in adult functioning to some degree, as well. Splitting is a natural sorting process by which the young child makes sense out of his world, and it is the beginning of

moral discrimination. A little child has no trouble differentiating between experiences that feel "good" and those that feel "bad," and it is
these perceptions, loosely linked in time and logic, that form the substrate of his morality. The mother who provides the comforting and
nurturing breast is "good" and "righteous" while she's doing that; at
the same time, when she leaves him or participates in his discomfort,
she is judged as "bad" and "evil," at least for that moment, hour, or
day.

While it is vital and normal, splitting is a primitive cognitive process,
which causes some problems intrapsychically and interpersonally, later
on. In the first year of life, good and bad experiences cannot be integrated because of the child's limited cognitive capacity. The infant thus
experiences either "good mommy" or "bad mommy" but not both
simultaneously. He may hate mommy and love daddy and then switch,
by the minute or by the hour. Splitting is normal and necessary in
infancy and early childhood, but with increased cognitive development
and, given some patience and consistency on the part of the parent,
considerable integration of good and bad objects can be expected to take
place during the course of the first three years.

In later childhood and adulthood, when the cognitive capacity of
the individual is theoretically such that integration of polarized objects
is possible, splitting will still be resorted to as a defense under conditions of psychic stress. Klein said splitting serves the defensive function
of "dispersal of destructive impulses" (1956/1986, p. 216), while later
object relations theorists saw splitting as a process designed to relieve
tension, not just from destructive impulses but from other painful internal conflicts as well (such as wanting to be close but fearing to trust
because of the threat of abandonment).

Everyone splits sometimes, and borderline personalities do so frequently (Kernberg, 1975). Splitting is the hallmark of the borderline who
cannot contain or integrate contradictory feelings and impulses but is
forced to experience one or the other in isolation with great intensity.
Because of his tendency to "split," the borderline can only see moral
issues in black and white, good or bad, terms.

Splitting makes **justice**, **responsibility**, and **egalitarianism** hard to
achieve and sustain. As long as I see *only* the bad parts of myself or
another and the good parts are split off, I will feel highly punitive toward myself or toward the other. As long as I only see the good parts of
myself or of another, and the bad parts are split off, I will excuse immoral behavior in myself or the other. If, in dealing with two people, I
see one as all bad and the other as all good, I am probably being unfair
to the one I am seeing so negatively.

Splitting is a group as well as individual phenomenon, and is a cause of misunderstandings, pain, and hurt on the family, community, and international levels. Tragically, humans are constantly prone to seeing the world in terms of "good guys" and "bad guys." We see the sad consequences of splitting in Europe today, where the break-up of the Soviet Union, instead of leading to peace, has released pent-up hostilities among nationalist groups, which have been festering for centuries.

In the case vignette from Chapter 6, where group members were expressing racist stereotypes, Edward, the therapist, made an effort to help the group "own" the split-off parts of themselves, which they attributed to blacks. He did this not just because he did not want to appear to condone racism, but because splitting is unhealthy for the psyche. As long as negative parts are split off from the self, we have no control over them. Those split-off parts can "do their thing" without mediation or inhibition from our more rational, conscious, or humane parts, as happened with the Nazi doctors interviewed by Lifton (Chapter 5), and with Rick, the HIV-positive young man (Chapter 5) whose fearful and rageful part was so split off from the rest of him that he endangered others with his promiscuous behavior.

Resolving splitting takes enormous conscious emotional and mental effort, a difficult challenge for anyone at any time, but particularly when we are under stress. Splitting, like other defenses, is resorted to because *it works*, at least for a while. When we engage in splitting, we can temporarily move from feelings of powerlessness and anxiety to righteous indignation, superiority, or sadistic satisfaction. The price we pay for this is severe, however, for underneath, we tend to feel any number of unpleasant sensations: emptiness, dissatisfaction, resentment, guilt, shame, or envy, to name just a few. Only if we can own the parts of us that are split off can we feel whole and satisfied. This, of course, means facing things about ourselves that we would rather attribute to others. I might have to admit that not only was the other person greedy, mean-spirited, and stubborn, but *I* was as well. While "owning" my faults may temporarily cause me shame and guilt, it ultimately will help my self-esteem and feelings of connectedness with others, for I will realize that my faults are part of what makes me human, that no one else is perfect either, and that the proudest moments we have are when we can acknowledge our complete self, liabilities and all, without fear.

Resolving splitting does not just mean admitting one's faults, but accepting one's good qualities as well. In therapy we are called upon, or should be called upon, to face the parts of us that are loving, generous, and moral. For some clients, exposing their goodness is excruciatingly painful, for it means revealing their deep caring for others, which they feel renders them vulnerable to hurt and rejection.

The conditions for learning to resolve splitting in childhood are similar to those necessary to learning how to feel appropriate guilt. In families where it is possible for children and parents to "screw up," apologize sincerely, be forgiven, and make amends, the child will begin to integrate the good and the bad, realizing that he and others have their bad parts and good parts, that one can love and hate the same person, and that the same person can be destructive and loving at different times.

Abusive parenting, by contrast, exacerbates and encourages splitting. In such a home there is a chronic lack of safety, trust, consistency, and space and time to think things out. Conflict management strategies are nonexistent and the child is often forced to take sides instead of encouraged to try to see two or more points of view simultaneously.

Splitting accounts for the strange sense of accountability in the minds of many people who have neglected and/or abused as children. Many patients in therapy seem to have the "good guys" and "bad guys" reversed. Some of them continually blame themselves for the abuse they suffered. Others seem fixated on the perception that they are totally blameless and take no responsibility for anything that happens to them. The first tendency is known as "introjective identification" and the second "projective identification."

Introjective Identification. When a child has parents who are frequently aggressive, corrupt, unreliable, and uncaring, her young psyche must work hard to dissociate from these experiences and to scrape together an idealized image of the parent so that she can feel safe and loved. The more unrealistic the idealized parent image, the more splitting must be resorted to in order to protect it. When someone uses splitting to protect a basically untenable idealization, it is called "introjective identification."

Taking the badness into oneself and attributing goodness to the other starts as a defense against the realization that one has no safe, nurturing parent. Splitting then becomes the person's routine way of dealing with any abusive authority figure. Fairbairn called this form of identification with the aggressor identification by means of introjection, a "way of dealing with an object that feels bad, by taking it inside and controlling it there by pushing it out of consciousness" (Scharf, 1992, p. 57). With the person who is stuck in introjective identification, morality will be a matter of what she perceives will make the abusive parent love her or disapprove of her less. She is stuck in Kohlberg's Stage 3 or, as Kegan puts it, "interpersonal morality," which is completely guided by the need to feel loved. She will define herself as selfish and irresponsible and her parent (lover, boss) as altruistic and responsible, and will have little notion of the unfairness of the situation for her, even when others try to point it out. This person, often identified as "codependent" in addictive relationships, has an unbalanced virtue profile. She is far too **altruistic** in her intimate personal relationships to the point of losing her self altogether, and she takes too much **responsibility** for the behavior of the "introjected" idealized object. On the other hand she is not at all **responsible** or generous to herself or to other people in her community. Furthermore, she is usually quite **dishonest**. She engages in self-deception at every turn and is all too willing to distort the truth to others in order to preserve her idealized picture of the authority figure.

Projective Identification. To willingly blame others for what one knows are one's own failures is **dishonest**, ungenerous, **irresponsible**, and unfair. Unfortunately, however, the mechanism of splitting makes it quite possible for a person to blame others unjustly and maintain complete oblivion with respect to his own culpability. Projective identification is a form of splitting in which unwanted feelings are unconsciously split off from the self and projected onto another person; the self then acts in reaction and response to those feelings supposedly emanating from the other. When projective identification is operating in a situation, accountability becomes very unclear.

Projective identification can make for some confusing interactions and generates responses that do not seem to make sense in a given context. Therapists are likely to feel the effects of projective identification in the presence of clients, an experience that at first may baffle the therapist but, when understood, reveals important information about the client. A woman is being mistreated by her husband and the therapist feels furious, while the woman seems to feel nothing. The woman picks up on the therapist's anger and starts defending her husband against the therapist. The therapist, initially irritated and confused, realizes that it is the *client's* anger at her husband that he has been feeling, anger that she has split off from her own consciousness and projected onto the therapist.

Another client, having just obtained a divorce in order to marry another woman, is telling the therapist how happy and relieved he is. The therapist, although he believes the divorce to be positive for the client, feels a sudden and powerful feeling of sadness, almost despair. The therapist realizes that he is experiencing the split-off despondency of the client. He questions the client as to whether he is feeling any pain about the divorce, but the client denies it. The therapist becomes concerned that the client needs to defend so intensively against these feelings. The therapist knows that should this client not be able to acknowledge and verbalize this pain, he will be vulnerable to a cataclysmic depression when the split-off feelings of loss and guilt finally come "home to roost."

Projective identification is an interpersonal as well as intrapsychic phenomenon. Therapists frequently encounter it in couples. A woman who is unconsciously furious herself somehow manages to get her spouse into a rage, and then feels frightened of him; or, one partner, sexually conflicted and inhibited since adolescence, professes to be sexually liberated, while her lover, sexually active and confident with partners prior to their relationship, "just happens" to develop a problem with sexual arousal, frustrating the supposedly eager partner.

Racism is a consequence of projective identification on the social level. One group sees itself as possessing all virtuous qualities and projects the attributes they find repulsive or frightening onto other ethnic or racial groups. We saw this in Edward's group; the members projected their rage and destructiveness onto the mischievous black boys with the water gun and felt justified in hating them.

Projective identification is at the heart of the self-fulfilling prophecy, for when one is the recipient of another's projections, one often finds oneself "acting the part." In my book (1984), I described how this occurred for quite some time in one of my therapy groups. A woman who had been sexually abused by her father sat smiling while she defended her sadistic boyfriend's mistreatment of her to the group. So successfully did she project her own rage onto the men in the group that they became uncharacteristically angry and sadistic toward her. A great deal of the therapy for the men and for her involved owning these disowned parts—she, her fury, and the men, their previously denied anger at other people in their lives, which they had displaced onto her.

Projective identification is the chief enemy of **egalitarianism** and **justice**, and is usually what gives the green light for aggression by one person or group against another. If the badness in a situation is perceived as located out there, the "I" or the "we" may feel justified in rooting it out by hurting or destroying the "other" in which the evil is thought to reside.

A major purpose of therapy is to resolve splitting—to identify with what we have projected out and disclaim what we have erroneously introjected. It calls for relentless questioning of much that has previously been taken as morally incontrovertible, including knee-jerk attributions of responsibility and blame. In this way, the search for psychological truth through psychotherapy is, as Kitwood (1990) says, a moral venture.

Spreading Goodness beyond the Home

While object relations theory helps us understand the genesis of goodness, very little is said in object relations literature about what needs to happen for the loving child to be able to take his positive morality out of the home and make a constructive impact on his community or the larger world.

Carrying object relations theory to its logical conclusion, Sagan (1988) believes that, as the child gradually makes moral sense out of his relationships with parents and siblings, his concerns automatically broaden to include people who are "farther from home." If attuned to them at home, the child will become alert to the inequities existing in her world and the larger world as well. How she then responds to them becomes a function of her early moral training at home combined with the influence of school and peer relationships.

Under optimal conditions, Sagan says, the growing adolescent continues the process already begun—learning to dis-identify with the aggressor, to identify with the victim and then gradually, to identify with the compassionate nurturing position. If encouraged in this direction by the outside world, the young person learns to "suffer with" an increasing number of others, not with masochism, possessiveness, or overprotectiveness, but with a love that is "distanced" enough to allow "the expression of pity, compassion, and solace without having to [actually] become the victim" (Sagan, 1988, p. 178).

Positive and rewarding childhood experiences with loving adults whom the child can idealize are necessary but not sufficient determinants of social morality. True social morality consists of values that are applied beyond the boundaries of one's family or intimate circle of friends. Morality begins at home, but if it stops there, society suffers, for when one only applies love and compassion to one's own, insularity and subgrouping result. The segregation of racial, ethnic, or economic groups generates opportunities for projective identification, fear, devaluation of the "other," rage, and powerlessness, as the riots in Los Angeles in 1992 demonstrated.

A child who learns at home and in her neighborhood to identify with the compassionate nurturer will, as her cognitive processes move to the formal operations stage during adolescence, become gradually more able to generalize this intuitive stance into a stable system of well thought-out moral values. Acting as a representative of her family's values, she will usually act in fairly compassionate and socially responsible ways, even when tempted toward malevolent action by less socially responsible peers.

When a thinking adolescent is challenged to defend his family's values in society, he will inevitably encounter some opposition and alternative views, forcing him to think things through on his own and to clarify his own feelings. He must work to iron out inconsistencies and fill in gaps in his moral thinking, and work toward application of his values in the larger world. Provided the family and the culture provides some support for questioning and autonomy, and provided the family's values and the society's values are not too widely divergent, the adolescent will probably be able to integrate them to his satisfaction. If the parents are not too threatened by the adolescent's autonomy and do not frustrate the young person's need to experiment and challenge constructively, the result will usually be an even stronger commitment on the adolescent's part to a morality based on love and compassion, which he learned at home in the first place (Sagan, 1988).

Educational opportunities, formal and informal, including the role-taking and group challenges suggested by Kohlberg and the social constructionists, are of great importance in continued moral education beyond the home. Exposure to the larger world is crucially important as well; a person cannot develop a moral presence in the world if he never gets a chance to leave his neighborhood, nor can she make independent moral decisions if she is spoon-fed what she is supposed to think and not allowed to independently observe her world.

FROM DEMORALIZATION TO "REMORALIZATION" THROUGH PSYCHOTHERAPY

Chapter 8

SHAME, GUILT, APOLOGY,

AND FORGIVENESS

Many people who enter therapy report feeling "demoralized." While they may mean they are in a general state of malaise, i.e., "disheartened," they may, in some instances, mean literally "demoralized"—having lost their moral bearings. In addition to the more defining characteristics, many forms of psychopathology carry as secondary features particular deficiencies in the five virtues.

In the chapters that follow I discuss the moral components of some common clinical syndromes, and suggests ways that effective psychotherapy can lead to "remoralization"—resolution of these moral difficulties and an increase in the level of goodness on the public and private levels. It begins with a discussion of two essential links between problems that are defined as moral and those defined as psychological—*shame and guilt*—and goes on to explore the roles of *apology, forgiveness, and making amends* in psychotherapy.

Shame and guilt are very different phenomena.

In recent years, therapists have determined that shame is a big problem for many who seek psychotherapy (Harper & Hoopes, 1990; Karen, 1992; Kaufman, 1985). Shame comes from the failure to live up to one's ideal or expectation of one's self and involves loss of self-esteem (Lewis, 1971). Shame is a wretched, pervasive emotional reaction, which is quite primitive; Erikson (1963) noted that shame seems to emerge in the earlier toddler years (anal stage). Beginning with dissatisfaction regarding one characteristic in oneself, shame quickly leads to other negative self-attributions, and usually generalizes to an overall sense of self-hatred and disgust (Tomkins, 1963). As Karen (1992) says, in shame, one regards oneself with the "withering and unforgiving eye of contempt" (p. 43).

Shame does not motivate change but, rather, acts to paralyze all efforts at self improvement. Often an ashamed person will semi-deliberately act in ways that will make him feel more ashamed. This is best explained by "consistency theory," which holds that people will strive to reconcile contradicting external and internal perceptions (Festinger, 1957; Kaufman, 1985). The shamed person may feel compelled to humiliate himself out of a need to validate his already dismal view of himself.

Self-other confusion and projection are essential components of the shame experience. The person who is ashamed is always convinced on some level that others view him with disgust or disapproval or would, if they knew the whole story. When people are ashamed they often become involved in projective identification, imagining themselves to be criticized by others, or encouraging actual criticism from them, and then responding defensively. They may even project the actual feelings of shame into others, while they take on the critical and lofty, or even abusive role. Introjective identification and masochism are also common tendencies in people who are ashamed. Their already low self-esteem makes it seem quite natural to attribute the negative qualities of significant others to themselves or to feel they deserve bad treatment from others.

When we feel badly that we have hurt or neglected another person or persons, what we are feeling is *guilt*. Guilt is interpersonal in its focus (Yalom, 1980). While shame is a narcissistic experience, guilt emerges from concern for others. Unlike shame, which launches an undifferentiated ballistic attack against the whole self, guilt targets specific misdeeds and their effect on others for which we feel regret. Consequently, guilt is usually far more manageable and potentially much more constructive than shame. While dissatisfaction with the total self offers no remedy, concern about specific "crimes" one has committed against others can lead to attempts to apologize, make reparation, and attain forgiveness.

It has been my observation that patients are frequently confused about whether they are feeling shame or guilt. Patients may say they feel "guilty" about not living up to their potential, for example, or for eating or drinking too much; what they are experiencing in these instances is shame. As we will see in the cases presented, people can become so steeped in feelings of inadequacy (shame) that they cannot face the specific ways that they have hurt others (guilt) and, therefore, cannot motivate themselves to make amends. This is very often true in the addictions—an individual feels he has made such a fool of himself while he was actively using, that it is difficult for him to acknowledge his actual moral abrogations. As we will see in Chapter 10, the "moral inventory" of addictions therapy breaks this stalemate.

To complicate matters further, I have observed there to be two dimensions to both shame and guilt: *moral and nonmoral*. Table 3 depicts the distinction among moral guilt, moral shame, nonmoral guilt, and nonmoral shame.

As we discussed, shame occurs when an ideal that one holds dear is not reached. If the ideal has to do with responsibilities to other people, the shame is moral; if it has only to do with the self, the shame is nonmoral. People can feel ashamed for any number of things that do not particularly hurt other people—gaining weight, failing an exam, spending too much money, being poor, saying something stupid, wearing the wrong clothes to a party, getting drunk, not getting the job one wants, not having a nice house, being disabled, disfigured, or unattractive, to name just a few. Even when we bring other people into it, imagining we have disappointed them, or being ashamed on their behalf for their failings or inadequacies, the shame is not moral, because the failures being focused upon have nothing to do with the virtues or interpersonal moral concerns.

When the ideal that has not been achieved has to do with the quality of one's relationships with others, then the shame is moral. Shame can

Table 3

	SHAME	GUILT
MORAL	did not meet highest standards in the five virtues e.g., did not do much for worthy community causes, should have tried to be a more responsible parent	violated another person's rights, safety, trust
NONMORAL	abrogated an ideal that does not have to do with goodness or interpersonal morality e.g., failed an exam, gained weight, lost job	did something that affected another but that one could not have prevented and did not intend e.g., was happy when mother was depressed, made more money than father

occur when one feels inadequate in one or more of the five interpersonal virtues of **altruism, responsibility, honesty, egalitarianism,** or **justice**. No immorality has been committed (for this would bring about *guilt*) but there is a generally negative self-appraisal with regard to one's moral standards. Even though shame usually stifles rather than promotes self-improvement, moral shame (in contrast to nonmoral shame) can sometimes spur some positive changes in the virtues if it is not too intense.

Nonmoral guilt is what I call it when someone mistakenly feels responsibility for having hurt or neglected another. When an individual feels guilty for something that either did not take place, was done by another and not himself, was unintended and/or could not have been prevented, he is feeling nonmoral guilt. A soldier who returns from a war unharmed having lost many of his buddies in battle may feel guilty for having survived when his friends did not, and may even may feel unworthy of a happy life when they have been deprived of any future at all. Some children are made to feel terribly guilty by their parents for acts that are not at all immoral. A client of mine recently married the man of her choice and suffered tremendous guilt right through the wedding. Her parents had made it clear to all their children that they (the children) were causing suffering to their parents whenever they took a step away from home and particularly if they chose to be happy when their parents were lonely and sad. Another client, the son of an abusive psychotic mother, told his group of being beaten up on the way to school and having the sandwich his mother had made for him stolen. He described the agonizing guilt he felt at the thought that he had been so careless with her precious gift to him.

Nonmoral guilt can be devastatingly painful. Nonmoral guilt, like shame, involves primitive mechanisms such as splitting, projective identification, and introjective identification.

Moral guilt is guilt for actual misdeeds committed against another. Unlike nonmoral shame and nonmoral guilt, moral guilt is a developmentally advanced emotion. Appropriate moral guilt requires fairly advanced cognitive processes, including some role reversal, which cannot take place until at least the preoperational phase of development. Kagan (1987) points out that children are not prepared to judge acts as right or wrong until they are able to infer possible motives and feeling states in others. Guilt may also involve understanding the meaning of symbols and a recognition of what one did as opposed to what one was supposed to do.

Patients in treatment should be actively assisted in learning to feel more moral guilt and shame and less nonmoral guilt and shame.

One type of patient who has guilt and shame, moral and nonmoral, confused, and needs help with this in treatment, is the bulimic. The bulimic feels as guilty for eating a bag of cookies as most people would for hitting someone with their car. She is ashamed of her size and her weight, but she is guilty for the act of eating the cookies. She is crushed by nonmoral guilt and nonmoral shame.

Meanwhile, her moral shame and moral guilt are minimal. Her desire for thinness is so powerful that it erodes virtues that she may have previously possessed in some measure. Her drive to lose weight may eventually cancel out her **honesty** (she lies); her sense of **altruism** and her sense of **justice** (she often does not care whom she hurts or frustrates), and her **responsibility** (to herself and others). Depending on the severity and stage of her disease, she may occasionally feel pangs of moral guilt at having abrogated the feelings or trust of others, but the drive to be thin usually eradicates any sustained effort to correct the damage she is causing in her relationships.

Chastising the bulimic for her narcissism and lack of virtue is, of course, not a useful treatment technique. It is possible to take a more positive approach in redirecting the bulimic's moral concerns. I believe that a fundamental learning that the bulimic must acquire in treatment is that she is needed out in the world. Her preoccupation with her weight and her abuse of her body to that end is sapping the strength and energy that might be directed to more constructive social endeavors.

On some level, the bulimic knows that her hunger is not for food but for love and acceptance. She needs to realize that much more love and acceptance will be forthcoming if she is involved with people, giving and receiving openly in very personal relationships and out in the larger world, than it will from staying "in the closet" trying to cultivate a perfect body, or from giving in to her mad cravings for fattening foods.

The prerequisite for the bulimic fulfilling her social role is **honesty**. She must face how empty her life is and how worthless she is to anyone, wasting all her energy bingeing and dieting. She must let herself feel the terrible sense of deprivation she felt as a child and still feels underneath her cravings for cake or hamburgers. She must let herself be nurtured by the support of her therapist and her group, if she has one. Without such emotional knowledge of her own needs, her efforts to give (**altruism**) and to be **responsible** to others will always be tinged with resentment. If she digs deeply, she will probably find serious **injustices** and inequalities (**egalitarianism**) existing within her family. There will almost always have been a devaluation of women, for example. To get well—to be remoralized—the bulimic will have to reckon with experiences of abuse and abandonment, which explain why she grew up so frightened, so hungry, and so inadequate. At that point, she can commit herself to a more meaningful life, which will inevitably involve an expansion of all five virtues in the public as well as the private domains.

LEARNING TO FEEL APPROPRIATE GUILT IN THERAPY

Most patients, if asked why they were going to therapy, would probably not reply, "to learn to feel guilty"; yet, to learn to feel appropriately guilty may be a very important by-product, if not goal, of effective therapy. As Judith Herman says of traumatized patients, "many struggle [in therapy] to arrive at a fair and reasonable assessment of their conduct, finding a balance between unrealistic guilt and denial of all moral responsibility" (p. 68).

Psychoanalysis, particularly Freud's version, gave guilt a bad name. The psychoanalytic perspective sees guilt as primarily psychopathological. As we noted in Chapter 7, Freud saw guilt as the artifact of the punitive and inhibiting structures of superego and conscience, which were geared to counteract man's drive to satisfy his sexual and aggressive strivings. While the object relations theorists countered with a positive view of guilt as the basis for concern for others, their ideas did not manage to counteract Freud's view in the mainstream. This was partly because Freud's assertion of the pleasure principle dovetailed so closely with the prevalent scientific concept of Darwinism (see Chapter 4).

It has been argued that the process of psychoanalysis basically works toward the reduction, if not elimination, of guilt in the individual. As Lowe (1969) points out, the attribution of intentionality to the unconscious tends to mitigate against one having to take **responsibility** for one's actions. If the impetus for our actions is thought to lie in the unconscious, then one does not have to worry if one is to blame. Further, the emphasis on feelings and free association as opposed to rational processes encourages avoidance of the conscious mental effort necessary to fairly decide accountability and determine the possible implications of one's actions on others. Psychoanalysis' focus on intrapsychic rather than interpersonal dynamics also serves to diminish the importance of guilt as a natural response to having hurt or betrayed another.

Humanistic psychologists, while differing with Freud on a number of other matters, tended to join with him in seeing guilt as a liability to individual freedom. Mental health for Maslow, Allport, and other "third force" psychologists involved self-actualization first and interpersonal morality second. No distinction was made between moral guilt and nonmoral guilt—both were considered encumbrances rather than resources. If anything, Maslow and Allport may have allowed for what we have called "moral shame," which they would frame very positively in terms of feeling the urge to expand one's virtues and values beyond the self. No allowance is made for the possibility that the ability to feel guilt when one has hurt or neglected one's commitments to others is part of living compatibly in the world.

The existentialist therapists have consistently tried to salvage guilt from what seems to have been a steady demise in psychology and psychotherapy. Existentialists have always recognized guilt as an essential part of life and of choice. As Vandenberg (1991) points out, it is guilt that, far from inhibiting freedom, makes freedom possible. Guilt is proof of our "freedom to violate parental [and other authority's] injunctions" and a reminder of "the sense of responsibility that such freedom entails" (p. 1283). Yalom (1980), in writing about the existential therapists' work, discusses two kinds of guilt—ontological guilt (guilt for existing), and secondary guilt (guilt for hurting another)—moral guilt, to use our term.

As we discussed in Chapter 7, ego psychology and object relations psychoanalysis espouse the view that guilt and interpersonal responsibility as mediated through love and attachment are an important part of mental health. Some therapists from this school have even recommended that moral guilt be fostered in treatment. Pattison (1968) stated,

> the task of the psychotherapist then is not to assuage guilt feelings, although that is often a necessary preamble to successful therapy. Rather the therapist seeks to help the patient to see himself and his relationships with others in the light of how the patient violates the relationships to which he is committed. (p. 207)

Only when the patient acknowledges his guilt can he begin to make reparation. Unacknowledged guilt blocks goodness, while guilt that is felt and reckoned with can liberate it.

People growing up in dysfunctional families are generally not given the proper tools with which to construct a sensible moral framework. As a result their moral judgments as adults tend to be illogical and inconsistent—too harsh, too lax, or both. On the one hand, they may condemn themselves excessively for insignificant deeds, while on the other, they may overlook glaring failures of responsibility and instances of selfishness, dishonesty, or unfairness. Patients who have been severely abused in childhood are particularly likely to be confused about their own and others' culpability. As their stories unfold in therapy, they often reveal situations of "lacerating moral complexity" (Herman, 1992, p. 69) that would take any philosopher years to unravel. Who was responsible for what? Who failed whom? Who is the victim and who the perpetrator? What if all are victims—does that mean there is no blame, no accountability?

A crucial part of the therapist's role in these cases is to teach the client how to rationally and compassionately appraise guilt and responsibility. The process starts with the therapist allowing himself to make moral judgments about the patient's behavior and/or about that of the patient's loved one. Judith Herman explains that, even in cases of trauma, far from hurting the patient,

> realistic judgments [on the part of the therapist] diminish the feelings of humiliation and guilt. By contrast, either harsh criticism or ignorant, blind acceptance greatly compounds the survivors of self-blame and isolation. (1992, p. 66)

Simply making and stating the judgment is not sufficient, however; in and of themselves, judgments might well be experienced by the client as cold and critical. It is teaching the patient to engage in a moral dialogue that is helpful, not telling her what is right and wrong. The therapist must convey to the patient the reasoning behind his judgment, letting her know that this is just *his* opinion and invite the client to dispute or build upon his ideas. Let us say, for example, a client has committed a violent act during a time of terrible stress. First, the therapist should state clearly that he does not condone violent behavior. Beyond that, however, he should encourage the client to think for herself about the degree of damage incurred by the victim in order to determine how much guilt is appropriate under the circumstances. Once an appraisal of the seriousness of the offense has been made by the client, the therapist can help the client look at other factors, such as: what her intentions were; what degree of volition was involved; what her state of mind was at the time; and what alternative ways she might have used to express herself and/or get her needs met other than resorting to violence. It is important that the exploration of motives, consequences, and extenuating circumstances not be used by the therapist or the client to *excuse* the violence. Attempts to "psychologize" moral issues away will simply result in more guilt, shame, confusion, and self-doubt for the client.

Many patients' core conflicts have to do with moral guilt on a subconscious level. These patients are among those who present themselves to therapists with complaints of depression and feeling very stuck in their lives. In each case, at some point in the treatment, it becomes clear that the patient harbors guilt with regard to a specific relationship or event in her life. It is only when this guilt is acknowledged that it can be analyzed as to whether it is shame or guilt, moral or nonmoral, and whether or not it is justified. If what the patient is feeling is moral guilt, then recognizing it opens up possibilities for apology, forgiveness, and making amends or, at the very least making peace with the self. Even when these actions are not possible, however, the simple acceptance of one's own guilt can make a person feel more honest and more whole, as happened with Tina in the case described below.

Tina was a 30-year-old married Catholic paralegal who lived next door to an esteemed judge, Horace, whom she also knew from work. Although she was attractive and friendly and people seemed to like her, Tina had few close friends and was quite lonely both as a child and as an adult. Tina came from a very large and highly traditional Catholic family where the boys were loved and respected more than the girls.

Tina's husband, Al, was several years older than she and was a depressed and angry man. His surly ways were one of the primary features that initially attracted Tina to Al, for she believed that he needed her love and care and that marriage to her would change him into a happy man. When, after they married, Al became even more irritable, Tina tried all the harder to cheer him but to no avail. She finally concluded that what the marriage needed was a baby, something she desperately wanted anyway.

Tina was firmly embedded in Kohlberg's interpersonal stage of morality. What was right and wrong for her was dependent on which course would result in the least loss of love. Despite her considerable success in her profession, homemaker and mother were the only roles with which she could identify. She and Al tried to conceive a child for several years with no success and finally initiated infertility procedures. Al continued to be gloomy and disinterested, while Tina labored strenuously to reassure her parents that the grandchildren they expected from her were just around the corner.

About two years later, still infertile, Tina began an affair with Horace, who was also married and had three children. At this point Tina entered therapy, feeling anxious and very angry at her husband for his lack of support and interest in her over the years. Horace was attentive to Tina when they were together but had no intention of leaving his wife and children. In fact, he was trying to get his wife pregnant. While Tina expressed to the therapist frustration about Horace's lack of commitment to the relationship, she did not seem to feel guilty for her role as the other woman in his life, nor for "cheating on" Al.

About three months after the affair began, Al, who knew nothing about the affair, decided that the infertility treatments were failing and suggested that he and Tina begin the process of adoption. Tina agreed and presented the plan to the therapist as if there were no Horace and no affair.

"But Tina," said the therapist. "What about Horace? Will you continue to see him?"

"Maybe I won't want to if I have a baby coming. Or maybe Al will be more into our relationship now, and I'll be able to forget about Horace." She then launched into her typical romantic rhapsody about how much Horace loved her, longed to be with her, but could not leave his little children, and so on. There was still no acknowledgment of guilt on Tina's part. The affair continued throughout most of the long adoption proceedings. It finally ended when Horace's wife found a letter from Tina among his clothes. She said she would not tell Al on the condition that the affair end immediately. Horace and Tina agreed to stop seeing each other, but Tina continued to work for Horace. Al and Tina struggled on with their marriage, waiting to adopt a baby. A few months later, Al decided he was not happy in the marriage and abruptly filed for divorce.

One year after the divorce, Tina was still in therapy, still pining for Horace. The therapist wondered, though he could not see any sign of it, whether Tina felt guilty for her role in the deterioration of her marriage and her deception of Al and Horace's wife. When he asked her this, she always changed the subject to how much Horace still loved her, and how sad it was that they could not be together. The therapist became more and more convinced that the missing piece in Tina's therapy was her guilt. "There is no way," the therapist thought, "that this conservative, 'good-little-girl' Catholic woman does not feel guilty for having tried to steal another woman's wife and for committing adultery in her marriage." In object relations terms, the guilt was "split off," primarily out of her awareness, where it plagued her far more than if it were conscious. Finally, the therapist, brought this up with Tina. "I just don't believe you don't feel guilty, Tina," he said.

Tina's eyes filled with tears. The therapist guessed that this response was not guilt, but hurt and shame. Tina had taken his comment to mean that he thought she was disgusting and bad.

"Now Tina, you know I'm on your side, here," said the therapist. "I am *not* criticizing you. If I were going to disapprove of you and put you down for having an affair, I would have done it a long time before this. I am simply concerned that you are ducking something very important here. Something that, if you faced it, would allow you to go on with your life. I *know* you feel guilty, Tina, and I want to hear about it, just like I want to hear about all your other feelings.''

"*I can't,*" said Tina, vehemently. The look of shame had disappeared and been replaced by a look of terror. She was trembling and her eyes were closed tight as if she did not want to see what was in front of her.

"It's okay, Tina," the therapist reassured her. "Guilt is nothing to be afraid of. It's a feeling like all the others."

"That's why I haven't gone to confession," Tina began to sob. "I feel worthless."

"What do you mean?" asked the therapist, wondering if it was guilt or shame that Tina was experiencing.

"I don't know. I feel so bad. She [Horace's wife] must have been so hurt when she found out what we were doing! What if I had gotten pregnant and Al had done that to me! I can't believe how terrible it was." This was clearly moral guilt and not simply shame, for the concern was for the person whom she had hurt, more than for herself.

"Why do you suppose you would not let yourself feel this before?" asked the therapist.

"I guess I kept thinking of confessing to the priest and getting absolution, and I didn't think I deserved to be forgiven," said Tina.

"Was this conscious, Tina?" the therapist inquired. "Did you know you felt guilty, but chose not to go to a priest or to tell me about it?"

"Not really," said Tina. "I knew I was holding something in and not telling you, but I didn't know what it was. I knew I felt loss and anger and disappointment, but I didn't know how much guilt I felt. You would think a Catholic like me would know guilt when she felt it, wouldn't you!"

It emerged in further discussions, that, in Tina's split-off guilt, were hidden some other unpleasant feelings she had not been aware of that were crucial for her to understand in order for her to get past these two unfortunate relationships. First, she realized how jealous she had been of Horace's wife, not because she had Horace, but because she had babies. She was appalled to admit to herself that, to some extent, the intent of the affair *had* been to hurt Horace's wife. She then could see that some of that jealousy and desire to punish was displaced from her mother and her sister, for the same reason—they had children and she did not. As guilty as she felt, understanding this vengeful behavior helped her realize the extent of the rage and misery she had been feeling, both in her marriage to Al and in her affair with Horace, who could not commit to her. She had never felt recognized and appreciated for herself; she had always felt like a second class citizen compared to her brothers and, now, compared to all women who had children.

Tina had felt so ashamed and unloved that she had acted against her own value system, which had resulted in a tremendous amount of guilt that she then repressed. She had to defend against the guilt, partly because to admit it would bring her too close to feelings of rage and helplessness that she could not control. With the therapist's help, she was able to face these strong emotions. Tina returned to the church, having forgiven herself for the pain she had caused Horace's wife, and ready to be forgiven by the priest. She quit her job with Horace and got another position and began to go to law school at night.

Given the fact that narcissistic preoccupations often counteract interpersonal concerns, it is hardly surprising that nonmoral shame frequently overrides moral guilt. As we have discussed, shame is the dreadful experience of total inadequacy. It is very hard to be generous or to meet one's responsibilities to another when one is filled with feelings of self-doubt and self-hate. Shame often brings with it a strong desire to hurt the person whom we perceive is making us feel ashamed. This urge to punish the "shame-er" can emerge suddenly and power-fully from a place very deep in the brain. As such, it is quite likely to wipe out **altruistic** and **responsible** impulses and to dismantle the cognitive processes needed to reason out issues of moral accountability. The punitive response of someone who has been shamed is often misdi-rected; "messengers," innocent by-standers, even people who are try-ing to be supportive are frequent victims of the shamed person who is frantically struggling to exorcise self-blame by placing it on another.

Therapy, especially group therapy, can greatly assist an individual in transforming the hideous and useless feelings of shame into feelings of guilt, which at least have the potential to foster positive changes in attitude and behavior.

The following anecdote shows group members, with admirable honesty and forthrightness, struggling with their respective legacies of shame, in order to understand more clearly the responsibilities of one of the members, Diane, who had found herself in an interesting moral dilemma at work.

A new member of a therapy group, Diane, age 27 and white, worked as a social worker in a hospital. In the therapy group also is John, 50 and black, and also a member of the helping professions. Both were children of alcoholics and both were in therapy for depression. Both are college graduates, but John has additional academic degrees.

Diane started off the session. "Well, remember last week we were talking about how hard it is to deal with being told you're wrong, even when you're sure you didn't do anything? Well I had one of those, and I can't believe how hard I'm taking it, even though I know in my head I didn't do anything wrong.''

She continued, ''Well, I was telling a co-worker, Barbara, who's white, about an incident where a black male patient was lurking around in a white female patient's room. I really didn't pay any attention to the fact that Sandra, a black co-worker was listening to Barbara and myself. I said to Barbara, *'So this big black man was in her room and it scared the shit out of her!'* Sandra, the black co-worker, became enraged, burst into tears, and said, 'Diane, I can't believe you said that. That was a racial remark.' And she ran from the room.

''I was just floored!'' Diane exclaimed. ''I went after her to talk to her, but not only would she not talk to me, she hasn't spoken to me since, and it's been over a week. I talked to Barbara and to my supervisor (also white) about it, and they assured me that I didn't do anything wrong. I mean it was a racial remark, but I didn't mean it that way. It was descriptive. I was simply describing the man as black, and Sandra took it the wrong way. Everyone at work said she overreacted, and that she does this frequently, and that eventually it will blow over. I'm still mortified, though, and I was up all night worrying.''

Bob, a 45-year-old librarian in the therapy group, was immediately sympathetic to Diane and said, ''I know what you mean. I, too, will go to great lengths to make amends when I didn't do anything wrong.''

Jack, a 33-year-old businessman with a degree in management, said, ''Sandra was out of line. Definitely.''

Linda, a 50-year-old nurse, said, ''I've seen lots of situations like this. It was your supervisor's responsibility to get the two of you discussing this and see if you can't work it out.''

John, meanwhile, was silent until Jack said, ''I don't think her being black had anything to do with it,'' at which point both John and Diane said in unison, ''Oh yes it does!'' At this point Bob and Linda argued vociferously that it did not, and the room fell silent again.

The therapist decided to address the inherent moral issues that were camouflaged for Diane by her shame at having been caught up short by her colleague. She said, ''I can understand the embarrassment you must have felt, Diane, to have a remark that you did not mean to hurt someone, result in such an explosion of feeling from Sandra. On the other hand, I don't want to gloss over the racial implications of this thing. You say that your remark was not 'racial' and cannot understand why it was perceived that way by Sandra; yet, you said you wanted to 'make amends.' I doubt your efforts to make amends will feel real to Sandra if

what you really feel is that you did nothing wrong and that she need-
lessly humiliated you."

"Diane did nothing wrong," Jack said adamantly.

John spoke slowly: "I wasn't going to say anything, but now that
[the therapist] has given me an opening, I have to say that I do understand why Sandra was so upset. You happened to describe the situation
in a way that fits a stereotype. The implication is that the female patient
was much *more* scared by the male patient because he was black. The
way you said it must have been heard with a parenthetical 'of course'
by Sandra. *Naturally,* the female patient was scared, because the guy
was *so big and black.* I am not saying you meant it that way, nor am I
saying you are racist, Diane. But unless we acknowledge that your remark buys into or reflects the stereotype, even though you, yourself,
may not hold that stereotype, it's like refusing to acknowledge the racism in society. And we can't deal with something we don't acknowledge."

Morissa, who is Jewish and had not yet spoken, then said, "I think
it's the casualness with which remarks like that are made. It used to
happen to me often in college. A friend would say something about
Jews being cheap right to my face, as if either I wasn't there, or I wasn't
Jewish, or it was so much a part of common knowledge that it wasn't
even supposed to be an insult. I have an Indian friend now, male,
whom I care for and trusted, until I heard him say to somebody *right in
front of me,* "[so-and-so] is Jewish and he'll get every penny out of you."

Morissa began to sob, "He has been wonderful to me. How can
someone be so good to you and then abuse you like this? When this
happened I felt devastated!"

In conveying the pain she had felt in being the object of prejudice,
Morissa had brought Sandra from Diane's story into the room so that
we could really step into her shoes as well as Diane's. The initial irrita-
tion many members had expressed about Sandra's "overreaction" began to be transformed into empathy for her position. The group began
to see that maybe some guilt on Diane's part was warranted. This alone
was an extremely valuable lesson in **egalitarianism**, but more such
learning followed in that session.

The therapist mentioned to Morissa that her mother, who had been
cruel and rejecting toward Morissa, seemed to have spared the Jewish
part of her, allowing her to be proud of being Jewish and not, as the
therapist said, "skewering her on that the way she did on just about
everything else."

"That's right, she joined with me on that—for obvious reasons,"
Morissa replied.

"What do you mean obvious reasons?" queried John.

"Because she was Jewish," the therapist said.

John replied, "Well, my mother was black, but she skewered me on race all the time. I remember when I was finished with the service and I grew an Afro and went back to visit. My mother ranted and raved. 'You look black!' she screamed. 'Get out of here and don't come back till you get a haircut.' She pushed my suitcases off of the porch and continued to scream. I left and came back later. One of the few times I stood up for myself. She let me in but she didn't speak to me all week."

The therapist said, "Well, here we are talking about making assumptions, and I just found myself making a big one. I assumed that Morissa's mother wouldn't be anti-Semitic because she's Jewish. Of course, I know that homosexuals can be homophobic and blacks can be anti-black and Jews can be anti-Semitic, but I forgot and had to be reminded. I wonder how many other similar assumptions we make that serve to deny that there is prejudice all around us."

At the end of the session, Diane was asked how she felt. With energy in her voice, Diane said, "Much better. Sort of enlightened and relieved, because I realize it's not so much about me, but what's right and wrong here. I want to do my part to make sure things are right and not be part of the problem."

In the course of this session, each and every member, including the leader, realized he or she carried assumptions that were implicitly, albeit subtly, racist. The virtue of **egalitarianism** was certainly fostered in the session. I am sure that no one present will be quite so quick to assume that persons of color or of an ethnic minority are "overreacting" when they complain of prejudice.

In Diane's family, no one, particularly not her alcoholic parents, knew any other way to respond to feeling shamed other than to shame someone else. Diane's reaction to being "called on the carpet" by Sandra was to want to shame Sandra more, but this was mixed with fear that, should Sandra continue to feel shamed, she would further humiliate Diane. Diane's nonmoral shame and fear of Sandra's shame initially kept her from understanding how and in what way she had hurt Sandra. John's confrontation and explanation of Sandra's feelings helped her feel appropriately guilty for her part in the misunderstanding. If John had not confronted her, her shame might have been generalized to include other blacks on her job, and perhaps elsewhere as well. As it was, Diane was able to recognize her own prejudices and to see how they reflected the racism in society. The experience greatly strengthened Diane's resolve to fight such biases in the future.

The therapist's role in this incident, similar to the situation with

Tina, was to help Diane's moral guilt to emerge. She did this by simply mentioning that there was an issue of **egalitarianism** and **justice** involved in the situation. This gave the group permission to think and speak in moral terms, something that clients are sometimes embarrassed to do in therapeutic contexts. She also let herself be educated by the process, by allowing her own prejudicial assumptions to be confronted by John.

THE ROLE OF APOLOGY IN THERAPY

A story is told about Lawrence Kubie being called upon to interview a very difficult patient at Austen Riggs Hospital in Massachusetts many years ago. The patient had been paranoid and angry for days, and had taken to uttering over and over the words, "Say you're sorry!" The patient was very agitated as he was brought in front of the staff and continued his demand at a great volume. Quietly, Dr. Kubie approached the patient, sat next to him and caught his gaze with his own. "I'm sorry," Dr. Kubie said sincerely. "I'm really sorry."

Many times in therapy I have committed an empathic failure of some kind, apologized sincerely, and been surprised at how amazed the patient was when I did so. Many patients have said, "My father/mother/parents *never* said they were sorry."

In my opinion, a necessary experience for adequate moral development is the experience of receiving and accepting a sincere apology. Often in treatment a client confronts a parent who has been abusive or neglectful and, instead of receiving the rebuff she expects and would have received in the past, she is given a heart-felt apology. Better than all the insight in the world, it is often this experience that helps the client move off "dead center" in her emotional and moral growth. When one receives that longed-for apology and request for forgiveness, one's view of the world can change from a place where no one is accountable to anyone else, to one in which people can, however belatedly, feel remorse for what they do, express it, and move on.

Receiving a sincere apology not only gratifies a legitimate and often desperate need, but also serves as encouragement to make one's self accountable for one's own misdeeds toward others. It is not an exaggeration to say that the experience of receiving an apology can be a gateway to remoralization for the patient.

Apologies do not need to be dramatic to have important moral consequences. As Winnicott (1965) pointed out, no matter how caring a parent might be, empathic failures on the part of parents happen frequently throughout the parenting process—a rough gesture with the infant, an undeserved outburst at a child who is in the wrong place at the wrong time when we are in a bad mood, an ill-timed laugh when a preadolescent child is feeling ashamed. Provided the errors are reasonably unintentional and the parent is not psychotic or abusive, such experiences constitute a necessary part of growing up—as long as the parent apologizes when she is wrong. These interactions are the vehicle by which the child learns to moderate his expectations of others and, by extension, of himself. If others are not perfect, perhaps one need not try so hard to be so oneself.

One difference between "good enough" parenting (or therapy) and *not* "good enough" parenting (or therapy) is not the frequency of the little hurts the parent (therapist) incurs upon the child (patient), but the way the parent (therapist) handles himself after they happen. If the parent cannot manage his own guilt, he may project blame onto the child for the injury that he himself has inflicted. Instead of apologizing, he may abuse the child more. The opposite reaction—almost as dysfunctional—is the parent who becomes so ashamed and anxious when she inadvertently hurts her child that she falls all over herself with guilt, leading the child to worry about *her* and to speculate that he (the child) has done something to hurt the parent. The optimum response when one has hurt a child is a prompt and sincere apology. Unless the child is preverbal, anything other than a spoken apology is experienced as a deflection of responsibility from the self. When a therapist has temporarily failed to be attuned to a patient, his apology can have therapeutic results, helping the patient to regain trust to a greater degree than existed prior to the mishap.

Apologizing takes practice. A person's failure to apologize even when he feels appropriate guilt may be due to his lack of spontaneity or to a fear that the apology will not be accepted. In group therapy particularly, therapists see many instances in which they know one member wants to apologize to another for hurting her feelings or insulting her in some way, but instead sits ashamed and mute. When asked what he is feeling, the client will say he feels guilty. If he is encouraged to apologize, he may be reluctant, recalling feelings of being humiliated when forced to say he was sorry as a child. Taking the risk in group and having one's apology accepted can be an important healing experience.

An opposite problem is demonstrated by the person who cannot apologize authentically for something she has done to someone else, because she is so busy apologizing for things that are not her responsibility. This person confronts the same task as the person who never apologizes, namely to feel appropriate remorse, and to acknowledge her responsibility and regret to people whose rights or feelings she has abrogated.

FORGIVENESS

After receiving a sincere apology, it is often, but not always, morally and emotionally desirable to forgive. Forgiving is deciding not to punish someone for an injustice against us even though we are clear that there has been an injustice committed. Mona Affinito (1990) claims that forgiveness is basically healthy for individuals and relationships. It is something that you do for yourself as well as for the other person. Forgiving helps you let go of anger and hatred, which are unhealthy for the body and soul. It is liberating to the forgiver as well as the forgiven. Forgiveness tends to decontaminate a relationship of envy and bitterness and to strengthen the relationship against future misunderstanding and hurt. It makes a relationship much more relaxed because it diminishes the fear of failure for both parties. If one knows one can make a mistake and be forgiven, one is more likely to take risks and be open, whereas the fear that one has no room for error in the relationship cuts down on spontaneity and expression.

Forgiving is a complicated matter, requiring considerable thought, soul-searching, and autonomy on the part of the forgiver, as well as some degree of mutuality in the power balance between the forgiver and the forgiven. The context of the act of forgiving must be understood in order to determine if it is valid or not. Often what passes as forgiving is the inappropriate condoning of another's injustice to the self. Some people forgive others too casually because they are overly invested in appearing kind, generous, and undemanding. Inappropriate forgiving is often characteristic of one who is highly dependent on the person he is forgiving for any or all of the following: physical care, financial support, love, and/or approval. Forgiveness is not genuine if it takes the place of taking care of oneself or of standing up for what one believes.

Susan Forward (1989) strenuously warns victims of abuse by parents to avoid the "forgiveness trap" (p. 189).

Responsibility can go only one of two places; outward, onto the people who have hurt you, or inward into yourself. Someone's got to be responsible. So you may forgive your *parents* but end up hating *yourself* all the more in exchange.

I also noticed that many clients rushed to forgiveness to avoid much of the painful work of therapy. They believed that by forgiving they could find a shortcut to feeling better. A handful of them "forgave," left therapy, and wound up sinking even deeper into depression or anxiety. (p. 187)

Forward, like many other therapists, believes strongly in the therapeutic power for the patient of confronting the parent who has been harmful or "toxic" to him. This encounter, while valuable in and of itself as a catharsis for the patient, also opens up an opportunity for the parent to express contrition and for the patient to forgive the parent if he chooses. The patient should remember that forgiveness is always optional. He should keep in mind that there can be no forgiveness unless there is remorse. If the patient clearly states what the parent has done to hurt him and how it has affected his life, and the parent does not seem truly moved and remorseful, then forgiveness is not appropriate. Even if the parent is genuinely remorseful, the patient may deem the parent's misdeeds too heinous to be forgiven, in which case he should feel no compunction about withholding his pardon. The patient can simply thank the parent for listening respectfully to what he has had to say. The moral decision regarding what is forgivable and what is not is the right and responsibility of the patient/victim, not the perpetrator.

In confronting the toxic parent, or any other abuser, and deciding whether or not to forgive, the patient is called upon to face challenges in the areas of assessing accountability (**responsibility**), maintaining **honesty** with himself and the other, and deciding what it is possible to forgive and what is not (**justice**). Forgiveness, if it is genuine, is an **altruistic**, unselfish act, for it gives a very sweet relief and peace to the other person. To confront another person honestly with what one believes to be an abrogation on her part, or to ask another for her forgiveness, requires that neither party be in a superior position to the other; otherwise, coercion seeps in and forgiveness is not freely given. In other words, for genuine forgiveness to occur, the value of **egalitarianism** must be assumed by both parties.

Janice, a 30-year-old woman in treatment, had often decried her family for their unforgiving ways. Janice's father had had an irrevocable argument with his siblings and his mother ten years before his treatment and never saw them again. When his children asked the nature of the dispute that had caused the rift, their father seemed vague about the details, but he was adamant that they deserved to be shunned. When his mother died, he did not even attend her wake. Similar vendettas characterized Janice's mother's family as well. Janice became aware in therapy of how terrified she was of displeasing her parents, since it was clear that forgiveness from them was not an option. When Janice got divorced, she was sure that her parents would cut her off and side with her husband against her. That did not happen; instead, they cut off the husband and never spoke to *him* again.

Janice was very close friends with Nancy, a single woman in her therapy group, and they talked to each other outside the group very frequently. In one group session, without discussing it with Janice first, Nancy expressed concern that her outside relationship with Janice might be detracting from their respective therapies. Janice was at first dumbstruck at Nancy's remarks and then furious. She had grown to trust Nancy, she said, and saw Nancy as her first close female friend ever. Janice felt betrayed by Nancy. This was no way to treat a friend, Janice insisted. Nancy should have expressed her concerns directly to Janice instead of publicly rejecting her in the group.

Several people in the group wondered why Janice was taking Nancy's need to protect her therapy as a personal rejection, but Janice could not see it any other way. She strongly considered quitting the group and never speaking to Nancy again. Fortunately, however, she became curious about the intensity of her reaction and agreed to explore the issue in treatment.

Meanwhile, Janice's initial blast of anger had hurt Nancy deeply. Nancy said resentfully that if Janice were really her friend, she would not want to jeopardize Nancy's therapy and would understand Nancy's desire to temporarily put some distance between them. She had never anticipated being expelled from Janice's life simply for putting forth her own needs in the relationship. She felt angry and misunderstood.

It took several weeks of discussion in group with Nancy for Janice to realize that her knee-jerk response had been to want to punish and abandon Nancy before Nancy punished and abandoned her. She was feeling full force the threat of rejection she had learned from her family, while acting out the hostile and rejecting part herself. Neither forgiving Nancy nor being forgiven by her seemed even a remote possibility for Janice for quite a while.

Nancy, in turn, realized how abrupt and dismissive her remarks had seemed to Janice. Lo and behold, Nancy recognized that the quality of her insensitivity to Janice bore a great resemblance to the manner in which Nancy's parents routinely dismissed her (Nancy's) feelings.

To the credit of both women, they valued their friendship and their therapy enough to work through these obstacles in the group sessions. Gradually, each was able to understand how they had hurt the other, to express their regret, and, eventually, to forgive and be forgiven by the other.

Once Janice had learned, through her therapeutic work with Nancy, that banishment was not the inevitable consequence of one person expressing her own needs in a relationship, she was able to be a strong and flexible friend to Nancy and to others as well. She had learned that forgiveness is not just a possibility but one of the greatest privileges afforded by a trusting and mutual relationship.

MAKING AMENDS

Some people harbor feelings of guilt that are so deep that even willingly proffered forgiveness from the person(s) they have hurt is nowhere near adequate to heal their wounds of guilt and shame. In the view of such a guilt-ridden individual, a verbal apology, while important, does not sufficiently compensate the injured person for the damage that she, the guilty party, has inflicted. As we learned from the work of Melanie Klein (see Chapter 7), the need to make reparation when we feel we have been destructive to others runs very deep.

As a general rule, making amends does not seem to be something that people in our culture are encouraged to do. When it comes to "expiation," our society has tended to rely on the legal and religious institutions to mete out punishment and determine criteria for forgiveness. Except for some clinicians in forensic work, therapists have tended to let the law punish the perpetrators of abuse, while they themselves have tried to comfort and aid the victims. Few therapists or psychology researchers seem interested in letting the perpetrator "off the hook" by helping him resolve his guilt. Even fewer have encouraged patients who feel guilty to pay attention to these feelings and to transform them into constructive virtuous action on behalf of others.

Alcoholics Anonymous has long recognized that the recovering addict needs to go beyond "I'm sorry" and to actively seek to correct his past errors when possible. One of the twelve "steps" of A.A. states: "We made direct amends to such people wherever possible, except when to do so would injure them or others" (A.A., 1952/1981, p. 83). In addition to helping clients learn to hold themselves and others properly accountable for their actions, and in addition to addressing dilemmas regarding obtaining and granting forgiveness, professional psychotherapy should follow the lead of the twelve-step programs by incorporating the making of amends into treatment. (Needless to say, making amends should be recommended for clients who actually have committed hurtful acts against others and not those who only *think* they have.)

The importance of making amends as a part of therapy has been recognized by David Johnson, Ph.D., the ward chief of a four-and-a-half month voluntary inpatient psychiatric unit at the Veteran's Administration Hospital in West Haven, Connecticut. Dr. Johnson's unit treats nonpsychotic male veterans with post-traumatic stress disorder (PTSD). PTSD is a frequent result of having experienced first-hand the brutality of human beings, whether it be through war (the majority of Dr. Johnson's patients are Vietnam veterans) or through other forms of physical, sexual, or emotional abuse (in childhood or subsequently). Its symptoms include: rage attacks, depression, panic disorder, phobias, flashbacks, and psychosomatic complaints. Repeated or chronic trauma, particularly when incurred in childhood, often produces a syndrome known as complex PTSD, which includes personality and addictive disorders in addition to the acute symptomatology described above (Herman, 1992).

We noted earlier that moral confusion is frequently associated with trauma (Herman, 1992). Trauma victims often attribute blame to themselves instead of their abusers for the injuries they have incurred, while overlooking the abuse they themselves might have inflicted, or might still be inflicting, upon others.

The level of moral complexity of PTSD surges, however, when—as is the case with Dr. Johnson's veterans—the trauma that launched the PTSD involved the patient committing, rather than just being the victim of, atrocities. This situation is not at all uncommon: Herman (1992) reports a study in which *all* soldiers who reported committing atrocities against civilians during wartime later suffered from PTSD. The task of helping the veteran work through guilt for his barbarous behavior in the context of war provides a stiff moral challenge for the therapist. As David Johnson (Johnson, personal communication) puts it,

> How do you as a moral therapist respond when the patient has consciously committed heinous acts from which they are now suffering? The fact that they are suffering helps you to feel empathy for them, but you cannot ignore what they have done and that they have a right to feel guilty. All soldiers, but particularly Vietnam veterans, struggle with what is sort of the ultimate moral question: "Is war moral or immoral? Is the warrior moral or immoral? Is he the hero or is he the pawn?"

Most of Dr. Johnson's patients grew up in abusive environments in the first place, but all of them either participated in and/or witnessed atrocities (usually in Vietnam, a few in previous wars). In his program both the staff and the patients are, as he says, constantly evaluating the right and wrong of it all, while, in the war itself, you just don't get into it. Once you start asking these questions it just becomes a morass. Some people dive into the morass, try to resurrect a moral self, and make an inventory of what was okay and what wasn't—killing a Vietnamese soldier to save a buddy was okay; killing a civilian wasn't, etc. But this doesn't work, because there are no answers.

Johnson says that PTSD veterans become adept at garnering forgiveness from staff and from each other; this is not particularly helpful and is often counterproductive. It is all too easy for them to talk about their war crimes, feel guilty, and then to withdraw and get even more depressed than they were before treatment.

"These veterans feel as if their soul died in Vietnam—that there is no goodness left in them," David Johnson explains. His program attempts to galvanize these veterans' paralyzing feelings of guilt into something vital and positive. Because he has participated in the destruction of others, the veteran must now become involved actively in helping others to make up for it. He may do this by being a better father or employee, or by undertaking some altruistic endeavor in his community.

Johnson and his staff insist that veterans begin to become constructively involved in the outside world beginning a day or two after they check into the hospital. This is terribly hard for most of them, since they are socially phobic. At first, the patients just go out into the community in pairs or alone or with staff—to a museum or to walk around a particular neighborhood. Within three weeks, they begin doing community service—working with inner city children, in soup kitchens, for Habitat for Humanity, building a fence in a park, coaching a kids' softball team, or cleaning yards.

Johnson says, "They're great at this type of thing; of course, they have no problem with hanging out in dangerous neighborhoods. Violence doesn't scare them. People do!"

On the unit the veterans are encouraged to feel and express their pain and their explosive rage about the ghastly and unfair things that happened to them, their war buddies, and innocent citizens. At the same time, however, they are out in the real world, working to counteract the destructiveness of their war deeds by acting with **responsibility** and **altruism**. One of the PTSD veterans decided during his treatment to become a police officer, and a year later reached his goal. This man had killed 42 people, and he was determined to save a life to make up for each one.

Part of Johnson's veteran patients' community work involves play-ing the role of "bard"—letting the community know in creative ways about the nature of war. The veterans have a public art show, a public poetry reading, and a play troupe, which tours Connecticut towns. Johnson's veterans urgently want to counter the glorification of violence that seems to pervade in our culture by informing adults as well as children of the painful consequences of brutality, not just for its victims, but for its perpetrators as well.

In their final weeks, every veteran has to talk in a high school about their Vietnam experience. Johnson notes,

> It's amazing—we think of Vietnam as a recent event, but many kids at the high school level don't even know when it was. This is actually a big relief for the guys, because they aren't stigmatized, which is one of their big fears. These vets' stories really make an impression on these kids and really make them reconsider their attitudes about war and violence.

Johnson points out that reaching these kids makes the vets feel very good but also extremely scared. It's a total identity change for many of them.

> They are not used to feeling like good people, but suddenly they realize they could do something like this every day, and their whole self-concept begins to shift. Most of them get happy and excited and use it as a base to move forward.

Chapter 9

ETHICAL FAILURES IN DEPRESSION

One generally known but rarely discussed fact about depression is that people who are in a clinically depressed state are rarely, if ever, very "good" to others. Their **responsibility**, **altruism**, **justice**, **egalitarianism**, and **honesty** are apt to be at a particularly low ebb. The depressed person fails to take responsibility either for himself or for others. As his depression worsens, he becomes a "taker" even if he was once a "giver" and often makes unfair demands of people. He is usually not particularly truthful or reliable, making promises he fails to keep and luring people into giving him advice which he then rejects out of hand.

The acutely depressed person is, by definition, narcissistically preoccupied. Such self-absorption naturally precludes a high degree of attention to the needs and rights of others and renders a high degree of goodness or virtuous behavior impossible. The pain of depression inevitably diverts a tremendous amount of psychic energy toward the self, even in the case of one who is not normally particularly narcissistic, even more so in the case of one who is. It is hard not to become frustrated with a depressed person, even though one might feel truly sympathetic with him at the same time. The tension for therapists, as well as for those who love the depressed person, is between listening empathically to his gloomy feelings versus making reasonable demands in order to coax him both out of his house and out of his narrow and pessimistic world view. It is very hard to know when a depressed person needs a little shove to get motivated and when pushing him will simply increase his resistance and/or damage his self-esteem, thereby exacerbating the depression.

Another reason why the depressed person is so hard to live with and to treat is that she shows little respect for others' attempts to be good to her. When one goes out of one's way for the depressed person (**responsibility, altruism**), she will likely respond by doing even less to help herself. If one feels one is being treated unfairly (**justice, egalitarianism**) by the depressed person and one asserts reasonable demands or says how one feels (**honesty**), one is usually made to feel guilty. One might also find oneself routinely hiding or distorting the truth in the presence of the depressed individual, thereby compromising one's own integrity (**honesty**). In the best of all possible worlds, virtue is its own reward. In dealing with the depressed person, however, one's attempts to be good to her are frequently frustrated, sometimes to the point where one begins to wonder, "Why bother?"

Lewis Andrews, psychotherapist, minister, and author of *To Thine Own Self Be True* (1987), takes a hard moral line with all his depressed patients. Although I am not at all comfortable with his approach, he makes some interesting points about the moral aspects of depression. Andrews sees depression (indeed, all psychopathology) as the consequence of trying to evade life's three major ethical responsibilities—*honesty, tolerance,* and *self-reliance*. In Andrews' view, each complaint associated with depression is a function of a particular ethical failure. For example, he defines feelings of worthlessness as the perfectionist response to low self-esteem. Living with a constant fear of death, Andrews says, is a defensive attempt to avoid dealing with a smaller but more immediate problem, such as a bad job review. A depression characterized by disappointment and frustration with others, he says, arises out of the foiled attempt to manipulate others into doing what one wants them to do. Andrews sees even loneliness as an ethical failure, claiming that lonely people are obsessed with social norms and expectations and lack authenticity. He says that lonely people seem to spend a lot of time devising criteria that will serve to eliminate them from any social gathering (too intellectual, not intellectual enough, too direct, too indirect, too formal, not formal enough).

Andrews believes that syndromes of depression and anxiety stem from an underlying self-centeredness, or narcissism. He offers some harsh prescriptions for dealing with what he calls the "ethical failures" that lead to mental illness. According to Andrews, psychotherapy should involve "ethical self-therapy"—ferreting out and dispensing with one's own manipulativeness, dishonesty, and laziness. Andrews assumes that these processes or behaviors are available to consciousness and that the therapist can shine the light on them if the patient is not able to do so through intensive self-scrutiny.

His routing out of unethical behaviors in depressed patients consists of a head-on attack—telling the depressed person he's lazy, dishonest, or whatever, decrying his selfishness, and challenging him to pick himself up by his bootstraps and be a better person. Aside from being crude, Andrews' approach ignores the biological component of a great many depressions, a factor that is clearly beyond the patient's control and that can only be addressed with medication. To blame the depressed patient for her unwanted and crippling condition is cruel and certainly will not induce any motivation to change. It also ignores the whole issue of defenses, which I will address shortly. I believe that Andrews has cause and effect reversed—that ethical failures stem *from* depression rather than cause it. I think it is extremely unfair as well as erroneous to assume that depressed people bring their misery on themselves.

Nonetheless, it is clear that ethical failures *are* indeed part of any depressive condition and, therefore, should be addressed as part of treatment. The depressed individual's unethical behaviors are substantially contributing to a deterioration of his interpersonal relationships, a situation that can only aggravate his depression. How can we—as therapists or friends—overlook the obvious ways that depressed people manipulate others? Should the depressed person not be held accountable for the pain he may be causing others? Should we let his dishonesty with himself and others slide, not confronting him when he claims to feel guilty for hurting others when he is taking no steps to change? Should we pretend not to notice how angry and hostile his behavior seems to us? Should we feel sorry for him if he breaks social engagements with us in order to isolate and feel sorry for himself? Should we excuse his reneging on work and financial responsibilities and putting unfair burdens on others? Should we forgive his demanding selfishness and disregard for the feelings of others? Should we let him make *us* feel guilty for *his* unethical treatment of *us*?

On the one hand, the answer to this question would seem to be a straightforward "no." On another level, however, the situation is far more complicated. Taking Andrews' highly confrontive approach with a depressed person runs the risk of stripping that person of his narcissistic defenses, which will certainly cause shame and, in some cases, great harm.

Narcissistic defenses are defenses employed (unconsciously) to ward off shame. Many, if not all, depressed persons already feel ashamed, a feeling that they try to diminish by convincing themselves and others that they are *entitled* to be passive and miserable due to some failure of life or other people to come through for them. To attack those defenses in someone who is strong enough to tolerate the confrontation may be useful, leading the person to rise to the challenge and stop wallowing in self-pity. To attack the defenses of someone who is fragile, however, is always a bad idea; it is dangerous to attack the narcissistic defenses of a person whose entire sense of self rests upon these defenses (whether that person is depressed or not).

According to Kohut (1971) and others, people with narcissistic personality disorders (people who are chronically narcissistic) have suffered a lack of parental attunement throughout childhood. For a variety of reasons they have received inadequate supplies of attention, empathy, and positive reinforcement, leaving them with extremely fragile self-esteem. Before challenging the depressed person it is important to determine if her depression is secondary to a narcissistic personality disorder. If the person has enjoyed some reasonably satisfying and mutual relationships, a good work history, and an absence of extreme difficulties with authority, then it is unlikely that a serious narcissistic disorder exists, in which case, some degree of confrontation of the depressed person on the ethics of her behavior is likely to be safe and constructive. If there is a history of narcissistic problems, the ethical aspects of the depression must still be addressed, but much more gingerly, and with consistent empathy for the feelings of distrust and shame that the individual feels underneath her narcissistic protestations.

Some defenses are like rusty pieces of armor, just waiting to be knocked off by the friendly poke of a therapist or a loved one, while other defenses seem sewn onto the person and can only be removed with surgical delicacy. To be able to discern when a depressed person's unethical or immoral behaviors can be confronted, one must have a sense of what level of psychic defense is operating.

PRIMITIVE DEFENSES VERSUS "RACKETS"

The defenses of *introjective identification* and *projective identification*, both functions of splitting, have been discussed previously. These are primitive and unconscious processes, which protect a fragile ego. These defenses need to be approached with particular care. People "split" objects (people, affects, ideas) because they cannot accommodate the whole object; they cannot bear to see the whole picture. Perhaps they cannot stand to face the truth about how terrible the parent was/is, so they split her into good and bad parts, seeing the idealized part only and identifying with the negative part as the "self," or vice versa. Perhaps they cannot tolerate the torrent of love and hate they feel toward one they have loved and lost, so they devalue the departed lover, vehemently denying the affection they once felt. While splitting provides a vehicle for avoiding intolerable parts of reality, the process of disowning unwanted parts inevitably creates feelings of emptiness and despair.

The defenses that involve splitting begin early in infancy and are unconscious and primitive. They are very difficult to confront in another person because they involve massive distortions of reality. Other defenses are more sophisticated, having evolved at later periods of development. Intellectualization does not involve wild distortion but merely places a comfortable distance between the individual and his feelings. Reaction formation, the attempt to master one's fear by engaging more, rather than less, with the feared object or activity, is also adaptive if not carried to great extremes (A. Freud, 1966).

Eric Berne described a "racket" as a feeling and the presentation of that feeling, which seems to have a great hold on the person experiencing it, but which is not quite authentic (James, 1977). The racket is a subconscious attempt to make a particular impression on people—to "pour it on," so to speak. Common rackets include feeling picked on or feeling outraged. Its target is rather nonspecific compared to projective identification, where the person onto whom the projection is deposited is precisely, though not consciously, selected. In contrast to the more desperate defenses, rackets have a decidedly deliberate tinge. Some degree of near-conscious dishonesty and manipulativeness is always involved in a racket. Confronting a person on his racket, if done with empathy and sensitivity, may incur anger but should not unduly hurt or insult the person. Rather it should give the patient a choice about whether to continue the racket or not.

One very effective way to confront a racket is to say to the person, "If you were not feeling angry (sad, victimized, fearful), what would you be feeling?" This gets at the feeling underneath the "rackety" feeling without accusing the person of being insincere.

The first two of the three case examples to follow illustrate two typical rackets (The "Angry Racket" and the "Helpless Racket") associated with depression and how they were addressed by a group therapist. (The two patients happened to be in the same group.) The third illustrates a not unusual situation in which a spurned lover uses his depression as an excuse to hurt the one who hurt him. In this case, confronting the ethics of the patient's behavior proved highly useful in resolving his depression.

The Angry Racket in Depression

Many depressed people seem always to be angry. They bristle arrogantly when someone implies that there is something they might be doing to contribute to their problems. They constantly blame others for their predicament—parents, spouses, siblings, children, friends, or therapists. Whether justified or not, their complaints have a carping "going-nowhere" quality that quickly becomes wearing to the therapist and has the effect of decreasing rather than increasing her empathy for the patient. These patients present a clinical and moral bind to the therapist, who can appreciate how much pain the client is in and, yet, recognizes that the client is willfully hurting people who do not deserve it. By employing his racket, the client is not only getting everyone frustrated with him, but he is failing to take responsibility for solving his problems.

Joe was a bright, recently divorced, and unemployed insurance executive in his late forties, who felt he was at the end of his personal and professional rope. While he was capable of great charm and empathy, Joe wielded anger with great skill to keep people from getting too close him. He was adept taking situations that could potentially be humiliating to him and turning them around in such a way as to make them uncomfortable for others. When Joe was confronted by his therapy group for being chronically late to meetings, he would become furious but in a slightly exaggerated way. Genuinely consternated to be sure, he would bounce in his seat and shout angrily: "Okay, if that's the way everybody feels, maybe I should just leave the group. I'm depressed and with depression comes disorganization, and maybe you think I can do something about it, but I can't." Occasionally, Joe would even leave the room in a huff, only to return shortly to see what the group's reaction was.

The therapist sensed a racket. Joe was indeed angry but was using his anger as a cover for fear, shame, and despair. The therapist also noticed that when Joe barked at the group and even when he stormed out, nobody seemed upset. The therapist surmised that if Joe were indeed rageful, people in the group would react by becoming frightened. Instead, patient, even amused, they acted as if they were calming down a younger sibling having a tantrum that would soon blow over. One member commented good-naturedly that Joe "really could be a big baby sometimes."

The therapist noticed that each of Joe's tantrums contained a reference to the fact that the group might reject him. When Joe said this, the therapist spotted what he imagined was fear in Joe's eyes. The therapist decided that the group was responding to Joe's terror, not to his anger. This made sense—Joe had been fired from a number of jobs. Joe was probably terrified that he would be "fired" from this group, too, and was doggedly testing the group to see if they would be loyal or reject him as his places of employment had done. Despite his angry tirades that no one cared about him there, the group was the only safe environment in Joe's world. If the therapist let him "blow the group away" with his anger racket, he would be letting Joe "kill off" his only friends in the world.

It is hard to confront the inauthenticity of a racket without implying that the patient is being a fraud for using it. To tell Joe he was a "phoney" would have been the last straw for this very depressed, already narcissistically depleted man. Joe did not see that he had the option of being more honest and vulnerable in the group. Rather than confronting Joe on his dishonesty, the therapist decided to give Joe every opportunity to be truthful in the group.

An interesting opening for this occurred when, during one session, Joe apologized to Margaret for making a cutting remark to her the week before. Such a direct and sincere apology was unusual for Joe and, the therapist thought, showed progress in his taking **responsibility** for himself. Another member, Tim, a timid man, who had seemed slightly annoyed with Joe for some time, took this opportunity to vocalize his doubts about Joe's sincerity. Not surprisingly, Joe instantly reverted to his angry stance. Loudly and sarcastically, he said, "Well, of course I wasn't sincere, Tim!" followed by, "Maybe I just shouldn't be here, then!"

"Do you mean that Joe?" queried the therapist. "I thought you were being sincere when you apologized."

"Of course I was," said Joe. "I think some feelings are okay to have in here and some aren't. Clearly my anger is not okay in here."

The therapist replied, "I'm not concerned about your anger one way or the other, simply that you tell the truth as best you can. If your anger is part of the truth then that's fine. Just as long as you say as best you can what is true for you."

Joe nodded. Moments later, Joe spontaneously began to cry and started for the first time to express how badly he really felt about himself and how frightened he was.

The therapist defused Joe's anger racket, not by disparaging him for being angry, but by giving truthfulness a higher value. She not only noticed and validated him when he was sincere, but told him straight out that **honesty**, rather than expression of any particular feeling was the goal of therapy.

The Helpless Racket in Depression

Stella was a single, 34-year-old banker who happened to be in the same group as Joe. She was just as depressed as Joe, but her racket was quite different. While Joe blamed everybody else for his troubles, Stella blamed herself. Joe's orgies of blaming the group for his problems gave Stella an opportunity to practice refraining from taking responsibility for other people's problems.

Stella was the dutiful youngest child in a traditional and very dysfunctional family with whom she had lived until she was about 30. While **altruistic** and **responsible**, Stella was less clear in matters of **justice**, **egalitarianism**, and **honesty**. Stella's mother, a very angry woman with no friends, always assumed that the purpose of Stella's existence was to make her mother happy, and Stella never disputed her. Stella's alcoholic father never stood up to her mother, either.

Stella's narcissism resided in her investment in appearing to be a good girl to her mother and to the outside world. To preserve this image, Stella developed the racket of presenting herself as powerless when, in fact, she was quite competent, a device she learned as a way to keep her mother from being threatened as Stella became older and smarter. Most of the time in group, Stella demonstrated strong interpersonal skills. She was refreshingly straightforward in dealing with Joe, refusing to feel guilty when he accused the group of not wanting him around. When it came to talking about her situation with her mother, however, Stella would dissolve in a puddle of tears, throw up her hands in despair, and insist she could do nothing about the situation.

The group was much more vulnerable to Stella's racket than to Joe's. There was something about the way Stella would cry when she would talk about how her mother treated her that got everyone furious at the mother rather than wondering why a competent woman such as Stella should be so at sea in dealing with one individual. Eventually, the therapist began to explore what the feeling was that lay beneath Stella's periodic displays of powerlessness.

The feeling that Stella was hiding behind her powerlessness was rage. When first asked about it, Stella denied any anger at all and cried all the harder. Gradually Stella realized that she was indeed furious, and that she dared not express it for fear that she might be cut out of her family forever. Given the mother's narcissism, this was a distinct possibility.

As with Joe, the group therapist explained that expression of raucous fury was not important, only seeing and telling the truth. The therapist urged Stella to take some time to evaluate her mother's morals. Over some weeks, Stella realized that her mother was selfish, irresponsible, and cruel. She continually abrogated the rights of others, stole from her place of work, lied continually, and tried to turn members of her own family against one another. Stella realized that she could not respect a person like this. It was this honest moral appraisal that cut through Stella's "powerless racket." She realized that it was appropriate to judge her mother negatively on her behavior, and that she, Stella, was entitled to feel rage for the way her mother had treated her over the years.

Stella next had to decide whether it was worthwhile to express this rage to her mother. She decided against it, opting instead to exercise what Andrews calls "ethical discipline" in the relationship. Over the next few years, Stella literally taught her mother the difference between right and wrong in relationships, rewarding her when she was kindly and humane and negatively reinforcing her when she was selfish, cruel, or dishonest. When she and her fiancé visited the mother and the mother was unpleasant, Stella and the fiancé would politely leave. If the mother tried to cause trouble between Stella and another family member, Stella would immediately call the family member and they would confront the mother with her manipulations. If her mother was demanding and unappreciative, Stella would insist on "thank yous," "pleases" and so on.

Stella is now happily married with a child, and her mother is behaving quite well. If she steps out of line, Stella and her husband respond firmly but gently with a piece of "ethical discipline" such as announcing that they will not bring their son to Sunday dinner the next week. Her mother's protests are few and far between now, perhaps substantiating Andrews (1987) claim that "Nobody can encroach on someone who is a beneficial presence in the world" (p. 160).

Stella's self-esteem soared when she gave up the helpless racket, facing and acting upon the realization that she, not her mother, had the knowledge, the skills, and the integrity to exert moral leadership in the relationship and in the family as a whole.

A Case of Misplaced Moral Outrage

Ned, a divorced narcissistic physician in his fifties, who prided himself on his professional competence, found his world turned around when he came back from a long trip to find that his girlfriend was breaking up with him and was already involved with another man. Totally forgetting how diffident he had been about this relationship and how devaluing of his girlfriend he had been before his trip, Ned became almost the caricature of the spurned lover. Agitated and extremely depressed, he stayed up until all hours of the night crying and writing his girlfriend long letters. He repeatedly parked near her house, spying on her, then ringing her doorbell and running away. He made numerous calls to her every night and, when she answered, would hang up or else beg her to come back to him.

This behavior went on for several weeks. Ned saw a psychiatrist for medication, which seemed to do no good, and he talked endlessly in group and individual therapy about the injustice of it all, which only served to get the group members and the therapist frustrated with him. Beyond shame, Ned could care less how undignified his behavior looked to the girlfriend, to the group, or to his grown children. When people urged him to let her go he steadfastly refused. She would "come around," he said. "Sooner or later she will feel guilty about how much she has hurt me, especially if I get really psychotic," he said with some relish. When he was not plotting revenge or harassing his girlfriend, Ned would lay paralyzed with depression on his bed for hours at a time, unable to eat or sleep. I shudder to think how his patients fared during this time.

Ned's condition had become severe enough to warrant hospitalization, when the psychiatrist tried appealing to Ned's morality as a way of breaking the logjam of his narcissistic depression. He hoped to reach Ned's "adult" part, which might still be capable of thinking and acting rationally.

"Do you think your behavior with Joanne is ethical?" the psychiatrist asked Ned.

"Ummm," Ned said. There was a long pause. "Ethical? Well, you mean I don't have the right to be crazy?"

"When you were with Joanne, did you ever let on that you could do these things?" the psychiatrist asked. "Would she have any reason to expect that you were the kind of guy who would spy on and harass a woman who did not return his affection?"

"Gosh, no," said Ned.

"Well she must be very frightened then," said the psychiatrist. "That makes what you are doing unethical, don't you think?"

After that session, Ned seemed transformed back to his "old self." He totally ceased bothering Joanne and stopped feeling sorry for himself. He began to remember how badly he had felt in the relationship and even to experience some relief that it was over.

Reporting on the session with the psychiatrist to his therapist, Ned said, "I was really caught between my lack of self control—I really wanted to act out—and ethics. He just laid it right out there, and I was brought up short. I was not prepared to think that my acting out was unethical and when he said it was—well, I had to agree with him, and then I just couldn't do it anymore."

Chapter 10

ADDICTIONS, CODEPENDENCY,

AND THE PROBLEM OF *HUBRIS*

Alcoholics and other substance abusers who engage in twelve-step programs, such as A.A., N.A. (Narcotics Anonymous) or O.A. (Overeaters Anonymous), commit themselves to a rigorous regime of self-healing that goes far beyond abstinence. An integral part of twelve-step programs is an explicit commitment to moral examination and moral change, beginning with what is called "the moral inventory." As *The Twelve Steps and Twelve Traditions* puts it, A.A. members "wish to look squarely at the unhappiness [we] have caused others and ourselves" (A.A., 1952, p. 43). Once this has been accomplished, the addict must take steps to confide in another about these misdeeds and to make amends to those whom they have hurt.

No method of treatment has been found to surpass twelve-step programs in the treatment of addictions. While other methods—cognitive-behavioral or rational emotive therapy, interactional group therapy, and psychodynamic treatments—can greatly enhance treatment, they have proved ineffective unless combined with A.A. (N.A., O.A., etc.). Consequently, few addiction treatment facilities today fail to include A.A. or N.A. meetings in their program. Twelve-step programs contain two major components that are not present in any of the psychotherapies: the moral and the spiritual. It can be speculated, therefore, that treatment of addictions necessarily involves a moral and/or spiritual component, if not both.

The Twelve Steps and Twelve Traditions gives the addict clear moral and spiritual direction. Additionally, however, it includes indispensable information about the addictive personality, much of which focuses on the problem of *hubris*, or inappropriate pride. If addiction treatment is to be truly successful, the addict must address this serious character flaw in himself. *The Twelve Steps* guides him in that effort and, secondarily, provides useful tips for the addictions therapist in understanding what makes the addict "tick."

Curiously, *The Twelve Steps* describes the character of the alcoholic in precisely the same way as Karen Horney depicts the "neurotic" in her book *Neurosis and Human Growth* (1950). (This may not be coincidence since the works are contemporaneous, but neither work makes reference to the other.) Putting Horney and the twelve steps together, I have found, gives one a profound sense of the demoralization involved in addiction and the inherent moral change involved in addictions recovery.

The essence of both the twelve-step program and Horney's psychoanalysis is the recognition and conquering of *hubris*. Referred to as "neurotic pride" by Horney, *hubris* has its genesis in childhood, when the child's basic needs for love and recognition are not met because his parents are too preoccupied with their own neurotic needs. This leads to a state of basic anxiety, which is characterized by an inability to manage oneself in relationships and a tendency to try to compensate for feelings of inferiority and not belonging by idealizing the self. This *idealized self* has standards that are not only unrealistic in their attainability but totally insensitive to the true psychic condition of the individual. The person can, thus, literally drive himself crazy trying to achieve perfection (adequacy is not nearly good enough) in many areas of his life. His choice of goal is not based on what he likes or what he truly wants to achieve but what he thinks will be respected by the outside world.

A.A. notices the same compulsive tendency to achieve a compensatory feeling of superiority in alcoholics as Horney notices in neurotics. The "soul-sickness" (A.A., 1952, p. 44) of the alcoholic, sober or active, is characterized as a tyrannical need for security in relation to others. This may lead one to go to great excess in the attempt to use "sex, material and emotional security or an important place in society" (p. 42) as a vehicle to feel adequate or, better yet, superior to others.

As with Horney's neurotic, it is pride, or *hubris* as we call it here, that drives the alcoholic, drinking or not, until he has achieved true humility through working the twelve steps. The grandiose alcoholic is plagued with "feelings of fear, frustration and depression" and therefore seeks "vainglory" and "foolish dreams of pomp and power" (A.A., 1952, p. 44). The depressive alcoholic allows himself to be "swamped with guilt and self-loathing . . . often getting a misshapen and painful pleasure out of it" (p. 45). This, A.A. points out, is the opposite of "true humility" and, in fact, "is pride in reverse" (p. 45).

Horney's "neurotics" and the pre-recovery or early recovery addict think they are quite moral, but their view of reality is highly distorted. "There is simply nothing that may not be invested with pride. . . . One person is proud of being rude to people; another is ashamed of saying anything that could be construed as rudeness and is proud of his sensitiveness to others . . ." (Horney, 1950, p. 93). He is also highly prone to what I call "turning a bad thing into a good thing." Horney states, "His capacity for this unconscious reversal of values is perfectly amazing . . . inconsistency turns into unlimited freedom, blind rebellion against an existing code of morals into being above common prejudice, a taboo on doing anything for oneself into saintly unselfishness, a need to appease into sheer goodness" (p. 94).

Both A.A. and Horney are aware that *pride* operates at a deep and often unconscious level and must be routed out from the deep recesses of the psyche for recovery to occur. Pride, says A.A., "leads the parade of the seven deadly sins. . . . For pride leading to self-justification, and always spurred by conscious or unconscious fears, is the basic breeder of most human difficulties" (pp. 48–49). Horney says, "It is necessary for therapy that the analyst gradually gain a clear picture of the particular kinds of pride operating in each individual patient. Naturally, a patient cannot regard a drive, an attitude, or a reaction as a problem to be tackled as long as he is unconsciously or consciously proud of it" (1950, p. 95).

The fourth step states "We made a searching and fearless moral inventory of ourselves." The step is explained as follows:

Step Four is our vigorous and painstaking effort to discover what these liabilities in each of us has been, and are. We want to find exactly how, when and where our natural desires have warped us. We wish to look squarely at the unhappiness this has caused others and ourselves. By discovering what our emotional deformities are, we can move toward their correction. Without a willing and persistent effort to do this, there can be little sobriety or contentment for us. Without a searching and fearless moral inventory, most of us have found that the faith which really works in daily living is still out of reach. (A.A., 1952, p. 43)

While *The Twelve Steps* never suggests psychotherapy per se, there is a constant awareness that the steps cannot be followed alone, and the need for an empathic "other" to bear witness in a supportive but objective way is essential. Step Five says, "We admitted to God, to ourselves, *and to another human being* the exact nature of our wrongs [emphasis added]." The book comments that after the initial feeling of acceptance one experiences when one first joins A.A., one realizes that "the isolation problem had been solved" (p. 57). As A.A. says in the fifth step, "Until we had talked with complete candor of our conflicts, and listened to someone else do the same thing, we still didn't belong" (p. 57). The book says that the criterion the alcoholic should use in choosing the "someone else" is not necessarily that they be alcoholic, but that they be trustworthy and objective, such as a clergyman or doctor. Unlike several years ago when A.A. members were discouraged from entering psychotherapy, many patients now choose to do the fifth step with their therapists.

The real reversal of pride Horney says comes when the patient can "assume a matter-of-fact responsibility" (1950, p. 69) for his actions. Taking responsibility means not just admitting shameful deeds but owning up to one's prideful intentions as well, recounting in detail how one has done the right thing for the wrong reasons and has done the wrong thing for the wrong reasons. The moral dialogue of therapy and the fifth step of the A.A. program both provide an opportunity to explore the moral and the psychological ramifications of one's actions with someone who is compassionate, but who is also willing to grapple with some of the moral complexities being presented.

So far, so good—but what happens when the patient or alcoholic decides it is actually time to make some of the changes suggested by the inventory? Has the individual's self-examination removed his faults and paved the way for effortless positive change? Not a chance, say Horney and A.A., realistically. It is precisely when we try to move beyond moral inventory to moral change that the alcoholic really sees how intransigent her faults are.

The sixth step states, "We were entirely ready to have God remove all these defects of character." The phrase "entirely ready" is almost paradoxical, for, the step goes on to say, no one is *ever* ready to give up *all* self-indulgences. In fact, we treasure a lot of them. Though they clearly cause us difficulty, our character defects do, however, net some immediate and powerful satisfactions, which are hard to relinquish, particularly if the rewards of characterological change feel remote. Feeling superior to our neighbor, for example, can be pleasurable—much more satisfying than feeling inferior. Being ambitious can be a convenient way to be greedy and get respect at the same time. Being envious is often a good excuse for laziness, and gathering resentments allows us to avoid seeing how many of our problems we bring upon ourselves.

Horney's interpretation of "resistance" in therapy offers the same explanation as that put forth by the sixth step for why it is so hard to achieve desired characterological changes. Pride makes us like ourselves the way we are, even when no one else does, and even when another part of us sincerely wants to change. Compensatory as this pride may have been in its origins, it is tenaciously rooted "in the core of . . . being" (1950, p. 23) and is very hard to unearth.

Resistance, driven by false pride, is acknowledged in the twelve-steps program, but few ideas are provided on how to resolve it. This is where psychotherapy becomes extremely useful, for it helps the alcoholic recognize and gain control over the unconscious parts of himself that will inevitably strive to sabotage his efforts to "work his program" effectively. Therapy will help the patient to recognize the basic anxiety and depression underlying the drinking behavior and to understand his own defenses against these feelings. He can then choose to dismantle these defenses and begin to divest himself of false pride.

In the final steps involved in the moral recovery from addictions, we "made a list of all persons we had harmed and became willing to make amends to them all" (p. 77) and then, "made direct amends to such people wherever possible, except when to do so would injure them or others" (p. 83).

All of the five virtues are tapped in this taxing process of moral inventory and subsequent moral change in the treatment of addictions. It requires **honesty** and **responsibility** above all. It requires the rooting out of prejudice and of feelings of superiority (**egalitarianism**). The inventory itself requires making moral judgments (**justice**) about oneself and evaluating the nature of one's abuses of other people. The individual's capacity for helpfulness and generosity (**altruism**) seem to be a natural consequence of the confrontation of pride endemic in the process of psychotherapy and twelve-step work.

Margaret's Moral Inventory

These days many A.A. members are in therapy and may choose to do their fourth step with their therapist. In this anecdote the therapist helps Margaret, a 48-year-old alcoholic therapy client, sort out her shame from her guilt in preparation for doing her moral inventory.

Margaret had gone to A.A. originally on the recommendation of her therapist, whom she had been seeing for help with the consequences of being sexually abused. Margaret had been in the program for four years and out of therapy for three years, when she was told by her sponsor one day that she really ought to hurry up and "do her fourth step." A few days later, Margaret, who had never been unfaithful to her husband, deliberately seduced a man of twenty. This experience left Margaret extremely anxious, ashamed, and perplexed, and she called her old therapist for an appointment.

The therapist and Margaret agreed that while her sexual behavior was highly uncharacteristic of Margaret's sober self, it would not have been unusual in her promiscuous drinking days. Mindful that the event had taken place on the heels of the sponsor's recommendation to do a moral inventory, the therapist suggested that Margaret might be afraid that she would feel a lot of shame if she began her fourth step. Margaret said she had been putting it off all these years for just that reason.

Margaret and the therapist also wondered if the choice of a much younger men for her "fling" had to do with unresolved issues about having being sexually abused. Margaret had been sexually molested by numerous male family members from the age of seven until adulthood and had received no protection from her parents. When Margaret was seven her mother caught her with her skirt up in the presence of an uncle and beat Margaret until there were bruises and welts all over her body. The therapist speculated that Margaret's seduction of the younger man might have been a semi-conscious attempt to master a situation that, when it happened to her repeatedly in childhood, had made her feel powerless and dirty.

Margaret admitted that her seduction of the young man had made her feel powerful and proud. Any guilt she felt was in relation to her infidelity vis-à-vis her husband, *not* in relation to the young man, for he, in contrast to herself as a girl, had not been a victim, but rather a confident and eager participant who had found the whole event enormously satisfying and flattering. After sorting out her *shame* (which mostly related to the past) from her *guilt* (about cheating on her husband), any lingering shame she felt over the recent incident receded rather quickly. She began to resolve her guilt by making an effort to improve her communication and her sexual interaction with her husband. Soon, the one-night stand became a pleasurable, but distant, memory.

A few weeks after returning to therapy, however, Margaret's shame burgeoned forth suddenly once again. This occurred when she revealed that her sponsor wanted her to do her moral inventory.

"I absolutely cannot do it," Margaret said.

"Why?" asked the therapist.

"Because I have done so many immoral things," replied Margaret, crying.

"You mean sexual things?" asked the therapist.

"Yes," said Margaret, mortified.

"Did you hurt anyone but yourself with your sexual behavior?"

"I guess not," said Margaret, confused.

"So how were you immoral?"

"I guess I wasn't, in the sense of hurting others. I feel ashamed though," said Margaret.

"That's different. You feel ashamed because you believe your behavior made you look badly to others and because you felt so terrible about yourself for having done these things."

In this interaction, the therapist helped Margaret shift her definition of morality away from the connotation of proper versus improper sexual behavior into the realm of the virtues used in our model. The criterion for immoral has become hurting others as opposed to doing things that are not socially approved of by others.

The therapist then directed Margaret's attention to the issue of *accountability*. "You know, Margaret, some people were deliberately hurtful to another during those sexual escapades—many males were hurtful—*to you*! In many of these episodes you were too young and too drunk to be in charge of your own behavior, and other people, older and more powerful, took advantage. I think in your case taking the moral inventory means not only identifying immoral acts for which you *were* responsible but also those for which you were *not*. It is not moral to blame yourself for something that was done to you as a child by a grown-up who misused his power and authority." In this way, the therapist was helping Margaret address the question of **justice** in the sexual encounters she had had while very young and drunk.

Margaret agreed, "Yes, I need to stop blaming myself. I was just a child, yet, on some level, I still feel ashamed, like I did something wrong. I did hurt myself—that's not moral."

"Yes, but did *you* do it, or did others do it?" demanded the therapist.

"I guess they did, but I should have stopped them and protected myself."

"You could not have done so then. You were too young and you had no allies. You learned early from your mother that if she found out about your problem, she would make things worse. Now let's get to what actual immoralities you yourself may have committed toward others while you were drinking. Immorality here means violating another's rights [**justice, egalitarianism**], being **dishonest** toward one who trusts you, abrogating your **responsibilities** to another, or being unusually greedy or selfish [**altruism**].''

Margaret understood the distinction immediately. ''I stole from the storekeeper for whom I was working. I stole money from him, and I stole merchandise. It must have amounted to thousands of dollars. I did it for years, and he never suspected a thing. I was on speed during those years. I didn't see anything wrong with it. He made a pass at me, too, when I was about sixteen. I think I just used that to give myself permission to steal from him some more. When I look back on it now, though, I feel guilty for what I did, even though he wasn't a very nice guy.''

When she spoke of the stealing, Margaret was not sobbing the way she had when she had discussed the sexual experiences. She seemed serious and purposeful. This clear-headed forthrightness is, I have noticed, characteristic of someone who is dealing with guilt, as opposed to shame.

''Okay, that's a clear immorality for which you accurately hold yourself responsible,'' said the therapist without judgment. ''I'm pretty sure that's the kind of immorality the moral inventory is supposed to ferret out, and, as you know, you have the option to make amends in some way at a later time.'' Margaret was able to come up with some other *bona fide* immoralities—breaking promises, lying to her friends, family, and children, neglecting some of her parental and employment responsibilities due to hangovers and drunkenness, and endangering human life and others' property by driving while intoxicated.

At a later session, the therapist introduced the notion of ''goodness'' into the moral inventory.

''Margaret,'' the therapist said. ''We also need to remember that the moral inventory involves searching out and labeling *positive morality* as well as negative. We need to look at areas in which you see yourself as being and acting as a good person.''

Here the therapist presented the virtues chart and invited Margaret to assess her ''goodness.''

''Well, I'm pretty unselfish [**altruism**] with my kids. I'm **responsible** toward almost everybody including all my friends and my community. I'm definitely *not* **honest** enough with my husband, although I never cheat anyone in business, and I would never steal from anyone whether I knew them or not. I need to make sure I get my rights in the marriage and the family and don't get treated like a second class citizen [**egalitarianism** and **justice**]. I feel used a lot, and then, instead of getting mad at *them*, I get mad at me.''

This discussion seemed to give Margaret energy and courage, which persisted in the treatment. Clearly, Margaret's self-esteem received substantial bolstering early in the treatment when, by using the virtues model, she was helped to see that despite her problems and her pain, her current self had a solid foundation of goodness at its core, goodness that was not represented in pious thoughts, but in daily and freely given action on behalf of others.

As this case illustrates, the moral inventory of the A.A. or of psychotherapy demands far more than confession of sins committed in a drunken state or during a hangover. It involves setting the moral record straight by clarifying accountability, sorting guilt from shame, identifying positive moral acts—as well as instances of immorality—and assessing levels of virtue.

To my mind, the moral inventory is, to some extent, a part of everyone's therapy, even when the client is not in A.A., and even if it is not labeled as such.

EMPOWERING THE ENABLER
WHO IS TRYING TO BE GOOD

There are two things that the addict and the person who continuously "enables" the addict have in common: the problem of *hubris*.

Someone who unwittingly aids and abets an addict or alcoholic in perpetuating his addiction is often termed an "enabler." The enabler is a frequent consumer of psychotherapy because his attempts to forge some normality out of a chaotic alcoholic environment have rendered him anxious and depressed.

Many enablers enjoy a reputation in their families or communities for being "good people." While the addict clings to other forms of false pride, the enabler is addicted to his "good guy" self-image. Enablers are frequently known and respected for being helpful to others in their professional lives, where they are very apt to be nurses or mental health workers. Even if they work in business, they are still the caretakers, the bosses with the "big hearts," or the people that everyone can depend on. Many enablers can stand almost any amount of pain as long as they are viewed as kind and generous. They need very little acknowledgment or appreciation from the addict in their lives, as long as they perceive themselves as being needed by others.

No matter how self-assured and controlling he may appear to be, the "good person enabler" who is struggling with an addict or alcoholic always feels two things deep down: ashamed and out of control. This he hides with all the strength that *hubris* can bring to bear. These normally negative feelings are particularly uncomfortable for the enabler, who is highly invested in appearing responsible and in charge. Trying to get the enabler to be less helpful, when being helpful is central to his identity, does not constitute constructive therapy for that individual.

Enablers value **responsibility** and **altruism** way above **honesty**, whereas, with therapists, according to Bergin's study (1988), it is usually just the reverse. When patients lie to protect their loved ones, therapists are apt to express disapproval. They may become frustrated when they are unable to persuade patients to see their "misguided" loyalty in a negative light. This discrepancy in moral priorities between the therapist and the enabler often leads the therapist to devalue the very qualities in the enabler, which he, the enabler, considers as crucial for his self-esteem—his loyalty and consideration for others. In stressful times, the enabler clings all the more strongly to an image of himself as being kind and concerned. When the therapist pushes the enabler to leave the alcoholic or to let the addict "sink or swim," she must be aware that what she is recommending is contrary to everything the enabler believes is "good."

Lately, there has been much talk of enabler's being addicted to people instead of to a substance, leading them to seek help from twelve-step programs to "break their addiction" and to form healthier relationships. I do not think that the enabler is addicted to the substance abuser; to me it has always seemed that what the enabler really seeks to preserve at all costs is his own moral self-image. For many enablers, clinging to an identity as caretaker involves exactly the kind of neurotic pride suggested by Karen Horney or *hubris* as described in *The Twelve Steps*.

Perhaps it is the enabler's *hubris* that engenders disrespect from others and often leads him to be blamed for the addict's behavior ("If I were with him, I'd drink, too!"). In any case, I think therapists tend to be too disparaging of enablers. While the motives of the enabler might not be one hundred percent pure, the desire to help others is a laudable motive, which psychotherapists should applaud, not discourage. It does not seem therapeutic, not to mention socially responsible, for therapists to devalue the **altruism** and **responsibility** of anyone they see in therapy, no matter how misdirected these virtues might seem to be.

Rather than being discouraged from helping others, enablers should be taught to become *more effective and efficient in their virtuous efforts*. Enablers need to be helped to detach a bit from the addicts in their lives so that they might be able to help them better and so that they can free up their energies to expand their generous endeavors to a wider range of recipients. Enablers need to be helped to become even more **responsible** in their personal relationships and to expand their sense of (*public*) **responsibility** in the work environment and in their communities.

The therapeutic message to the enabler should be the following:

The world needs what you have to offer. Your alcoholic spouse (child, partner, parent) needs you, but in certain specific and limited ways. She needs you to set boundaries; she needs you to save yourself so you can be with her when (if) she gets sober. Meanwhile, your (other, nonalcoholic) children need you, and your community needs you. The most responsible thing to do at this point is to attend to their needs, give them the attention they have been lacking lately, refresh yourself so you can be there for them.

The tendency of enablers to lie in order to protect their addicted loved ones can be quite frustrating for the therapist, but, in my experience, it is useless to try to get the enabler to value truthfulness (**honesty**) more than **responsibility** or **altruism**. For the enabler, who is fixated at Kohlberg's Stage 3 of morality, lying to spare someone else pain is moral behavior. If it is a choice between being honest and doing what is perceived as one's duty to a loved one, there is little question which the enabler will choose. The therapist must accept this about the patient and try to respect it, or he risks causing the patient shame, which, as we have discussed, is never useful. Rather than attempting to change the enabler's moral priorities, the therapist can hope that, in the course of the therapeutic relationship, the patient will absorb the value of **honesty**, either through identification with the therapist or by seeing for himself the fruitfulness of being forthright and truthful in the treatment.

Once the therapist has learned to respect the difference in moral priorities between herself and the patient, the "good person enabler" can be very rewarding to treat. For one thing, he is as responsible and giving in treatment as he is in his other personal relationships. He is prompt, pays regularly, and always tries hard in treatment. He is responsive and, of course, tries to be helpful in a therapy group. He "hangs in there" in treatment when things get stormy or frightening, just like he does with his loved ones. The only way he will terminate prematurely is if he is being forced to choose between treatment and the addict in his life, in which case he will politely but firmly choose the latter.

While the therapist may not be able to get the client to value **honesty** more than **responsibility**, she may well be able to help him become *more honest in the interest of becoming more responsible.*

Josephine was an attractive, single, intelligent woman in her early thirties, who worked as a hospital nurse. She came from a substance-abusing family, with an alcoholic father, and at least two siblings out of five were addicted. The addict in her current life was her boyfriend, with whom she lived and whom she supported financially. Josephine's boyfriend was verbally abusive to her when he drank, which was virtually every night. Josephine sought therapy after a violent altercation during which her boyfriend had accused her of having an affair with one of her friends from work and pushed her roughly against the wall. By this time, Josephine had amassed a number of symptoms of depression and anxiety including sleep disturbance, chronic stomach pains, and tearfulness.

A few months before starting formal psychotherapy, Josephine had joined a self-help group for "women who love too much." It was apparent to the individual therapist that it was this group experience that had given Josephine the support she needed to begin to branch out and begin to socialize with people besides her boyfriend. Clearly, the boyfriend realized this, too, and before too long was able to convince Josephine that the support group had instigated trouble in their relationship.

At her third meeting with the therapist, Josephine announced, "I have decided, now that I have you, I don't need the group anymore."

"What a set-up!" the therapist thought. "It's just a matter of time before the boyfriend attributes their problems to me and she quits therapy." She said nothing about this, but simply acknowledged Josephine's decision.

From long experience, the therapist knew that any attempt to get Josephine to separate from the boyfriend would simply result in her separating from the therapist instead. Trying to get Josephine to see that her depression and anxiety stemmed from her boyfriend's behavior was useless, because to see him as the root of their problem would remove the problem from her potential control, exacerbating her feelings of powerlessness and shame. The therapist decided instead to reframe the problem in terms of Josephine's strongest suit: her sense of **altruism** and **responsibility**.

Looking at the chart, the therapist could see that Josephine was greatly involved in **altruistic** and **responsible** activities in her personal and professional life. By contrast, her sense of **justice** was very weak; she could not even see the manipulativeness of her boyfriend, much less hold him accountable for it. She alternated between seeing herself as superior and as inferior in relation to her boyfriend (**egalitarianism**). As with many enablers, she did not put much priority on truthfulness (**honesty**). It was clear that these other three virtues were necessary for Josephine's very survival. If she did not soon learn what is fair and what is not (**justice**), she would allow her boyfriend's abusiveness to escalate to the point where her physical safety, not to mention her emotional well-being, would be permanently jeopardized. She had to learn to see herself and her boyfriend as equal, with the same rights and responsibilities (**egalitarianism**). This stance is necessary to be able to establish or maintain boundaries or rules in relationships. Finally, she had to learn to be assertive (**honesty**) with herself, with him, with her family, and with the community; if she did not learn to be truthful, no one will trust or like her, and she will become more isolated in her relationship with the abusive boyfriend. It would be particularly difficult to teach her to be honest, since Josephine did not particularly value truthfulness.

As we have discussed, virtues are such core parts of the personality that it is difficult if not impossible to infuse them into a patient, especially during the course of a short-term therapy. What can be done, however, is to encourage the virtues that the patient does exhibit and to reframe them in such a way as to encompass the virtues that seem to be lacking. For example, the therapist might say any or all of the following over the course of the treatment.

"Josephine, I know how important it is for you to be responsible. Given that, I'm surprised that you would so easily give up the group. That does not seem like taking responsibility for *yourself*."

"It is not like you to so easily forgo your responsibilities to your group. It sounded like many people value, perhaps even need you there. Have they contributed so little to your life that you can just walk away from them?"

"You are very proud and rightly so of being a person who gives to those she loves. We need to consider whether what you are doing with your boyfriend is helpful, or whether there is something else you might do that might help him more."

"You always try to take responsibility for your behavior. Have you thought about whether it is responsible to lie? Is it more giving in this instance to lie or to tell the truth?"

"When you give to someone who demands from you, does it feel like as pure a gift as giving to someone simply because you want to?"

"Is it responsible to take responsibility away from another person?"

There are probably many other routes, but the purpose of all the above interventions is to reframe **honesty**, **egalitarianism**, and/or **justice** into terms of **responsibility** and **altruism**. This preserves the positive intent of the enabler's behavior and gives options for behaving virtuously in new domains. Whenever I have tried this approach with enablers I have had considerable success. They have been far more amenable to my suggestions to set boundaries, take care of themselves, and "detach," when I have framed the advice in terms of **responsibility** and **altruism** than they are when I simply frame it in terms of "what works" in alcoholism treatment or what might build their self-esteem.

The interventions suggested should not be made in a cynical or sarcastic way but, rather, should be based on an authentic respect for the person's moral priorities. In sorting through the debate between Kohlberg and Gilligan, we found that the difference Gilligan hypothesizes between the morality of care and the morality of justice might actually be more semantic than functional. Male or female, the "good person" enabler demonstrates for us how this might be the case. While the enabler may lie too much, he is doing so in an attempt to take care of others. His nonegalitarian view of the world stems not from prejudice and hate but from a sincere desire to be strong in order to protect the vulnerable. He correctly perceives the unfair behavior of others towards him as a symptom of their pain and need. He doesn't like it, but if he thinks that another will feel safer or happier for treating him that way, he may let that person continue. While his stance and behavior might be, in effect, masochistic, his intent is virtuous.

The purpose of therapy for the enabler, therefore, is not to learn to stop helping, but to learn to pursue his virtuous endeavors with more clarity and at less cost to himself.

Chapter 11

THE MORAL COMPLEXITY OF THE

NARCISSISTIC AND BORDERLINE

PERSONALITY DISORDERS

The terms "personality disorder" or "character disorder," as typically used by therapists, suggest that a person's entire personality is pathologically tinged. The names of most of these disorders, as listed in *The Diagnostic and Statistical Manual of Mental Disorders* (APA, 1987), describe patterns of behavior generally considered to be undesirable: *passive-aggressive personality disorder, avoidant personality disorder, paranoid personality disorder, histrionic personality disorder, schizoid personality disorder, and antisocial personality disorder*. In my opinion, these are not diagnoses, but insults. They say nothing about personality but simply apply a derogatory label to an habitual style or way of relating.

In the psychodynamic frame of reference, however, the term "character" or "personality disorder" is not just a behavioral description but suggests a serious and chronic condition embedded in the personality—one that has its genesis in infancy or early childhood. Psychodynamic therapists in the past twenty years have paid very close attention to two personality disorders: the *borderline personality* and the *narcissistic personality*. The moral aspects of these two disorders will be the focus of this chapter.

Borderline personalities, by definition, have severe object relations impairment, characterized by splitting, projective identification, and introjective identification (all described in Chapter 7). A hallmark of the borderline personality disorder is sudden vacillations between idealization and devaluation of others, which is linked to fears of being abandoned and of being smothered. The borderline's behavior is character-

191

ized by intense clinging when he feels the threat of abandonment and hostility as a means of distancing when he feels one is getting too close. Symptoms can include dissociative phenomena, rage attacks, paranoia, feelings of being unreal, and phobic anxiety. All of these tendencies and symptoms render goodness difficult for the borderline personality who is prone to unfairly blaming others for his own problems (**justice**), being totally unaware of the feelings and needs of others (**altruism**), reneging on commitments (**responsibility**), acting superior to and humiliating others (**egalitarianism**), and presenting radically contradictory and inaccurate information (**honesty**).

People with borderline personality disorder are often very narcissistic (Kernberg, 1975). The narcissistic personality disorder *per se*, however, shows a particularly excessive preoccupation with and emotional investment in the self (Kernberg, 1976). The virtues of **justice, altruism, responsibility**, and **egalitarianism** are even less developed in the narcissistic personality than in the borderline personality who is not highly narcissistic.

Narcissistic and borderline personalities are very apt to have grown up with parent figures who punished them too inconsistently, too severely, or not at all. This leads to the development of a weak, erratic, or overly harsh superego. Superego problems make one prone to antisocial behavior. In the terminology of this book, we can define antisocial behavior as "not virtuous," i.e., selfish, irresponsible, dishonest, unfair, inegalitarian. Superego problems can add to the moral problems caused by the object relations difficulties (splitting, introjective identification, projective identification) of the borderline and narcissistic personalities.

It is the combination of superego and object relations pathology that determines the degree and nature of antisocial behavior that can be expected from the character disordered person. In his book, *Severe Personality Disorders*, Kernberg (1984) identifies six levels of superego/object relations pathology—I will call it moral pathology—that he has found to be characteristic of patients with severe to mild personality disorders. These levels are paraphrased and commented upon below.

LEVEL 1: THE PSYCHOPATH

The most severe moral pathology seen among the character disorders is represented by the *psychopath*.[1]

[1]I (not Kernberg) am making a distinction between psychopaths and sociopaths. Eliasoph (1963) has said that "psychopaths" are character disordered people for whom antisocial behavior is ego-syntonic (does not make them feel guilty) but whose impulse control is poor. "Sociopaths," according to Eliasoph, are individuals whose antisocial behavior is ego-syntonic, but who have good impulse control. Eliasoph suggests that if you want to rob a bank successfully, you would want to bring the sociopath and leave the psychopath at home.

Table 4: Levels of Moral Pathology in the
Character Disorders (from most to least severe)
(from O. Kernberg, 1984)

Level 1	The psychopath (feels no guilt)
Level 2	Narcissistic personality with antisocial traits (feels virtually no guilt; feels justified as a victim)
Level 3	Severe borderline who is not very narcissistic (dishonesty as a defense)
Level 4	Narcissistic personality who is not very borderline (denies responsibility; seeks others to collude)
Level 5	Mild borderline who worries about committing immoral acts (and probably won't)
Level 6	The person with repressed guilt (commits antisocial acts in order to get caught and punished)

People who are psychopathic have no moral standards and are not really aware that other people do. They may pay lip service to the fact that moral standards exist, but they really do not understand that the moral requirements they encounter in society represent any kind of authentic, mutually agreed-upon system of morality that other people have internalized. If they pay any heed to moral restraints at all, it is only in the interests of avoiding punishment.

Psychopaths rarely enter therapy voluntarily, but when they do, they make a lasting impression, particularly on therapy groups. One of my teachers once told me, "You can tell you have a psychopath in the group when all the women have fantasies that they are going to be raped."

Jake, a 23-year-old salesman wished to be in group therapy because, he stated, he needed to meet more women. The cotherapists explained to him that the purpose of the group was not to provide dates but to help members improve their interpersonal skills. Jake said this sounded like just what he needed. With considerable skepticism, the cotherapists accepted him into their group.

On the night of his first session, Jake entered the room, winked at one of the women and made a suggestive remark to another. He then pulled from his briefcase a huge package of bright pink match books with people's names written on them, party favors that he sold for a living. He began tossing them at people, presumably as a way of being friendly or breaking the ice, but in the process he hit two people in the face—one of them in the eye. When his victims cried out, Jake uttered a loud sadistic laugh.

In discussing his relationships with women, he related violent sadistic fantasies, seeming to take pleasure in the discomfort he was causing his audience. Most of the women in the group were afraid of him from the beginning, with the exception of one histrionic woman who found him attractive, although even she became intimidated after one or two group sessions with him. He said he never raped anyone, but many in the group were not convinced.

Probably because all of the men in the group were considerably older and larger than Jake, Jake kept a respectful distance from them, although he exuded disdain. Jake liked to encourage the men's baser inclinations. A member, George, was talking about his angry feelings toward his wife, and Jake intervened with a harsh laugh, "I'll bet you'd like to skewer her, wouldn't you, George! I hope you don't wimp out this time." It is hard to convey the savage coldness that emanated from Jake at such moments.

The therapists encouraged the group to be as honest as they could with Jake, pointing out that he had joined the group in order to learn what he was "doing wrong in his relationships." The group members became extremely angry with Jake and were very direct with him. Jake glowed when he received this feedback, so much did he enjoy the attention. He never came close to remorse, but he was not particularly defensive, either, so the group got a chance to practice assertiveness. His lack of defensiveness suggested even more severe superego pathology than if he had engaged in splitting or had been more paranoid. In object relations terms, it seemed there were no internalized good objects that could be mobilized to struggle against the bad ones. In Freudian terms, the level of superego development was minuscule. A glimmer of fear crossed Jake's face once—when one of the larger men in the group began roaring at him in fury after Jake insulted him; however, no hint of conscience was ever visible.

Lindner, who studied criminal psychopaths in the 1940s, wrote of their prevalent fantasies of being dismembered (1944). One night, when Jake had been in the group for two months, the therapists introduced a warm-up exercise, in which members were to imagine themselves as statues in a museum and then describe their statues to the group. Jake described his "statue" as having had the legs and arms torn off; it was bloody and misshapen. Before the session was over, Jake excused himself quietly and never returned to the group. A year later he wrote a vengeful and threatening letter to the female therapist—in red ink.

One can speculate that, instead of an integrated, controlled and in-control superego, Jake had frightening, punitive, and cruel monsters in his head, rageful parent parts that, when mobilized during his fantasy, threatened metaphorically to "tear him limb from limb." Perhaps in the statue exercise, Jake experienced a few moments as the victim of his own terrifying and bloodthirsty superego part, and he had no choice but to flee in order to prevent those self-annihilating forces from rising up inside of him again.

LEVEL 2: NARCISSISTIC PERSONALITY WITH ANTISOCIAL TRAITS

The second most severe moral pathology is demonstrated by persons whom Kernberg calls the "narcissistic personalities with ego-syntonic antisocial behavior." Translated, this means a severely narcissistic individual who does not feel guilty when he behaves immorally toward others because he sees himself as a victim. He may be "borderline," which means he is prone to splitting, rage, and/or paranoia, but his characteristic feature is that he feels he has the monopoly on morality. Such people know there is a morality that other people in society "buy into," but they feel they have the ultimate say about what is right and wrong. They have the beginnings of what Kernberg calls "idealized superego precursor integration," meaning they at least *have* a value system, but the moral messages they have internalized from parent figures are inconsistent, moralistic, self-serving, and idiosyncratic.

Narcissistic people of this type are not only extremely grandiose, but they are highly judgmental of others, making them most unpleasant to deal with. They feel morally justified in doing what they want to do, and they become completely enraged when they feel they have been treated unfairly. They massively distort interpersonal interactions after the fact in order to assign blame to others for whatever difficulties have occurred. They will frequently devalue and try to displace blame for their problems onto therapists and others who have tried to help and may alternate between rage and paranoia in treatment. This is the type of patient who "takes and takes" from the therapist, but is never satisfied, and who may, when the treatment ends or becomes stalemated, sue the therapist on spurious grounds.

The narcissism, rigidity, and periodic cruelty of these patients reflects their internalization of omnipotent and cruel parents who abused them. Kernberg mentions that these patients often have learned to take out their frustration on younger siblings, or perhaps animals or other younger children. They got away with this because there was no accountability in the household. Feelings of remorse or mature guilt are rare in this type of patient, for they were not exposed to adults from whom they could internalize a benevolent superego part. When mean things were done to them by parents, they never received an apology, so they have never learned to feel guilty, make reparation, or forgive.

While these persons are very difficult to help in therapy, the treatment, to the extent that it is successful, will help the person learn to reverse roles with others—to "get into the other person's shoes" a little bit. Long-term group therapy, if it can be tolerated by this kind of patient and if the therapist and other members can tolerate him, is particularly useful in helping this type of narcissistic personality learn that he is not always the victim, but can take responsibility for some of his own problems.

LEVEL 3: SEVERE BORDERLINE
WHO IS NOT VERY NARCISSISTIC

Kernberg's third category of moral pathology is represented by borderlines without excessive narcissism. This person is dishonest out of desperation. Her dishonesty is not totally calculated and usually has a self-protective purpose. She is apt to be demonstrate immoral behavior in the context of the therapy and in other close relationships.

This person chronically lies in therapy about things she knows are important to discuss. When she commits antisocial acts, it is out of frustration or fear. She will tend to "confess" to the therapist or a loved one what she has done and then report feeling cleansed; but she does not process her own behavior in any kind of thoughtful or critical way.

The therapist of one such patient found she had no choice but to confront the dishonesty of her patient, even though it was unconscious. In doing so, she may have saved the patient's life.

Chris had been seen in therapy by an experienced social worker for six months, when he began cutting his wrists, a behavior he had engaged in in previous years. The cutting seemed to be related to Chris's confusion and fear in his relationship with his girlfriend who, like Chris, had poor boundaries and who was prone to cutting her wrists as well. As the relationship became more toxic and enmeshed, Chris's suicidal behavior escalated, and he tried locking himself in the garage with the car motor running. Fortunately, he changed his mind and got out at the last minute.

The therapist was suitably alarmed and tried to hospitalize Chris, but he had no medical insurance and refused to go to a state facility. He stated he no longer wanted to die, so the therapist asked him to sign a contract that he would not hurt himself and that he would call the therapist if he became desperate. Four weeks later, after his girlfriend made a suicide attempt, Chris again cut himself and then sat in the car in the garage, determined to "do it this time," again jumping out only at the last minute.

The first time Chris remembered the contract was when he walked into the therapist's office for his next appointment with bandaged wrists.

The therapist was faced with two dilemmas: the first was that Chris was extremely dangerous to himself; and the second was that she could not trust his word. She was surprised that he had forgotten the agreement, given how responsible he had seemed to be about paying for sessions and being truthful about other matters. She asked him whether he thought he would have kept his pledge if he had remembered it. Chris said, "I think it would have been hard for me to do what I did if I had remembered the contract."

The therapist said, "Chris, I think you should go to the hospital, but you will not. If I got a psychiatrist to commit you, you would be out very quickly. What's more, the risk is not now but later on, when you are feeling depressed and lonely or when you have had another struggle with your girlfriend. I cannot treat you if you are not willing to keep yourself safe. Psychotherapy only works on people who are alive. I also cannot treat you if I cannot trust your word. I will give you 24 hours to convince me that you are trustworthy and can be treated outside of a hospital. You can do that by leaving a written statement in your own words that reiterates the promise you made last month not to hurt yourself and to call for help. You must also put into this document that you understand that if you do hurt yourself, I will terminate your case."

The therapist was quite surprised to find a lengthy letter from Chris in her office mailbox hours before the appointed time, one that conveyed a sincere desire to continue treatment with her and a willingness to forgo suicide or any form of self-mutilation as an option. The document was surprisingly thoughtful and self-reflective, evidencing an "observing ego" that he had not seemed to have at his disposal before. Two months later, when a crisis occurred and Chris felt despondent, he talked at length about his suicidal feelings. He then looked the therapist straight in the eye and said, "I can't betray my promise to you. I'd quit before I did anything."

The therapist correctly judged that Chris was capable of making and keeping a moral commitment and hoped that this would provide the necessary deterrent to his killing himself. In fact, this was the case; within six months, while some suicidal ideation persisted, the inclination to act on it was greatly diminished.

Borderlines who are not excessively narcissistic may seem morally "wishy-washy." Their poor boundaries and low self-esteem makes it difficult for them to differentiate from others enough to take a moral stand. While they may have strong moral principles, which can be tapped in the treatment, as Chris's therapist was able to do, these may fade in the face of internal and interpersonal pressures.

Cassandra was a borderline woman in her thirties whose strong antisocial tendencies were totally split-off from the rest of her personality and would emerge in bizarre ways under stress. A nurse with the best of manners, Cassandra presented as proper and well-behaved. At her second therapy session, Cassandra announced that, in going back to work after the first session, she had experienced strong feelings of anxiety and had purposely rammed her car into another automobile in the parking lot. Before the therapist could respond, Cassandra breathed a sigh of relief and said, "I'm so glad I told you this. I feel much better!" Other incidents like this popped up frequently in the next few weeks—stealing a little bit of money at work, deliberately scratching someone's car. After Cassandra's confessions, the therapist would firmly tell her that this behavior had to stop. Cassandra would become very tearful and contrite and would feel more stable for a couple of weeks, only to find herself suddenly committing some other randomly destructive or dishonest act.

Unfortunately, this patient terminated treatment due to lack of funds. The therapeutic objective, had the therapy continued, would have been to help Cassandra accept and establish control over the angry and antisocial part of herself, starting with recognizing and labeling her angry feelings as they would inevitably emerge in the transference with the therapist.

LEVEL 4: THE NARCISSISTIC PERSONALITY WHO IS NOT VERY BORDERLINE

The fourth level of moral pathology is represented mostly by narcissistic persons without any overt borderline features. These patients do not overtly lie to therapists and loved ones; rather, they consistently deny responsibility for their actions and try to get others, including their therapists, to collude with them in antisocial endeavors. As patients, they are apt to make an innocent revelation to the therapist about doing something that would seem to be completely against their value system and yet, will seem "clueless" that they have done anything wrong. They will demonstrate a lack of concern about their behavior and a lack of capacity for a sense of moral responsibility and guilt.

Such persons may take the "innocent bystander" position, completely overlooking their own moral responsibility. Jane in Chapter 2 is a perfect example of Level 4 moral pathology. When her father-in-law insisted on driving the car even though he was practically blind, she never thought to call the police. With an ingenuousness that was frustrating, she would engage in immoral behavior in an attempt to catch other people in theirs. She saw nothing wrong with spying on her husband or violating the privacy of her son's bureau drawers or her daughter's diary. She denied moral responsibility for her violence when she tracked down her husband's ex-lover and slapped her in the face.

Because these people were not treated particularly cruelly in childhood, their object relationships are not markedly impaired. On the other hand, because they were not fully loved or appreciated by parent figures, they suffer a limited capacity for in-depth object relationships. Because they have not experienced the strong love from and toward parent figures necessary to achieve a thoroughgoing internalization and identification with parental beliefs and values, they have not achieved superego integration, which means they demonstrate blind spots in their moral thinking. They may be quite guiltless, but compared to the psychopath described earlier, they are much more organized and have better social reality-testing. The denier of responsibility knows quite well that there are rules in society that other people believe are important, but he would just as soon beat the system if he can.

Because he knows the "lingo," the denier can rationalize his antisocial behavior to his therapist with disarming logic, which can occasionally cause the therapist to stray from his own value system. A young male patient of this type, a person of great charm, almost persuaded his usually ethical therapist to lie for him about his whereabouts on the day he had arranged to get his car stolen for the insurance money. The therapist, in discussing the case in his peer supervision group, was appalled at how close he had come to complying with the patient's request. (Projective identification at work!)

In my experience people who are antisocial at this level are highly amenable to confrontation by people whom they know really care about them. Consequently, if the therapeutic bond is strong, this patient is quite susceptible to the moral influence of therapy. This was certainly the case with Jane. The therapist may be able to help the patient see that ultimately his antisocial behavior is detrimental to his own self-esteem and relationships and that acting more in line with the five virtues will make him feel much better about himself and will lead others to like him better as well.

All persons with narcissistic disorders (severely character disordered or not) suffered as children from the experience that their needs were secondary to those of their parents and that approval and love was contingent on performance (Kohut, 1971). When a narcissistic personality behaves in antisocial ways, he is rebelling against authority figures in his childhood who made and enforced rules capriciously, without reference to his needs. Such an individual has been a victim and so can be helped to identify with the victim. He can even take the position of compassionate nurturer and voluntarily advance his activity in the area of the five virtues. In a firm and caring therapeutic relationship, he can learn, even late in life, that rules that are mutually agreed upon and that protect innocent parties are useful and affirming, and are different from the kind of the rules imposed upon him in childhood, the kind that were "made to be broken."

LEVEL 5: MILD BORDERLINE WHO WORRIES ABOUT COMMITTING IMMORAL ACTS (AND PROBABLY WON'T)

Persons at levels 5 and 6 of superego pathology have incorporated idealized superego precursors and a minimum of sadistic superego precursors. Their object relations are not disturbed, just weak—but not as weak as those of the people in Level 4. I would describe them as suffering from disorders of the self (Kohut, 1971), which render them incapable of experiencing continuity in their concern for others. They are not immoral, they are just not particularly good. They do not manifest dishonesty in their relationships nor are they antisocial, but their relationships are shadowy and insubstantial. Having strong feelings about others—desire, jealousy, envy—makes these people so uncomfortable, that they manage their lives in such a way as to minimize the demands and expectations of others, as well as their own longings for closeness and approval. They do not form close enough attachments to their fellow humans to care about being **altruistic**, **responsible**, or **egalitarian** or to get very excited about **dishonesty** or **unfairness**. They are likely *not* to "pull through for others in a pinch."

Level 5 persons have, Kernberg notes, contradictory ego and superego features as part of general borderline pathology. What this means is that people at this level of superego pathology are aware of strong and contradictory urges. They will express worry that in a different mental state they might do something "bad" toward others or their self. In the absence of strong object attachments to channel internal strivings, these people often feel at the mercy of intense libidinous and aggressive impulses.

The person in this category can learn, with psychotherapy, to take the good with the bad. He has ideals and he has prohibitions, but he has not had much opportunity to explore the ins and outs of his moral beliefs and immoral fantasies, since he has had only superficial relationships, which do not include talking about anything so intense. As a patient, if allowed to go at his own pace and to feel very safe, he is quite happy to discuss his morality because it is of great concern to him. While the therapist may not feel he is going to act out his antisocial impulses, the patient is quite worried that he might. "What's to stop him?" he feels. "Love? Don't know what it feels like. Responsibility? So far, but who knows how it would hold up if I really got crazy."

A perfect example of Level 5 was Mark, a quiet man in his mid-thirties who always felt he was valued by his parents only "as a thing" and not as a person. He experienced his parents as extremely domineering and critical, yet, also, impulsive and erratic in their behavior. Mark entered therapy with two pressing concerns. The first was that he felt he somehow lacked the emotional wherewithal to be in a relationship with a woman, and the second was that he thought he might kill his father. His father had a very serious and long-term disease, and Mark was the only family member available to take care of him, a task that he took on with diligence, despite his intense resentment toward his father for never paying any attention to him as a child. Mark felt rage building inside him and worried that he might act this out against his father or, if he became guilty and depressed enough, against himself.

In the absence of firm object relationships, Mark's impulses and superego coexisted in stark opposition to one another in his head. This made for great internal turmoil, which in Mark's case, might have accounted for his high level of somatic disturbance in the form of tachycardia, stomach problems, and muscle spasms.

The emotional distress of this type of person may be imperceptible to others, but he is in constant turmoil, for very little of his internal conflict is repressed from consciousness. Even therapists may fail to appreciate the intensity of his discomfort and may mistakenly think him healthier than he is. When, after a year of participation in his therapy group, Mark finally revealed that he had experienced such strong impulses to kill his father, other members were amazed at how "intense he was inside," as they put it. Mark was also amazed, and greatly gratified, that others could understand and accept his experience. This recognition helped Mark realize that he could "contain" his negative feelings and did not need to act them out.

Treatment with patients such as Mark involve building a strong and warm therapeutic relationship, which lasts over a long period of time. Group therapy is extremely beneficial as it provides the opportunity to form a number of such strong relationships. This is necessary for the resolution of the superego pathology as well as other problems. Only in the context of an authentic relationship in which Mark was valued for himself, could he let people matter enough to act genuinely on their behalf. In a world where people had emotional importance to him, the ideals that used to echo meaninglessly in his head now began to make sense, and he began to strive hard to achieve them.

LEVEL 6: THE PERSON WITH REPRESSED GUILT (WHO COMMITS ANTISOCIAL ACTS IN ORDER TO GET CAUGHT AND PUNISHED)

This last and least severe form of moral pathology is characterized by antisocial behavior expressing unconscious guilt. People with Level 6 moral pathology, if they are character disordered at all, are mildly so. As Kernberg explains it, the person's enactment of antisocial behavior reflects repressed fantasies involving masochistic submission to a sadistic, but well-integrated superego. In other words, his antisocial behavior has an unconscious self-destructive intent, reflecting the need for expiation of unconscious guilt. The genesis of this sixth type of superego pathology occurs later in childhood than the previous types and in a context of more stable object relationships.

The Level 6 person will exhibit, as part of his superego pathology, a high degree of inhibitions and symptoms reflective of unconscious or barely realized guilt, as opposed to shame. Because his object relations are more stable than those of persons in the previous levels, he will not engage in excessive splitting, introjective identification, or projective identification. Kernberg cites as an example the case of a researcher who falsified his data and then was so guilty he got himself found out. A woman who was in therapy with me years ago had not sufficiently worked through her feelings of guilt about having an abortion. Her way of handling her guilt was to promptly get herself pregnant again and have to have another one!

Ronald, a proud lawyer and community man, came for therapy after his wife filed for divorce. Though Ronald claimed he loved his wife and was happier with her than he had ever thought possible, he had recently had a one-night stand with a woman and was caught by his wife. Soon after his wife found out about the affair, Ronald uncharacteristically breached a client's confidentiality and was suspended from his law practice. Then, as if he had not made matters bad enough for himself, Ronald made a physical threat to his wife—something he had never come close to doing before—and his wife promptly had him arrested. Ronald was shamefully remanded by the court to group counseling for battering men in the very town where he held a number of prominent volunteer positions.

Ronald's therapist asked Ronald what he possibly could have done in his life that was so bad that he should deserve so much trouble. Ronald told a few stories that suggested that he might have been unconsciously feeling guilty: He had not visited his father for several years before he died; he had divorced his first wife just after she became ill with cancer; and he had been a largely absent parent who had not managed to attend any of his son's plays or football games. At first Ronald insisted that he did not feel guilty about any of these situations, but his self-punitive behavior suggested otherwise. Eventually Ronald had to agree that somewhere deep down he must have been feeling guilty, for there was no other way to explain the retribution he had brought upon on himself lately. Just recognizing his guilt and really feeling it instead of acting it out helped Ronald gain control over it. Instead of unconsciously torturing himself for his "sins," Ronald learned through therapy to feel the guilt instead of acting it out and then to try to make amends to people he had hurt.

Chapter 12

HOW THERAPY FOSTERS GOODNESS

Does therapy foster goodness? The answer is probably yes and no.

Given the amoral biases inherent in psychology and psychotherapy (Chapters 3 and 4), one would think that psychotherapy would not foster goodness at all but, rather, increase patients' alienation, hardheartedness, egoism, and individualism at the expense of a sense of relatedness, community, social responsibility, and the five virtues in the private and public domains.

Indeed, as Bellah et al. (1985) have said, therapy can be quite a self-centered pursuit. As Jungian writer Hillman (Hillman & Ventura, 1992) says, some of our society's brightest people may have spent too much time in therapy working on the "inside soul" rather than the soul of society at large. By emphasizing the metaphor of the child, whether as the "primitive beast" of psychoanalysis or as the victimized "inner child" who needs comfort and nurturing, therapy may foster passivity and helplessness instead of appropriate outrage at deplorable world conditions and a zeal to change them. Therapy often encourages looking, even living, backward in time, diverting the individual from current and future social and environmental realities (Hillman & Ventura, 1992; Roszak, 1992).

Nonetheless, I believe therapy, in the hands of a skilled, ethical, and mentally healthy practitioner, frequently does foster goodness. In sorting through the complicated relationship among mental health, psychotherapy, and moral health, it has become clear to me that often, and in many ways, the holding environment of effective therapy represents and promotes many of the finest human qualities in clients. If lovers, parents, friends, families, communities, and nations could provide and facilitate goodness as consistently and effectively as psychotherapy does, the world might be a better place.

This final chapter suggests some ways that the process of therapy itself seems to me to foster goodness. These ideas are not meant to be inclusive, but to inspire the reader to think of others.

FREE AND EQUAL RELATIONSHIPS

Claude Steiner (1975), an early proponent of "radical therapy," defined oppression and mental illness as equivalent; he said both involve a combination of mystification plus alienation.

Alienation and mystification seem to be a part of the experience of each person who comes to therapy. The average therapy patient does not feel connected to his world and is confused about what is going on around him. Alienation breeds mystification and vice versa, creating a vicious circle through which the patient becomes increasingly powerless relative to others in his personal and public world; hence, the oppression that may have started out as limited in scope, intrapsychic or affecting a very small proportion of one's social contacts, can broaden to affect one's entire relationship to society.

Therapy has the moral function of reducing the oppression of the client and others in his world by helping him to restore or institute more **egalitarian** and mutually satisfying relationships. Two ways that this occurs in therapy is through the demystification and rejection of inequitable power arrangements, and by countering alienation through community and belonging.

Educator Paolo Friere (1970) said that the rectification of power imbalances takes place only through a rigorous, often painful dialogue between the oppressed and the oppressor. In intensive therapy, whether or not the client confronts his real-life oppressor(s) directly, he is in constant dialogue with the introjects of those who hurt or neglected him. If the patient is dealing in therapy with his role as oppressor, he will, in one way or another, have a dialogue with his victim. This "moral education" that clients receive in therapy is, in my view, an excellent example of what Friere calls "the pedagogy of the oppressed." Friere indicates some basic principles, which must be kept in mind if oppressive relationships are to be transformed into **egalitarian** ones. These principles seem to be inherent in the process of psychotherapy.

1. *Education is the only route to freedom.* Without education, the oppressed will inaccurately conceptualize liberation in terms of reversing

roles with the oppressor and securing the power to do the oppressing himself. The slave fantasizes that he will be free only when *he* becomes the master and his master becomes his slave. As we have written in the section about splitting and projective identification (Chapter 7), the result of such a reversal is no change at all, but simply a perpetuation of oppression with different subject and object. When they first arrive in therapy, many patients harbor fantasies of bringing their parents into therapy and verbally "flattening them," with the therapist cheering them on. Therapists who collude with such vengeful fantasies are perpetuating, rather than correcting splitting and, hence, oppression. The opposite of oppression/splitting is a situation in which there is freedom and equality for all parties and mutual love and appreciation, freely and authentically expressed. When the complementarity of roles ("top dog" and "underdog") is obliterated, both the motivation and the opportunity for either party to be slave or master is eliminated.

2. *The only people who can* really *educate oppressors are the oppressed.*

This is a hard concept for therapists to remember. We often think we are educating our clients, when, in many cases, it is their dialogue with their oppressors that is the greatest teacher.

As Friere explains it, the education of the oppressed begins when they rise up in revolt. This gets the oppressor's attention and gives her a taste of what it is like to feel powerless, threatened, and afraid, which is how the oppressed have been feeling all along. Knocking the oppressor off her pedestal is only the beginning of the educational process, for this equality of power is highly temporary. The disarmed oppressor could snatch back the power, or the formerly oppressed could take over and become abusive themselves. Either of these simply constitutes reverting to the former state of inequity. On the other hand, if the oppressed takes advantage of this opportunity to really articulate their experience at the hands of the oppressor, the oppressor, in her weakened state may well be able to really hear and feel the pain and misery she has caused. The oppressor's response may be to feel remorse, and to wish to give love and appreciation instead of abuse to the oppressed.

Often, the therapy client begins his education when he enters therapy; therapy may be his "revolt." He is saying, "The situation I am in is oppressing me, and it is not okay." The therapist may encourage the client to break the cycle of abuse by confronting his abusers with the harm they have done. While these encounters are often charged and angry, people who have confronted an abusive parent have realized that, as well as being an act of self-preservation, it is an act of love toward the oppressor. No matter how painful, the confrontation allows the oppressor an opportunity to come down from his isolated and superior position and relate in a mutual and honest way with his former victim. If the oppressor does choose to step down and listen, he will receive an unparalleled moral education. Once enlightened about the horrors of oppression, he is likely to join with his former victim and other ex-victims and oppressors to try to prevent abuse in their families and communities.

A crucial part of what makes group therapy effective is that the members are considered equals in the group, regardless of what positions they hold in society. Within this highly democratic and **egalitarian** setting, each participant brings to the group painful experiences of oppression, which play themselves out in the group. An authoritarian father may find himself oppressing a man who is easily intimidated because of his experiences with his own father. Unlike in his home, however, the younger man is encouraged rather than discouraged from letting the authoritarian man know how disparaging and cruel he sounds. The feedback process of a therapy group is a moral dialogue in Friere's terms, because it is conducted in a context of equality, not oppression. True dialogue, according to Friere, "does not impose, does not manipulate, does not domesticate, does not sloganize" (1970, p. 168). No one person, even the therapist, is the authority in a group, and no one is seen to have the monopoly on truth.

3. *Freedom is defined as "wholeness" and "authenticity."* These qualities are exactly what we help our patients strive for in therapy. In any psychodynamic theory or its derivatives, it is axiomatic that a divided self cannot be free; the parts of the divided person are consigned to conflict or at least to work at cross-purposes with one another. A divided self cannot be good to others, because the unintegrated selfish, hateful, greedy, and rageful parts will always sabotage the other parts' loving and generous efforts. Therapy tries to mend the splits in the self and to permit the reowning of parts that have been projected or denied, so that at least one has the freedom to act virtuously. This does not mean that virtuous behavior will necessarily result, but at least the potential to do so is liberated.

THE SEARCH FOR TRUTH

. . . ultimately the best way for a person to discover what he ought to do is to find out who and what he is, because the path to ethical and values decisions, to oughtness, is via "isness," via the discovery of facts, truth, reality, the nature of the particular person. (Maslow, 1971, p. 111)

The truth that is sought in therapy is the truth of the heart as well as of the head. The contract a client makes with the therapist upon entering therapy is to join with the therapist in a rigorous search for the truth, which involves being honest in the relationship with the therapist as well as with oneself.

Kegan (1982) sees the development of personality itself as an ever widening search for truth, and psychotherapy as isomorphic with this process. In his view, the self evolves through endless cycles of assimilation (taking in new information to fit old paradigms) and accommodation (forming new paradigms to accommodate the information that will not fit into the old ones). Growth involves emerging from embeddedness in a succession of perceptual and social fields, each of which brings forth a new set of moral viewpoints and responsibilities. With increasing cognitive and social maturity one is able to encompass larger social and moral fields, moving from self-centeredness to other-directedness, to institution-dependent, to interdependence. The psychotherapy relationship is seen as cycling through successive levels of truth in the same way as the child does in the course of his moral development.

Truth tends to join people with one another in positive and loving ways, leading to increased **altruism, responsibility, egalitarianism,** and **justice** in the relationship. This is particularly noticeable in group therapy, where a notable effect of authentic self-disclosure is always increased closeness in the group. This closeness tends to extend beyond the relationships between the discloser and other members to encompass others in the person's life as well. Even in individual therapy, however, the "aha" experience, in which the patient realizes something new or in a new way always enriches the therapeutic relationship. Whether the truth is a feeling, a thought, or a perception; whether it is about oneself or a relationship; whether it is pleasant or painful—facing it opens up more possibilities for genuine affection than could ever exist when there were secrets or blocks, not to mention unspoken resentments. Often, expression of the truth brings with it a vulnerability on the part of the discloser, which encourages others to respond in warm, comforting, and appreciative ways.

Even when the truth that is discovered turns out to be that a relationship is over, it usually leads to a more humane ending to that relationship than if the reality of the current relationship is denied. We have all seen a partner leave a spouse or lover with the claim that she "just wanted space," when the truth was she was miserable with him. We are always aware of how much more pain this causes the person who has been rejected than would a straightforward approach. A separation born out of honest soul-searching, no matter how disappointing the end result, is better for all concerned than staying together by means of lies. A host of difficult truths are faced by clients in therapy every day—truths that compel action commensurate with the insight. Such action, it seems to me, is usually moral.

Part of the search for truth involves the careful analysis of intent. Therapy helps people make the crucial distinction between failure and evil. Clients struggle continually with their own failures and those of their parents, trying to decipher the intent of the person who has perpetrated hurt, abuse, or disappointment. "Did I mean to hurt my child . . . ?" "Did my father have malevolent intent toward me as a child?" a client in therapy may query. Most of the time, through confrontation with the actual parent or with his own memories, the client concludes that the answer is no. Most of the time the client decides that he was loved, however badly and sporadically by the parent figure who has failed him. Sometimes, however, this is not the case. Some children are clearly not loved by their parents, at least in any way that could possibly be experienced that way by the child.

Throughout this book we have seen therapists struggling to come to terms with the moral issues inherent in their cases and to articulate them in ways that did not shame their patients. As Kitwood says, this is a highly moral responsibility.

> Paradoxically, this kind of relationship, which so resolutely abstains from all moralizing judgment, is one which is required to meet the most rigorous moral criteria. When it does so, here is the epitome of that respect for persons, fairness, truthfulness, and promise-keeping that make up the stuff of what is commonly meant by morality. . . . A therapeutic relationship, then, in its uncompromising regard for personhood and its resolute pursuit of psychological truth, has moral qualities that are conspicuously lacking in the everyday world. (Kitwood, 1990, p. 202)

PURSUIT OF LIFE, NOT DEATH

The pursuit of psychotherapy, by patient and therapist, is, by definition, a life-promoting endeavor. Whether we conceive of therapy in the medical model as healing the sick, or in more lay terms as improving coping and relationships, the intent is to preserve and enhance life. This, in and of itself, is at least good, and probably moral.

One prominent psychoanalytic theory, however, may have significantly impaired the moral thrust of psychotherapy: Freud's death instinct (*thanatos*). In 1920, weary and disillusioned after years of economic depression and the terrible destruction wreaked by World War I, Freud searched for an explanation for the misery that human beings seemed to experience and perpetrate upon one another. He concluded that everyone, including so-called normal people, possessed a "death instinct" (*thanatos*), which he defined as a biological tendency to return to an inorganic state. This literally morbid theory represented a radical departure for psychoanalysis, which had heretofore assumed that people strove for life, not death, and for pleasure, not pain.

It is unclear how Freud, the arch-Darwinian, justified the construct of *thanatos* in terms of the drive of the species to perpetuate itself. The only connotation of *thanatos* that makes sense in the context of evolution is Durkheim's suggestion (1951) that it is really the desire for peace and relief of stress through sleep or loss of consciousness. Durkheim saw this desire for "peace at last," when carried to an extreme, as the motivation for suicide.

Thanatos is an example of a psychological theory that is interesting, but not at all useful for therapy, particularly if one is interested in fostering goodness in the process. An enterprise that strives for health and growth can make little headway if therapists and patients adopt the idea that to get better they have to battle a fundamental drive for nonexistence.

Much of change in therapy comes from reframing what seem to be negative behaviors as actually positive and life-affirming. Even Freud, before he invented *thanatos*, saw compulsively repeated destructive behavior as an ongoing attempt to reconstruct a particular situation in accordance with desires stemming from the pleasure principle (Freud, 1920/1961). Object relations and self-psychology retained Freud's early perspective that much of anti-social behavior has a positive intent, namely the obtaining of love and attention. Systems theorists reframe negative behavior into efforts to perpetuate the family. All inclination to reframe is eliminated if we believe that our patients' self-destructive or destructive behaviors have no underlying motive but the wish to die.

Fromm (1964) radically reframed Freud's construct of the death instinct. Renaming it necrophilia, Fromm saw the death instinct as offering an explanation for both immorality and insanity. "Necrophilia," the desire for death, was, for Fromm, the opposite of "biophilia," attraction to life. Necrophilia is the desire to seek pain, depression, and lack of stimulation, and to gravitate toward places and situations and people who are deadened, mechanistic, apathetic, or negative. Necrophiliacs have anal sadistic characteristics and demonstrate little feeling and spontaneity and an obsessional concern with material things. With closed minds and closed hearts, they think and converse in intellectual abstractions and are virtually incapable of moral sensitivity.

> Necrophilia develops in one who grows up "among death-loving people [and is caused by] lack of stimulation; fright, conditions which make life routinized and uninteresting; and mechanical order instead of one determined by direct and human relations among people." (1964, p. 52)

By contrast, Fromm says, the development of biophilia requires that one be with people who love life; have warm, affectionate contact with others; enjoy freedom and an absence of threat; experience the availability of teachers who teach by example rather than by threat, and who "teach the principles conducive to inner harmony and strength"; have stimulating influences in one's life; and engage in a way of life that is genuinely interesting (p. 51).

For Fromm, necrophilia is the substrate of all psychopathology, and biophilia is the aim of therapy. Fromm (1964) defines what he calls the biophiliac ethic.

> Good is all that serves life; evil is all that serves death. Good is reverence for life, all that enhances life, growth, unfolding. Evil is all that stifles life, narrows it down, cuts it into pieces. Joy is virtuous and sadness is sinful. . . . The conscience of the biophilous person is not one of forcing oneself to refrain from evil and do good. It is not the superego described by Freud, which is a strict taskmaster, employing sadism against oneself for the sake of virtue. The biophilous conscience is motivated by its attraction to life and joy; the moral effort consists in strengthening the life-loving side in oneself. For this reason the biophile does not dwell in remorse and guilt which are, after all, only aspects of self-loathing and sadness. (1964, p. 47)

It would seem that the criterion for a therapeutic environment must be commensurate with the conditions necessary for producing biophilia. Necrophiliac conditions would surely be iatrogenic as well as immoral. It is likely that the extreme barrenness of the overly strict analytic situation veers toward necrophilia, since almost all of the above life-promoting conditions are absent. Successful therapy groups would seem to be exactly the opposite, characterized by all of the biophiliac principles (Nicholas, 1984). Most one-to-one and family therapy situations are full of life, warmth, and growth, despite periods of hostility and resistance, which may indeed feel "deadly."

In his book, *The Roots of Evil*, Staub (1989) identifies conditions in society that are nurturing of caring and prosocial behavior as opposed to selfishness, destructiveness, and evil. He says that a cultural norm that involves the valuation of human beings is a crucial variable in promoting prosocial action. Where valuing of human life is explicitly promoted and articulated, people conform to this as the norm. There needs to be a sense among people that others deserve to be helped, that they "deserve" your kindness. This theory has important implications for therapy. If the norm is to see patients as "specimens" they may behave as such, whereas seeing them as having the potential for goodness is probably the basic means by which therapists foster their positive morality.

Some clients in therapy are heavily infused with necrophiliac tendencies from their experiences with necrophiliac parents. To get rid of their own necrophilia, they have to grapple with the terrible reality that their parents did not want the best for them.

One patient, Janet, age 32, was perpetually down-in-the-mouth. In her therapy group, her relationships were distant and strained; she could be depended upon to stifle a group laugh and to see the darkest side of every issue. What Janet had to face in the course of her therapy was that her mother did not love her. Janet had hoped there was another explanation for why she never felt her mother had any benevolent intentions toward her, why she disparaged every one of Janet's accomplishments, and why she shamed her mercilessly when Janet disappointed her. Janet faced her own feelings of rivalry with her younger disabled brother, on whom the mother appeared to lavish affection, and tried to pretend that the rejection she experienced was not as monolithic as it was. Finally, however, she had to admit that the main feeling she received from her mother was that her mother wished she had never been born. She realized that the only reason she had even survived, given her mother's murderous rage, was due to the love she received from her father.

Janet wrote her mother a letter, stating very clearly how hopeless Janet felt about their relationship past and present. Her mother responded with an annoyed message on her answering machine, saying that she understood Janet was "going through a phase" and would "give her space" for a while. The total absence of guilt or concern on the mother's part served as final confirmation for Janet that her perceptions were accurate—that her mother could not take responsibility for her own failures as a mother, and that to continue the relationship would be sheer masochism on Janet's part. She wrote another letter suggesting that they have very minimal contact from then on.

Shortly after Janet removed herself from her mother's life, her relationships in the group became richer and deeper. She began to gather some self-esteem and met a loving man whom she is planning to marry, although the relationship is difficult for her because she has such trouble trusting anyone. Janet began to nurture her nascent sense of humor and joined many social activities.

This desire to continue to be eaten alive by that carnivorous part of the parent is the most frequently-seen and most potent representation of necrophilia. Janet's therapy involved extricating herself from her attraction to the dark, lugubrious world of her mother, reversing her trend toward necrophilia and choosing biophilia instead. Necrophilia, when wrought against an innocent child, has been called by Shengold "soul murder" (1989).

"The sacrifice, the sacrifice, that is all I exist for," cried a young man to his therapy group. He had already made a serious suicide attempt and still wanted to die. "I have to sacrifice myself for my mother. I have to make up for all the men who failed her. I sacrificed my childhood to comfort her, and now I will sacrifice my life. Then she will know that at least *I* really loved her."

"I know what that's like," a woman in the group told the young man. "My mother and I had a pact of exclusivity," she said.

"And what did you have to give up to get exclusivity?" someone else in the group asked.

"Just myself," she said instantly. "And it was worth it at the time. Now I'm paying the price. I keep wanting to crawl back into that dark space and rest. I'm scared to live my life."

Many patients face the task in therapy of reviving and feeding their diminished and tortured souls, which requires facing the evil within themselves as well as in their parents. Kohn (1990) pointed out that in order to understand and prevent evil, "we need to grasp its appeal from the inside" (p. 157). The same client who stated his wish to sacrifice himself for his mother expressed a powerful desire to hurt animals and others who remind him of his vulnerability. A great many patients in therapy, and Janet was one of them, acknowledge their strong attraction to the deadest and deadliest parts of their parents. They learn that this attraction comes from having formed a defensive compensatory idealization of the aggressor to ward off the pain of having been used, abused, and often repeatedly discarded by the parent. Therapy strives to point individuals away from such dark pursuits, to help them find the self-esteem to seek more life-promoting, biophiliac goals.

LOVING MORE AND BETTER

In Chapter 7, we cited psychoanalytic perspectives that suggest that moral development is, in large part, the development of the capacity to care. As Kraft (1986) put it "morality is fundamentally and ultimately a transrational process oriented toward being together in love . . . to resolve conflicts in service of justice is indeed important, but the transrational option to love is the basis and source of justice" (p. 27).

A psychotherapy that does not open up options for love is, to my mind, a failure. If a person leaves treatment less loving than she went in, the therapy has hurt more than helped. By becoming more truly loving I mean not just having more loving feelings, but being able to think and act more lovingly as well, without sacrificing the **honesty** with self and others that a rigorous therapy inevitably promotes. A successful therapy will, I believe, expand or generalize the objects of one's love beyond one's intimates or children to include one's community and even to persons with whom one has no personal relationship. One has greater compassion toward one's fellow man, which automatically generates generosity (**altruism**) and fairness (**egalitarianism, justice**) toward persons less fortunate or more vulnerable than oneself, and as well as more **responsibility** in all kinds of relationships.

When 43-year-old banker Jacob entered therapy, one would hardly have described him as loving—just angry and misunderstood. Jacob was filled with complaints about his wife who, he said, ruthlessly humiliated him in public and treated him with unmitigated callousness at home. When Jacob joined a therapy group, it was easier to see his part in the marital problems. In the blink of an eye, Jacob managed to get most of the women irritated at him; the women who were angry at men anyway were furious at him for his constant put-downs of his wife. He greeted their responses to him with sexist jokes, annoying the men with a sort of "you guys understand, these women can't take a joke" attitude. When the group members or the therapist would try to get Jacob to listen to how critical and relentless he sounded, Jacob would interpret this as everyone taking his wife's side against him. When this occurred, Jacob would sulk, which would prompt the angry women to express sympathy for his wife for having to "put up with such a baby," which, of course, convinced Jacob that no one could understand his problems. When anyone did give Jacob sympathy, they would soon regret it, for this was the fuel he needed to tell another half-dozen stories about how he was mistreated, without taking a breath or looking up. When other people would talk about their own situations, Jacob was generally attentive and helpful for a while, but eventually would begin yawning and drop out of the conversation.

The therapist decided it was important for Jacob to learn how to get empathy from people. Clearly this was not going to happen in the course of any discussion about his wife, so he got Jacob talking about his childhood with his mother and father. It was abundantly clear to the group that Jacob's needs were last on everyone's list of priorities. Jacob's happiness and success were of no importance to his mother, who was a very narcissistic and chronically dissatisfied individual. His cleverness in business was very threatening to his father, who was highly competitive with Jacob. As he described his childhood, he cried softly. The group could feel the deep level of emotional deprivation Jacob had incurred. Some members wept with and for him, and many expressed sincere empathy and a new understanding of how deep his current unhappiness was. Jacob gradually began to take a real interest in other members and their problems; his support and insight was highly valued in the group. Over time, the group gave Jacob more validation and love than he had ever received in his life. He was openly appreciative and told the group that he experienced their empathy as permission to be happy.

At first, however, Jacob could only "sneak" his happiness. He engaged in an extramarital affair with a single woman who made him feel sexy and wanted. The group noticed a dramatic improvement in Jacob's mood and self-esteem, but were afraid he was on a self-destructive course, for it was clear that should his wife find out and seek a divorce, she would show him no mercy with respect to finances and child custody. Several people in the group were unhappy with his solution on moral grounds, feeling that Jacob needed to take responsibility for his mistake in marrying his wife and leave the marriage, rather than stringing along the new woman, lying to his wife, and possibly jeopardizing his relationship with his children.

While he was having the affair, Jacob was feeling so narcissistically gratified that he developed a new tolerance for his wife, which she sensed, and she was a little less hard on him for a while. While he had always been an attentive father, Jacob found himself even more involved and responsive with his children than usual.

Within a few weeks, this new, more loving Jacob began to have trouble reconciling his new and valued persona with that of a cheating husband. He stated that he liked the way he was acting in the marriage and wanted to preserve that way of being, if possible, whether the marriage lasted or not. He decided to stop the affair and give the marriage one last try.

Within a few weeks, Jacob was complaining about his wife in group again, and generating the same negative response from the group members that he had before. The therapist realized projective identification was at work in the group. Jacob was projecting the part of himself that believed he did not have any right to complain onto, or into, the group, and several group members were cooperatively playing that role while he responded with the defensive and misunderstood part. The therapist told Jacob that he not only had a right to be happy, but he also had a right to be unhappy. She said he did not need to make his wife wrong in order to justify feelings of unhappiness. The therapist advised that Jacob take a careful reading on his feelings, and decide for himself whether he loved his wife and wanted to be married to her or not.

A few weeks later, Jacob opted to end his marriage. With an almost total absence of rancor, Jacob proceeded with gentleness and patience to tell first his wife and then his children that he was moving out. He obtained an apartment near to his wife and took full responsibility for sharing child care and providing financial support. He avoided conflicts by being as pleasant and accommodating as possible, but without being a martyr. While the therapist and the group could not get the wife's side of the story, it was evident that Jacob was far more loving during his divorce than he had been for most of the marriage. The group could only marvel at how peaceful and contented the once contentious and resentful Jacob had become. His concern and caring for other group members was felt by even the most cynical of the women who had found him so obnoxious in the beginning.

As often happens in such a situation, once Jacob was available, his girlfriend was not interested in a relationship with him. Even this rejection Jacob handled with aplomb. He was so happy with himself as a loving, generous, responsible, and honest person, that he decided to just enjoy seeing his kids and his friends and not worry about having a woman in his life for a while.

Before he left the group, Jacob spontaneously expressed how happy he was in his life and how he wanted to share this happiness. "I am so fortunate," he declared. "I have health and love in my life and plenty of financial security. I think I am going to volunteer a certain proportion of my time to a cause I really believe in." After some consideration, he chose to finance and manage an inner-city sports project.

Jacob's therapy is a modest example of how therapy can enhance one's capacity to love. Jacob had difficulty loving anyone, including himself, because of his narcissism, his depression, and his unresolved guilt and shame. Confronting the "truth" of his situation—his own inauthentic behavior and his strong negative feelings about his marriage— was Jacob's first step to psychological and moral change. Then came the curative value of the group's empathy, which fed and soothed the hurt "child" within, so that Jacob could begin to find the peace and security within himself to think and behave in a more humane fashion. At the end Jacob was filled with and acted upon the desire to reach out and help others at home and in the community, which was a curative process in and of itself.

CHOICES OF THE HEART

The following is a transcript of a session of one of my weekly therapy groups comprised of eight adult members, ages 32 to 50, who have been in the group anywhere from two months to four years. They are in treatment for depression, anxiety, and difficulties in relationships. Three of the clients are active members of Alcoholics Anonymous.

Many themes discussed in this book, and particularly in the last chapter, are touched on in this session and its aftermath. Of particular note, however, is the group members' gradual realization, through their own dialogue, that the enactment of goodness is integral to psychotherapy.

Joe, the "protagonist" of this session, is a 40-year-old man whose father is in a convalescent home. Joe's father is chronically, though not terminally, ill, and Joe, as the only member of the family in town, has taken on the responsibility for care of his father's financial and other pragmatic affairs. For all of his adult life, Joe has resented his father for what he feels is his father's total neglect of his emotional needs growing up. His father, an extremely cold and narcissistic man, has expressed very little appreciation for Joe's efforts on his behalf over the past several years, which have included visiting his father several times per week before he went into the home, getting him into the home of his choice, hiring extra nursing care, and now, visting him twice a week in the home for short periods.

JOE: My father asked me if I would spend more time with him. I didn't answer because the nurse was changing the bed. When she left, I said no.

MARIE: Does he know why?

JOE: I thought about telling him while the nurse was making the bed, not sure what I was going to say. Then I just told him the truth. I said, if he was not ill, I probably wouldn't have any contact with him at all.

RACHEL: How do you feel about it?

JOE: Guilty, plus I'm still afraid he'll disinherit me.

PATRICIA: How come you don't want to?

JOE: (*adamantly*) It's a terrible, terrible feeling to be in his presence. We never talk.

PATRICIA: Well, if you don't have to talk to him, then why don't you just do what he asks?

JOE: I just feel so isolated with him.

PATRICIA: I feel bad for him.

RACHEL: (*smiling*) You want to do to him what he did to you. Ignore him and leave him alone.

JOE: (*not smiling*) Yeah. Payback's a bitch, isn't it!

MARIE: Sounds like it.

DANA: You sound pretty mad. Are you uncomfortable with this?

RACHEL: You're just trying to take care of yourself.

JOE: It doesn't feel like he really wants me there for me. He's just trying to control what I do.

BEN: Must be scary for him. He's not in control now, and he doesn't know why you're doing this.

JOE: (*angrily*) I don't know what he knows or remembers. I just remember all the lying and the games and it feels really terrible.

BEN: It's a hard situation. He finally wants a relationship with you and now it's too late.

JOE: (*defensively*) I see him a lot—at least two times a week. He's pretty ill. No one can really have much of a conversation with him. His speech is really slurred.

VIRGINIA: I see you as really angry. I think that's the issue more than his illness. I'm glad you're talking about this, because I never realized how angry you are—about this, or maybe in general.

RACHEL: Well, if you are, that's okay. You have a right to be.

JOE: The worm has turned—flip-flop.

ART (*new member*): Could you explain to me what you're paying him back for?

JOE: He was not there for me when I was young, not at all. The way I feel now is he's not my child, he's not my responsibility. I was his and he blew it.

MARIE: Don't you think that down the road he might say something that will start a relationship?

JOE: No.

PATRICIA: How do you feel about that?

JOE: Sad . . . I can't say that I love him and I can't say how angry I am. I wish he would just die, frankly.

PATRICIA: That sounds so heartless.

JOE: I know. It's true.

BEN: I feel I'm being really judgmental in saying this, but I feel like your soul might be in jeopardy.

JOE: Well, he made his own bed, so to speak (*short laugh*).

PATRICIA: But what are you doing in that bed?

DANA: But he did sacrifice a lot for his father already.

PATRICIA: I feel differently—that an opportunity, however small, was wasted.

JOE: I've tried to engage him in a dialogue, and he's never responded. He just puts the paper up in front of his face. It's hopeless.

PATRICIA: (*excitedly*) But it's never hopeless. So, he is egocentric, so what? He's dying and he's reaching out. Why not start where you stand, even just for that night—once he takes that, he'll take more.

GEORGE (*co-therapist*) (*looking toward the group*): Patricia seems to be proceeding on the assumption that things are not hopeless.

ART: My relationship with my mother *is* hopeless. I'm sure of it.

PATRICIA: Okay, but you're there anyway, Joe. Why not try to make things more pleasant.

RACHEL: You don't think you should feel bad, do you? I agree, Joe. Why should you take even more abuse now just because he is sick.

BEN: Gosh, if some situations are beyond hope, what does that imply?

PATRICIA: That's as bad as it gets. The only time I felt there was no hope was when I was drinking. If I felt that way now, I'd have to go back to drinking. That's scary.

BEN: That's just what I was thinking. I don't want to ever go back there.

VIRGINIA: I was thinking that, too. But I can also understand your position, Joe, having lived with a mother who was chronically ill. Maybe that's why I'm picking up on your anger. I was furious all the time my mother was ill and dying. She had abused me and she was not going to change, *plus* I was stuck taking care of her. I couldn't accept that. Have you *really* accepted that your father is not going to change, Joe? I don't think you have, because if you had, you would not be so angry. I know for me, I don't want you to have that kind of anger as a parent. I don't want you to be so angry as an old man that your kids don't want to have anything to do with you and you are left all alone.

JOE: Yeah but his wanting to be with me *has nothing to do with me*. Any companionship will do. It's not *me* he wants to be with.

MN: Okay, but what if by some chance you're wrong?

JOE: What?

ART: What if he really meant he wanted to be with *you*, this one time, and you missed it.

MARIE: Yes!

PATRICIA: I can't believe how strongly I feel about this! I think you gotta get the closeness you can.

RACHEL: You could ease your guilt that way.

PATRICIA: But why do it out of guilt? Just do it for that moment.

GEORGE (*noticing Marie twisting in her chair*): I would like to hear what Marie has to say.

MARIE: When I think about moments . . . (*starts to weep*), I try to do what makes the heart feel good. When my mother was in Hospice the last few days, she barely knew us. I know how you feel—full of resentment and anger—but when all is said and done, you want to go through it the right way. I would just find this small little square, and do what would make her feel good in that little square. I remember I only had a few hours left, but I rushed out and got a haircut, just the way she liked me to wear it . . . and when she opened up her eyes, she saw it and smiled a little bit. All those little moments, so I would know her the best way I could. My Dad, he didn't get it . . . he gets *nothing*. . . . He couldn't figure out why I wore a print dress to her funeral, 'cuz she loved prints (*laughs*). I go back to Hospice to visit sometimes just to remind myself to pay attention.

JOE: I feel what I have done already is monumental.

GEORGE: I think what you have done *in here* is really great. I know how hard it has been for you to talk about yourself, and you have been very open.

MN: A real gift to the group, Joe. Thank you.

PATRICIA: Yeah. I realized something about myself. I do not give up on relationships. Now that has been one of my problems, but I think it has its good points. I think I like that in a situation like Joe's I wouldn't hold onto the bitterness, but just be spontaneous . . .

MN: I like that about you, too, Patricia. But you pay your price for that. Like in your relationship with Jack, which just went on and on, despite how badly he treated you.

ART: Yes—spontaneous. Back a while, Mary said, "What if you were wrong?" I think that was a crossroads of this discussion, just like you had a crossroads with your father. For me the opportunity you have is to take the anger and do something with it. . . . Maybe tell him how angry you are.

MN: I see what you mean, yes. Not being spontaneous is a problem you have been working on in here and shutting down is a problem you have had in many relationships in your life. When you have ended relationships you have done it rather crudely and brutally without giving the woman any idea beforehand that anything was wrong. Maybe you can take advantage of "those moments," as Marie suggests, in other relationships if not with your father—to be angry, to be loving, just to be honest.

The next week, a discussion ensued about the previous week's session.

PATRICIA: Of all the sessions we've had in here in three years, I thought about this one the most. I really feel I learned something important about me.

JOE: You mean about always having hope?

PATRICIA: Yes. I realize I like that about myself, but that I have to be willing to take my lumps for it.

MARIE: Well, I thought I probably talked too much, or was totally incoherent.

SEVERAL MEMBERS: No, we heard everything you said.

MARIE: Maybe if I had said it differently it might have had more impact.

JOE: Who did you think you didn't have impact on?

MARIE: Well, you, I guess.

JOE: Well, you're wrong. I heard all that and thought about—about the minutes and stuff. And I think it made a difference—probably not in my relationship with my father, but in other relationships.

Groups and sessions where the members do so much of the work are truly a joy for the therapist. The high quality of the interaction reflects the thoughtfulness, imagination, and good communication skills of the individual members as well as their cohesivenesss and trust as a group. We therapists intervened minimally—to clear a path for Marie to talk; to support the self-disclosure and receptiveness of Joe, who was taking a risk by opening himself to the possibility of moral judgment by the group; to confront Joe's assumption that he always knew exactly what his father was thinking and feeling; and to link what was transpiring to Patricia's and Joe's ongoing therapy. For the most part, however, George and I sat back, listened, and learned.

The group, with caring and curiosity, explored the moral ramifications of "those moments" when one has the choice to "do what makes the heart feel good," whether it be to make the other person feel better (Marie's and Patricia's choice) or to take one's truest feeling and "do something with it" (Art's suggestion), in the interest of a fuller and more real relationship.

THE MORAL INFLUENCE OF THE THERAPIST

Only sporadic attempts have been made to assess the effect of therapist values on patients. Research on the interaction of therapist and patient variables in therapeutic outcome by Truax and Carkhuff (1967) suggested that therapist empathy and nonpossessive warmth, as well as the ability to be genuine and transparent, are essential prerequisities for successful outcome. More recently, Kelly and Strupp (1992) found that the patients in treatment with therapists whose values were moderately similar to their own showed the most improvement in treatment.

Despite the small amount of empirical evidence, however, few seasoned therapists would disagree that the therapist's personality, including what he thinks is important and what he believes about life, are factors which guide the thrust of therapy. Given therapists' considerable moral influence over their patients, it is important that therapists and consumers of the therapy become aware of the values therapists are transmitting.

One way to to determine a therapist's underlying values is by his choice of method.

Moral Ramifications of the
Therapist's Choice of Method

Consciously or unconsciously each therapist will gravitate toward a method of practice the inherent moral premises of which are compatible with her personal moral biases and preferences among the virtues. The selection is by no means objective. As Herron (1978) put it, "the choice of psychotherapeutic orientation to stand by for some lengthy period in one's professional existence is really the choice of the truth you like best, rather than 'the truest truth'" (p. 398).

Grant (1985) suggests that in selecting a psychotherapeutic theory or method, the therapist decides "whether he wants to live in a world populated by the sorts of humans" it describes—and "whether we value the goals, opportunities, ways of relating to each other, and the life projects" the theory makes possible (p. 147). A clinician's choice of therapy theory and technique, whether in general or in the context of a given treatment, is a moral choice, having to do with what she values in human beings.

We have talked about the kind of human portrayed by the behaviorists (man as a product of the programming of reinforcement, devoid of an inner life) versus the classical Freudians (man as beast who needs to be tamed; a cauldron of unconscious drives and primary process) versus the object relations theorists (the need for love and attachment are the strongest motivating forces) versus the ego psychologists (humans, like other living beings, strive for growth through adaptation). Each of these perspectives will lead the therapy in very different directions—the latter two (object relations and ego psychology) being much more likely to enhance goodness than the first two (Freudian and behaviorist).

Different therapies elicit different aspects of goodness from clients. Psychodynamic therapy demands **honesty** and **responsibility** on the part of the patient. In working to go past his own defenses, the client is called upon to be truthful with himself and others, on the emotional as well as intellectual level. Other methods are perhaps less rigorous in the demand for honesty and responsibility, but are more **egalitarian** than psychoanalytic models. Some therapists prefer humanistic models in which the therapist is less of a "doctor" and more of a guide or companion on the therapeutic "journey." In humanistic methods (e.g., existential, Gestalt) the authentic creative expression of the client is viewed as healing in and of itself, rather than the achievement of a particular kind of cure based on preordained paradigms of what is healthy. Group therapy, whether psychodynamic or humanistic, values the contribution members can make to one another's healing as much, or perhaps more, than the therapist. As we discussed in Chapter 5, **altruism** is inherently fostered by group therapy. In the past decade, therapists have become sensitive to the role of gender, race, ethnicity, and class in the problems brought to therapy, and have realized that issues of power and oppression (**egalitarianism**) cannot be ignored in treatment. Recent "feminist" therapies explicitly foster an awareness of these issues as a part of treatment. As we discussed in Chapters 6 and 8, therapists who help clients deal with acountability are inevitably sensitizing clients to issues of **justice**.

The therapist's choice of methods and techniques will foster change in the direction the therapist thinks is desirable for the patient and his significant others. London (1986) espouses the following credo:

> I want to reshape people's lives so that they will emulate values I cherish for myself, aspire to what I wish humanity to be, and thus fulfill my need for the best of all possible worlds. (p. 9)

The Therapist's Responsibility to Promote Goodness

Since no theories can be deemed "correct" or "true" inclusively, therapists should be trained to pay close attention to the moral direction of the methods they employ and to ask themselves what aspects of human functioning they promote. If they are overemphasizing one virtue at the expense of another, they should consider learning other methods that will enhance goodness in the dimension that has been lacking.

Personally, I believe therapists have a conscious moral responsibility which goes beyond simply admitting and neutralizing their biases. I believe they must, when possible, consciously work toward fostering goodness, not only over evil, but over apathy and negligence as well. If the patient has a choice between **altruism** and selfishness, the therapist should be open in his preference for altruism. Therapists should actively try to cultivate **responsibility** and **honesty** and encourage **egalitarianism** and **justice** over prejudice, violence, and exploitation. They should try to do this without shaming the patient (see Chapter 8). Therapists should be aware that even though they are committed to goodness, they are not necessarily authorities on what that is. Taking this modest position allows therapists to engage in an open dialogue with the client as to the relative moral merits of the situations and choices being discussed.

Therapists should openly show delight when a new level of goodness is achieved by a patient. It is appropriate to appreciate the many ways that an increased generosity of spirit (**altruism**) is evoked by successful treatment, and the many other ways virtues are manifested as well. Perhaps the client is sensitive to others' feelings in a way he never would have been before. Perhaps he goes out of his way to take **responsibility** in an interaction, which he heretofore would have tried to use as a way to cast blame upon others. Perhaps he begins to see the therapist as a person, as an equal, instead of "big, bad wolf-mama," or "wolf-papa" (**egalitarianism**). Perhaps he exhibits an increasingly dependable sense of (**justice**), becoming more assertive when his rights are infringed upon and protecting the rights of others as well. Perhaps he is able to say he is sorry and make amends when he has hurt or neglected another. Therapists should recognize and take pride in their clients' increased **honesty**, not only about their thoughts and feelings in the context of treatment, but in their behavior in the therapeutic relationship and elsewhere.

Throughout this book we have touched on many moral components of the therapist role. The therapist tries to sensitize the client to moral issues and to encourage increasingly sophisticated levels of moral reasoning; this often involves "making talkable" the implicit moral aspects of situations described by the patient or enacted in the therapeutic relationship. The therapist strives not to be morally neutral but, rather, to be fair and compassionate. He tries to help patients learn to assess moral accountability and helps them with the processes of moral inventory, apology, forgiveness, and making amends. He helps his clients understand to what extent mental illness does and does not serve as an excuse for immoral behavior or for avoiding goodness. He recognizes the ethical failures inherent in some of the problems brought to therapy (e.g., depression, addictions, codependency, and the narcissistic and borderline disorders) without discounting the role of defenses in human functioning. He positively reinforces goodness when he notices it emerging from the client. He encourages clients, when possible, to expand their newly found goodness beyond the boundaries of intimate and family relationships into the larger world.

The Moral Influence of the Therapist's Use of Self

The therapist's primary influence over her patients, however, stems from the way she uses her total self—who she is and what she believes in—in the therapy. If the therapist is strong in all of the five virtues in the public as well as the private domains and is a good communicator and a good listener, then she will probably find that many of her patients, particularly those in long term treatment, will improve in many of these areas during the course of therapy. Psychiatrist Richard Rubin, a friend and colleague of mine, eloquently describes how he consciously transmits his own moral values to his patients.

> I hold as a jumping off point two assumptions: that ultimately the currency of love is a higher order of interaction than the currency of power; and that living in harmony and balance with the universe is better than trying to live separately from and/or trying to control the universe.
>
> I don't proselytize that. It influences how I interact, and I just keep questioning. For example, if someone says, "My goal is power and money." I say, "Why do you want power? What will it give you? Who do you want power over? Why?" *Over and over and over* until their beliefs fall apart, and what they realize they really want is that higher order of interaction—love. If they are struggling to win, to control, to gain revenge, I always find, upon questioning, that what they *really* want is the harmony that comes after the struggle.
>
> I use my beliefs to help them begin to question theirs, to help them clarify their own philosophical position; and while I rarely tell them my philosophy, ineveitably their ideas seem to move in the direction I have described. I don't believe that this is because I lead them there, but because these conclusions are moreor-

less inescapable when we struggle with our goals and purposes in life.

Every real teacher seems to guide students toward this higher order (of love and harmony): Ghandi, Jesus, Buddha, many of the saints. Other people have been charismatic and put forth some powerful ideas, but were not teachers. Machiavelli, for example, was considered smart, but not really a teacher. I think as therapists we are, at least potentially, teachers.

CONCLUSION

Improving life on the planet in the twenty-first century will require marshalling forces of goodness to counteract the forces of greed, violence, and prejudice so prevalent in the world today. But goodness cannot be mobilized unless it is first understood.

In this book, we have proposed that psychology and psychotherapy offer tools, if we will only use them, for getting at how goodness works—how it starts, how it grows, what promotes it, what stifles it. We have seen how the process of therapy itself enhances **honesty**, moral reasoning, and moral sensitivity, and opens up avenues for **altruistic** action. We have seen how closely linked psychopathology and "demoralization" can be, and how successful treatment almost inevitably liberates an individual's desire to be a "better person" in the context of his close relationships and in the world at large. We have seen how therapy can promote a zest for freedom and for love, can counteract oppression (**egalitarianism**, **justice**), and can build **responsibility**, a reverence for life, and a sense of community.

I hope this book is just the beginning of what will become a larger effort on the part of psychology and psychotherapy to probe the mystery of goodness.

REFERENCES

Adler, A. (1927/1957). *Understanding human nature*. New York: Premier Books.

Adler, T. (1991). In terms of evolution, altruism makes sense. *APA Monitor*, April, p. 11.

Affinito, M. (1990). *Eight steps to forgive: Preparing for the new miracle*. Unpublished manuscript.

Alcoholics Anonymous. (1952/1981). *Twelve steps and twelve traditions*. New York: Author.

Allport, G. (1950). *The individual and his religion*. New York: Macmillan.

American Psychiatric Association. (1987). *Diagnostic and statistical manual of mental disorders* (3rd ed.—rev.). Washington, DC: Author.

Andrews, L. (1987). *To thine own self be true*. New York: Doubleday.

Arendt, H. (1963). *Eichmann in Jerusalem: A report on the banality of evil*. New York: Viking.

Barbidge, B. (1988). Things so finely human. In C. Gilligan, J. Ward, & J. Taylor (Eds.), *Mapping the moral domain* (pp. 87–110). Cambridge, MA: Harvard University Press.

Bateson, G. (1979). *Mind and nature*. New York: Dutton.

Batson, C. D. (1987). Prosocial motivation: Is it ever truly altruistic? In L. Berkowitz (Ed.), *Advances in experimental social psychology* (vol. 20, pp. 65–122). New York: Academic Press.

Batson, C. D. (1990). How social an animal? *American Psychologist, 45*, 336–346.

Batson, C. D., et al. (1981). Is empathic emotion a source of altruistic motivation? *Journal of Personality & Social Psychology, 40*, 290–302.

Becker, E. (1973). *Denial of death*. New York: Macmillan.

Bellah, R., Madsen, R., Sullivan, W., Swidler, A., & Tipton, S. (1985). *Habits of the heart: Individualism and commitment in American life*. New York: Harper & Row.

227

Bellah, R., Madsen, R., Sullivan, W., Swidler A., & Tipton, S. (1991). *The good society*. New York: Knopf.

Bergin, A. (1980). Behavior therapy and ethical relativism. *Journal of Counseling & Clinical Psychology, 48*, 11–13.

Bergin, A. (1988). Mental health values of professionals: A national interdisciplinary survey. *Professional Psychology: Research and Practice, 3*, 290–297.

Bergin, A. (1991). Values and religious issues in psychotherapy and mental health. *American Psychologist, 46*(4), 394–403.

Blasi, A. (1980). Bridging moral cognition and moral action: A critical review of the literature. *Psychological Bulletin, 88*, 1–45.

Bloch, S., & Crouch, E. (1985). *Therapeutic factors in group therapy*. New York: Oxford University Press.

Blum, L. (1987). Particularity and responsiveness. In J. Kagan & S. Lamb (Eds.), *The emergence of morality in young children* (pp. 306–337). Chicago, IL: University of Chicago Press.

Bok, S. (1978). *Lying: Moral choice in public and private life*. New York: Vintage.

Brabeck, M. (1986). Moral orientation: Alternative perspectives of men and women. In R. Knowles & G. McLean (Eds.), *Psychological foundations of moral education and character development* (pp. 65–89). Lanham, MD: University Press of America.

Buber, M. (1966). *The way of response*. New York: Schocken Books.

Chodorow, N. (1978). *The reproduction of mothering: Psychoanalysis and the sociology of gender*. Berkeley: University of California Press.

Cialdini, R. (1985). *Influence: Science and practice*. Glenview, IL: Scott, Foresman & Co.

Clary, G., & Miller, J. (1986). Socialization and situational influences on sustained altruism. *Child Development, 57*, 1358–1369.

Clinebell, H. (1984). *Basic types of pastoral care counseling*. Nashville, TN: Abington Press.

Coles, R. (1986). *The moral life of children*. Boston: Houghton Mifflin.

Coles, R. (1989). *The call of stories*. Boston: Houghton Mifflin.

Csikszentmihalyi, M., & Rochberg-Halton, E. (1981). *The meaning of things: Domestic symbols and the self*. Cambridge, England: Cambridge University Press.

Damon, W., & Colby, J. (1987). Social influence and moral change. In W. Kurtines & M. Gewirtz (Eds.), *Moral development through social interaction* (pp. 3–19). New York: Wiley.

Darwin, C. (1871). *Descent of man and selection in relation to sex*. New York: Appleton.

Dewey, J. (1922). *Human nature and conduct*. New York: Henry Holt.

Dilman, I. (1983). *Freud and human nature*. New York: Basil Blackwell.

Dollard, J., & Miller, N. (1950). *Personality and psychotherapy*. New York: McGraw-Hill.

Dovidio, J. (1984). Helping behavior and altruism: An empirical and conceptual overview. *Advances in Experimental & Social Psychology, 13*(3), 195–205.

Durkheim, E. (1925/1961). *Moral education*. New York: Free Press.

Durkheim, E. (1951). *Suicide*. New York: Free Press.

Eisenberg, L. (1972). The human nature of human nature. *Science, 14*, 123–128.

Eisenberg, N., & Mussen, P. (1989). *The roots of prosocial behavior in children*. New York: Cambridge University Press.

Eliasoph, E. (1963, June). A paradigm for the classification of juvenile delinquents. *Berkshire Farms Monographs*.

Emde, R., Johnson, W., & Easterbrooks, M. (1987). The do's and dont's of early moral development. In J. Kagan & S. Lamb (Eds.), *The emergence of morality in young children* (pp. 245–276). Chicago, IL: University of Chicago Press.

Epstein, S. (1989). Values from the perspective of cognitive-experiential self theory. In N. Eisenberg, J. Reykowski, & E. Staub (Eds.), *Social and moral values* (pp. 3–22). Hillsdale, NJ: Erlbaum.

Erikson, E. (1963). *Childhood and society* (2nd ed.). New York: W. W. Norton.

Fairbairn, W. (1952). *An object relations theory of the personality.* New York: Basic.

Feather, N. (1982). Actions in relation to expected consequences: An overview of a research program. In N. T. Feather (Ed.), *Expectations and actions: Expectancy-value models in psychotherapy* (pp. 53–95). Hillsdale, NJ: Lawrence.

Festinger, L. (1957). *A theory of cognitive dissonance.* New York: Row, Peterson.

Flanagan, O., & Rorty, A. (1990). Introduction. In O. Flanagan & A. Rorty (Eds.), *Identity, character and morality: Essays in moral psychology* (pp. 1–15). Cambridge, MA: M.I.T. Press.

Forward, S. (1989). *Toxic parents.* New York: Bantam.

Frankl, V. (1969/1988). *The will to meaning.* New York: New American Library.

French, M. (1985). *Beyond power: On women, men and morals.* New York: Ballantine.

Freud, A. (1966). *The ego and the mechanisms of defense.* In *The writings of Anna Freud* (vol. 2). New York: International Universities Press.

Freud, S. (1914/1957). On narcissism. In J. Rickman (Ed.), *A general selection from the works of Freud* (pp. 104–123). New York: Doubleday.

Freud, S. (1917/1961). Mourning and melancholia. In J. Rickman (Ed.), *A general selection from the works of Freud* (pp. 124–140). New York: Doubleday.

Freud, S. (1921/1957). Group psychology and analysis of the ego. In J. Rickman (Ed.), *A general selection from the works of Freud* (pp. 169–209). New York: Doubleday.

Freud, S. (1920/1961). Beyond the pleasure principle. In J. Strachey (Ed. & Trans.), *The standard edition of the complete psychological works of Sigmund Freud* (vol. 18, pp. 3–64). New York: W. W. Norton.

Freud, S. (1921/1938). Totem and taboo. In A. Brill (Trans.), *The basic writings of Sigmund Freud.* New York: Modern Library.

Freud, S. (1923). The ego and the id. In J. Rickman (Ed.), *A general selection from the works of Freud* (pp. 210–235). New York: Doubleday.

Freud, S. (1925/1961). Some psychical consequences of the anatomical differences between the sexes. In J. Strachey (Ed. & Trans.), *The standard edition of the complete psychological works of Sigmund Freud* (vol. 19, pp. 257–258). New York: W. W. Norton.

Freud, S. (1930/1961). Civilization and its discontents. In J. Strachey (Ed. & Trans.), *The standard edition of the complete psychological works of Sigmund Freud* (vol. 21). New York: W. W. Norton.

Friere, P. (1970). *Pedagogy of the oppressed.* New York: Seabury Press.

Fromm, E. (1947). *Man for himself: An inquiry into the psychology of ethics.* New York: Henry Holt.

Fromm, E. (1955). *The sane society.* New York: Henry Holt.

Fromm, E. (1964). *The heart of man: Its genius for good and evil.* New York: Harper & Row.

Fultz, J. (1992). Resurrecting sympathy. Review of L. Wispe's *The psychology of sympathy. Contemporary Psychology*, 37(10), 1003–1004.

Gavrin, E. (1987). Moral choice. In W. Kurtines & M. Gewirtz (Eds.), *Moral development through social interaction* (pp. 135–151). New York: Wiley.

Gay, P. (1988). *Freud: A life for our time.* New York: W. W. Norton.

Gaylin, W. (1988). Love and the limits of individualism. In W. Gaylin & E. Person (Eds.), *Passionate attachments* (pp. 41–62). New York: Free Press.

Gaylin, W. (1990). *On being and becoming human*. New York: Penguin.

Gibbs, J., & Schell, S. (1985). Moral development vs. socialization: A critique. *American Psychologist, 40*, 1071–1080.

Gilligan, C. (1977). In a different voice: Women's conceptions of the self and morality. *Harvard Educational Review, 47*, 481–517.

Gilligan, C. (1982). *In a different voice*. Cambridge, MA: Harvard University Press.

Glad, D. (1959). *Operational values in psychotherapy*. New York: Oxford University Press.

Glantz, K., & Pearce, J. (1989). *Exiles from Eden*. New York: W. W. Norton.

Grant, B. (1985). The moral nature of psychotherapy. *Counseling & Values, 29*(2), 141–150.

Greenberg, J., & Mitchell, S. (1983). *Object relations in psychoanalytic theory*. Cambridge, MA: Harvard University Press.

Haan, N. (1978). Two moralities in action contexts: Relationships to thought, ego regulation, and development. *Journal of Personality and Social Psychology, 36*(3), 286–305.

Haan, N. (1985). Processes of moral development. *Developmental Psychology, 21*(6), 996–1006.

Hale, A. (1981). *Conducting clinical sociometric explorations*. Roanoke, VA: Ann Hale.

Harding, S. (1986). *The science question in feminism*. Ithaca, NY: Cornell University Press.

Harper, J., & Hoopes, M. (1990). *Uncovering shame*. New York: W. W. Norton.

Herman, J. (1992). *Trauma and recovery: The aftermath of violence—from domestic abuse to political terror*. New York: Basic.

Herron, W. (1978). The therapist's choice of psychotherapy. *Psychotherapy: Theory, Research & Practice, 14*(4), 396–401.

Hillman, J., & Ventura, M. (1992). The politics of self-pity. *Family Therapy Networker*, Nov/Dec, 38–43.

Hoffman, M. (1975). Empathy, role-taking, guilt and development of altruistic motives. In T. Lickona (Ed.), *Moral development and behavior* (pp. 124–143). New York: Holt, Rinehart & Winston.

Hoffman, M. (1989). Empathy and prosocial activism. In N. Eisenberg, J. Reykowsky, & E. Staub (Eds.), *Social and moral values* (pp. 65–85). Hillsdale, NJ: Erlbaum.

Hofstadter, R. (1944). *Social Darwinism in American thought*. Boston: Beacon Press.

Horney, K. (1945). *Our inner conflicts*. New York: W. W. Norton.

Horney, K. (1950). *Neurosis and human growth*. New York: W. W. Norton.

Hunt, M. (1990). *The compassionate beast: What science is discovering about the humane side of humankind*. New York: William Morrow.

James, M. (1977). *Techniques in transactional analysis*. New York: Random House.

James, W. (1920). *Collected essays and reviews*. New York: Longmans, Green & Co.

Jordan, A., & Meara, N. (1990). Ethics and the professional practice of the psychologist: The role of virtues and principles. *Professional Psychology: Research & Practice*, 107–114.

Kagan, J. (1984). *The nature of the child*. New York: Basic.

Kagan, J. (1987). Introduction. In J. Kagan & S. Lamb (Eds.), *The emergence of morality in young children*. Chicago, IL: University of Chicago Press.

Karen, R. (1992, Feb.). Shame. *The Atlantic Monthly*, pp. 40–70.

Kaufman, G. (1985). *Shame: The power of caring*. Cambridge, MA: Schenkman Books.

Kegan, R. (1982). *The evolving self: Problem and process in human development*. Cambridge, MA: Harvard University Press.

Kelly, T., & Strupp, H. (1992). Patient and therapist values in psychotherapy: Perceived changes, assimilation, similarity and outcome. *Journal of Clinical & Consulting Psychology*, 60(1), 34–40.

Kernberg, O. (1975). *Borderline conditions and pathological narcissism*. New York: Jason Aronson.

Kernberg, O. (1984). *Severe personality disorders*. New Haven, CT: Yale University Press.

Kimble, G. (1989). Psychology from the standpoint of a generalist. *American Psychologist, 44*, 491–499.

Kitchener, K. (1984). Intuition, critical evaluation and ethical principles: The foundation for ethical decisions in counseling psychology. *The Counseling Psychologist, 12*, 43–56.

Kitwood, T. (1990). *Concern for others*. London: Routledge.

Klein, M. (1935/75). A contribution to the psychogenesis of manic-depressive states. In *Contributions to psychoanalysis: 1921–1945*. New York: Delacorte Press.

Klein, M. (1946). Notes on schizoid mechanisms. *International Journal of Psychoanalysis, 49*, 662–677.

Klein, M. (1956/1986). A study of envy and gratitude. In J. Mitchell (Ed.), *The selected Melanie Klein* (pp. 211–229). New York: Free Press.

Koch, S. (1959–1963). *Psychology: A study of a science* (6 vols.). New York: McGraw-Hill.

Kohlberg, L. (1975). Moral stages and moralization: The cognitive developmental approach. In T. Lickona (Ed.), *Moral development and behavior* (pp. 31–53). New York: Holt, Rinehart & Winston.

Kohlberg, L., & Higgins, A. (1987). School democracy and social interaction. In W. Kurtines & M. Gewirtz (Eds.), *Moral development through social interaction* (pp. 103–128). New York: Wiley.

Kohn, A. (1990). *The brighter side of human nature*. New York: Basic.

Kohut, H. (1971). *Analysis of the self*. New York: International Universities Press.

Kraft, W. (1986). A phenomenological approach toward the moral person. In R. Knowles & G. McLean (Eds.), *Psychological foundations of moral education and character development*. Lanham, MD: Lanham Press of America.

Latane, B. (1970). *The unresponsive bystander: Why doesn't he help?* Englewood Cliffs, NJ: Prentice-Hall.

Levine, M., & Perkins, D. (1987). *Principles of community psychology*. New York: Oxford University Press.

Lewis, H. (1971). *Shame and guilt in neurosis*. New York: International Universities Press.

Lewis, H. (1990). *A question of values: Six ways we make the personal choices that shape our lives*. San Francisco, CA: HarperCollins.

Lickona, T. (1978). Critical issues in moral development. In T. Lickona (Ed.), *Moral development and behavior*. New York: Holt, Rinehart & Winston.

Lifton, R. (1976). *The life of the self*. New York: Simon & Schuster.

Lifton, R. (1986). *The Nazi doctors*. New York: Basic.

Lindner, R. (1944). *Rebel without a cause: The story of a criminal psychopath*. New York: Grune & Stratton.

London, P. (1986). *Modes and morals of psychotherapy* (2nd ed.). New York: Hemisphere.

Lowe, C. M. (1969). *Value orientation in counseling and psychotherapy*. San Francisco: Chandler Publishing Co.

Luks, A. (1992). *The healing power of doing good*. New York: Ballantine.

Macaulay, J., & Berkowitz, L. (1970). Introduction. In J. Macauley & L. Berkowitz (Eds.), *Altruism and helping behavior*. New York: Academic Press.

Mahler, M. (1975). *Psychological birth of the human infant*. New York: Basic.

Maslow, A. (1968). *Toward a psychology of being*. New York: Van Nostrand Reinhold.

Maslow, A. H. (1971). *The farther reaches of human nature*. New York: Viking.

Masterson, J. (1976). *Psychotherapy with the borderline adult*. New York: Brunner/Mazel.

May, R. (1958). Contributions of existential psychology. In R. May, E. Angel, & H. Ellenberger (Eds.), *Existence*. New York: Basic.

May, R. (1962, April 18). *Freedom and responsibility reexamined*. Paper presented to the American College Personnel Association, Chicago, IL.

May, R. (1969). *Love and will*. New York: Delta.

McDougall, W. (1908). *An introduction to social psychology*. London: Methuen.

Miller, A. (1984a). *For your own good*. New York: Farrar, Straus & Giroux.

Miller, A. (1984b). *Thou shalt not be aware: Society's betrayal of the child*. New York: Farrar, Straus & Giroux.

Miller, A. (1988). *Banished knowledge* (L. Vennewitz, Trans.). New York: Doubleday.

Mitchell, S. (1988). *Relational concepts in psychoanalysis*. Cambridge, MA: Harvard University Press.

Money-Kyrle, R. (1955). Psycho-analysis and ethics. In M. Klein, P. Heimann, & R. Money-Kyrle (Eds.), *New directions in psycho-analysis*. London: Tavistock.

Moreno, J. L. (1946/1977). *Psychodrama* (Vols. 1 & 2). New York: Beacon House.

Moreno, J. L. (1953). *Who shall survive?* Beacon, NY: Beacon House.

Moreno, Z. (1986). J. L. Moreno's concept of ethical anger. *Journal of Group Psychotherapy & Psychodrama, 38,* 145–154.

Morrison, A. (1986). Shame, ideal self and narcissism. In A. Morrison (Ed.), *Essential papers on narcissism*. New York: International Universities Press.

Mowrer, O. H. (1964). *The new group therapy*. New York: D. Van Nostrand Co.

Mullan, H. (1987). The ethical foundations of group therapy. *International Journal of Group Psychotherapy, 37,* 403–416.

Mullan, H. (1988). Horney's contribution to a rational approach to morals. *American Journal of Psychoanalysis, 48*(2), 127–137.

Mullan, H. (1991). Inherent moral practice in group psychotherapy. *International Journal of Group Psychotherapy, 41*(2), 185–197.

Neumann, E. (1969/1990). *Depth psychology and a new ethic*. Boston: Shambhala.

Nicholas, M. (1984). *Change in the context of group therapy*. New York: Brunner/Mazel.

Nicholas, M. (1993). How to deal with moral issues in group therapy without being judgmental. *International Journal of Group Psychotherapy, 43*(2), 205–221.

Nietzche, F. (1886/1985). On the history of moral feelings. In *Human, all too human* (M. Faber & S. Lehmann, Trans.). Lincoln: University of Nebraska Press.

Oliner, S., & Oliner, P. (1988). *The altruistic personality: Rescuers of Jews in Nazi Europe.* New York: Free Press.

Pattison, E. (1968). Ego morality as an emerging concept. *Psychoanalytic Review, 55,* 187–222.

Peck, S. (1983). *People of the lie: The hope for healing human evil.* New York: Simon & Schuster.

Piaget, J. (1936/1952). *The origins of intelligence in children.* New York: International Universities Press.

Piaget, J. (1948/1965). *The moral judgment of the child.* New York: Free Press.

Piliavin, J., Evans, D., & Callero, P. (1984). Learning to give to unnamed strangers. In E. Staub & D. Bar-Tal (Eds.), *The development and maintenance of prosocial behavior: International perspectives on positive morality.* New York: Plenum.

Pittman, F. (1992). It's not my fault. *Family Therapy Networker, 16*(1), 57–63.

Pogrebin, L. (1983). *Family politics.* New York: McGraw-Hill.

Polster, E. (1987). *Every person's life is worth a novel.* New York: W. W. Norton.

Pope Edwards, C. (1987). Culture and the construction of moral values. In J. Kagan & S. Lamb (Eds.), *The emergence of morality in young children* (pp. 123–151). Chicago, IL: University of Chicago Press.

Radke-Yarrow, M., & Zahn-Wexler, C. (1984). Quoted in E. Staub & D. Bar-Tal (Eds.), *The development and maintenance of prosocial behavior: International perspectives on positive morality.* New York: Plenum.

Rank, O. (1941/1958). *Beyond psychology.* New York: Dover.

Rank, O. (1954). *Will therapy and truth and reality.* New York: Knopf.

Reich, W. (1950). *Character analysis.* New York: Vision Press.

Rest, J. (1986). *Moral development: Advances in research and theory.* New York: Praeger.

Riger, S. (1992). Epistemological debates, feminist voices: Science, social values and the study of women. *American Psychologist, 47*(6), 730–740.

Rokeach, M. (1973). *The nature of human values.* New York: Free Press.

Rosenthal, T., & Bandura, A. (1978). Psychological modeling: Theory and practice. In S. Garfield and A. Bergin (Eds.), *Handbook of Psychotherapy and Behavior Change, 2nd edition* (pp. 621–658). New York: Wiley.

Roszak, T. (1992). *Voice of the earth.* New York: Simon & Schuster.

Rushton, J., Russell, R., & Wells, P. (1984). Genetic similarity theory: Beyond kin selection. *Behavior Genetics, 14*(3), 179–193.

Rutkowski, G., Gruder, C., & Rober, D. (1983). Group cohesiveness, social norms and bystander intervention. *Journal of Personality & Social Psychology, 44*(3), 545–552.

Safransky, S. (1991). The rainmaker fantasy. *Family Therapy Networker, 15,* 21.

Sagan, E. (1988). *Freud, women and morality.* New York: Basic.

Sarason, S. (1974). *The psychological sense of community.* San Francisco: Jossey-Bass.

Scharf, J. (1992). *Projective and introjective identification and the use of the therapist's self.* Northvale, NJ: Jason Aronson.

Seiz, R., & Schwab, J. (1992). Value orientations of clinical social work practitioners. *Clinical Social Work Journal, 40,* 323–335.

Shengold, L. (1989). *Soul murder.* New Haven, CT: Yale University Press.

Shweder, R., Mahapatra, M., & Miller, J. (1987). Culture and moral development. In J. Kagan & S. Lamb (Eds.), *The emergence of morality in young children* (pp. 1–79). Chicago, IL: University of Chicago Press.

Siporin, M. (1975). *Introduction to social work*. New York: Macmillan.

Skinner, B. (1971). *Beyond freedom and dignity*. New York: Alfred Knopf.

Slater, P. (1976). *The pursuit of loneliness*. Boston: Beacon Press.

Smith, M. B. (1991). Psychology in the public interest. *American Psychologist, 45*(4), 530–536.

Snodgrass, S. (1985). Women's intuition: The effect of subordinate role on interpersonal sensitivity. *Journal of Personality & Social Psychology, 49*, 146–155.

Staub, E. (1971). The use of role-playing and induction in childrens' learning of helping and sharing behavior. *Child Development, 42*, 805–816.

Staub, E. (1979). *Positive social behavior and morality* (Vols. 1 & 2). New York: Academic Press.

Staub, E. (1989). *The roots of evil: The origins of genocide and other group violence*. Cambridge, MA: Harvard University Press.

Steiner, C. (1975). Principles. In C. Steiner et al. (Eds.), *Readings in radical psychiatry*. New York: Grove Press.

Stern, D. (1985). *The interpersonal world of the infant: A view from psychoanalysis and developmental psychology*. New York: Basic.

Sullivan, H. S. (1953). *Interpersonal theory of psychiatry*. New York: W. W. Norton.

Sullivan, H. S. (1962). *Schizophrenia as human process*. New York: W. W. Norton.

Sulloway, F. (1983). *Freud: Biologist of the mind*. New York: Basic.

Szasz, T. (1961). *The myth of mental illness*. New York: Harper & Row.

Tarnas, R. (1990, Nov. 15). *The western mind at the threshold*. Audiotape of lecture presented to the Center for Psychological Studies in the Nuclear Age. Cambridge, MA: Center for Psychological Studies.

Tomkins, S. (1963). *Affect/imagery/consciousness. Vol. 1: The negative affects*. New York: Springer.

Truax, C., & Carkhuff, R. (1967). *Toward effective counseling and psychotherapy*. Chicago, IL: Aldine.

Turiel, E., Killen, M., & Helwig, C. (1987). Morality: Its structure, functions and vagaries. In J. Kagan & S. Lamb (Eds.), *The emergence of morality in young children* (pp. 115–243). Chicago, IL: University of Chicago Press.

Vandenberg, B. (1991). Is epistemology enough? An existential consideration of development. *American Psychologist, 46*(12), 1278–1286.

Veroff, J., Douvan, E., & Kulka, R. (1981). *Mental health in America: Patterns of help-seeking from 1957–1976*. New York: Basic.

Vitz, P. (1990). The use of stories in moral development. *American Psychologist, 46*, 709–720.

Walker, L. (1984). Sex differences in the development of moral reasoning: A critical review of the literature. *Child Development, 55*, 677–691.

Wallach, E., & Wallach, L. (1990). *Rethinking goodness*. Albany, NY: State University of New York Press.

Watson, J. (1930). *Behaviorism*. New York: W. W. Norton.

Watson, J. (1936). Manifesto. In C. Murchison et al. (Eds.), *A history of psychology in autobiography* (vol. 3). Worcester, MA: Clark University.

Watson, J. (1988). *Teachers' conceptions of morality and moral education*. Unpublished dissertation. University of Leicester, England.

Wechsler, H. (1990). *What's so bad about guilt?* New York: Simon & Schuster.

Weinberg, G. (1990). *The taboo scarf*. New York: St. Martin's.

Weiss, F. (1965). Psychoanalysis and moral values. In H. Kelman (Ed.), *New perspectives in psychoanalysis* (pp. 68–89). New York: W. W. Norton.

Welfel, E. (1992). Psychologist as ethics educator: Successes, failures and unanswered questions. *Professional Psychology: Research & Practice, 23*(3), 182–189.

Wilson, E. (1975). *Sociobiology: The new synthesis.* Cambridge, MA: Harvard University Press.

Winnicott, D. (1965). *The maturational processes and the facilitating environment.* London: Hogarth Press.

Wispe, L. (1991). *The psychology of sympathy.* New York: Plenum.

Yalom, I. (1980). *Existential psychotherapy.* New York: Basic.

Yapko, M. (1988). Individuation: Alone together. In S. Lankton & J. Zeig (Eds.), *Developing Eriksonian therapy* (pp. 237–256). New York: Brunner/Mazel.

Zimbardo, P. (1971). Coercion and compliance: The psychology of police confessions. In R. Perruci & M. Pilisuk (Eds.), *The triple revolution emerging: Social problems in depth.* Boston: Little Brown.

INDEX